The Extreme Cinema of Eastern Europe

To Nika Nazirova

The Extreme Cinema of Eastern Europe
Rape, Art, (S)Exploitation

Anna Batori

EDINBURGH
University Press

Edinburgh University Press is one of the leading university presses in the UK. We publish academic books and journals in our selected subject areas across the humanities and social sciences, combining cutting-edge scholarship with high editorial and production values to produce academic works of lasting importance. For more information visit our website: edinburghuniversitypress.com

© Anna Batori, 2024

Grateful acknowledgement is made to the sources listed in the List of Illustrations for permission to reproduce material previously published elsewhere. Every effort has been made to trace the copyright holders, but if any have been inadvertently overlooked, the publisher will be pleased to make the necessary arrangements at the first opportunity.

Edinburgh University Press Ltd
The Tun – Holyrood Road
12(2f) Jackson's Entry
Edinburgh EH8 8PJ

Typeset in Monotype Ehrhardt by
Cheshire Typesetting Ltd, Cuddington, Cheshire,
and printed and bound in Great Britain

A CIP record for this book is available from the British Library

ISBN 978 1 4744 4832 1 (hardback)
ISBN 978 1 4744 4834 5 (webready PDF)
ISBN 978 1 4744 4835 2 (epub)

The right of Anna Batori to be identified as the author of this work has been asserted in accordance with the Copyright, Designs and Patents Act 1988, and the Copyright and Related Rights Regulations 2003 (SI No. 2498).

Contents

List of Figures	vii
Acknowledgments	viii
Introduction	1
Extreme Cinema = Art Cinema?	3
Extreme Cinema = Exploitation?	7
Is Eastern *European* Cinema *European?*	11
Eastern Extreme: A Post-Socialist, (Post-)Colonialist Reaction	13
Post-Colonialist Sexuality: Eastern European Supererogation	16
About This Book	19
1. The Cradle of Eastern Extremism: Sexual Oppression and the Yugoslav Black Wave	22
Sexual Supererogation and Extreme Eroticism: The Case of Dušan Makavejev	25
2. The Political Transition and the Extreme: Cinema of Castration	37
A Gendered Transition	39
Emasculated Cinemas	44
Rape, Colonisation, Motherhood: *Pleasant Days*	48
Festival Triumph = Body, Commodity and Self-exotism	52
The Patriarchal Gaze and Sexuality: *She-Shaman*	54
Reception and Rape: Recipe for Success	58
3. Post-Socialist Animality: Towards an (Eastern European) Extreme Cinema	62
Eastern European Animalities: Metaphors of Sexual Objectification	70

vi THE EXTREME CINEMA OF EASTERN EUROPE

4. Eastern Extreme Cinema: (S)exploitation and Animal Death 82

Eastern European Exploitation: *Marble Ass* and *Baklava* 86

Balkan Exploitation, Transvestitism and Political Cynicism 89

Exploitation, the Extreme and Moral Concern: *Baklava* 92

5. Post-War Extremism: Subversive Serbia 99

Subversive Serbian Cinema 100

Family, Nation, Nationalism: The Route to Balkanism 102

Post-Yugoslav Cinema: The Cinema of Anger 105

Intermedial Torture: *The Life and Death of a Porno Gang* 106

S(n)uffocating Eastern Europe: *A Serbian Film* 115

Newborn Art? 117

Raping the Senses of the Spectator 124

6. Towards Contemporary Extreme Forms of Double Colonialism 127

Crisis of Neoliberalism in Eastern Europe 128

Populism and Self-Colonising Structures in Eastern Europe 129

Extreme Corporal Violence in Contemporary Eastern European Cinemas 131

"This EU, It Costs Us a Lot of Money": *Slovenian Girl* and *Bibliothèque Pascal* 134

Conclusion 139

The Future Dangers of Extreme Cinemas 142

Bibliography 144
Filmography 174
Notes 177
Index 187

Figures

1.1	Tuli Kupferberg (*WR: Mysteries of the Organism*)	27
1.2	Milky Way (*Sweet Movie*)	30
1.3	Chaos (*Sweet Movie*)	31
2.1	Connected to the past (*The Conjugal Bed*)	47
2.2	Torture by emasculation (*The Conjugal Bed*)	48
2.3	Un-erotic images (*Pleasant Days*)	50
2.4	Clinical inventory (*Pleasant Days*)	51
2.5	Subjugated (*She-Shaman*)	56
3.1	Femininity (*Somnambulance*)	73
3.2	Grasping perspectives (*Andel Exit*)	75
3.3	Feathers and femininity (*Alone*)	78
4.1	Goaty (*Marble Ass*)	88
4.2	Shockumentary (*Baklava*)	94
5.1	Family portrait (*The Life and Death of a Porno Gang*)	110
5.2	Balkan portrait (*The Life and Death of a Porno Gang*)	114
5.3	Hall of blood (*A Serbian Film*)	118
5.4	Spectatorship, intermediality (*A Serbian Film*)	119
5.5	Witnessing positions (*A Serbian Film*)	120
6.1	Western gaze (*Bibliothèque Pascal*)	137

Acknowledgments

This book was difficult to write. It was even more difficult to finish. The struggle – endless nights, nightmares, flashbacks and my always shaking-hands – prompted my family and friends to ask if, after my own rape trauma, I really want to go ahead and write a book on gender and sexual abuse in extreme cinemas. It is hard to explain and make people understand what is going on inside in someone after such a trauma, but this research helped me to find some answers and understand victim-blaming and society's blindness when it comes to sexual abuse.

Most importantly, the book helped me to see that even in the deepest darkness, I have people who lift me up. A select few who did not disappear. I dedicate this book to them. But I also wish to send my gratitude to those who turned their back to me. You helped me in my growth. To be more than you are.

I am obliged to Csibi László at the Babes-Bolyai University for his understanding and support. I am also grateful to the Hungarian Academy of Sciences and their Premium Postdoctoral Programme in Budapest, Hungary. I also feel obligated to the Russian, East European and Eurasian Center at the University of Illinois, USA and University of Pécs in Hungary for letting me conduct research at their institutions.

Special thanks go to Sam Johnson and Richard Strachan from Edinburgh University Press for their immense patience, empathy and understanding. I am also grateful for the reviewers' comments.

Finally, I hope this book can change something. To help academics, scholars and students understand certain social dynamics and aim for a gender-equal future. I know this book is imperfect. But I hope it can start a debate on the (artistic) value (if there is such a thing) of rape representation in cinemas.

Introduction

On 23 May 2011, *Vice* published a thought-provoking article on the meaning and value of modern art. In 'I'm Sick of Pretending: I Don't "Get" Art',[1] Glen Coco shares her experience of the exhibition opening of the new Tracey Emin retrospective at Hayward Gallery in London. Shocked by the vision of 'unskilled art' that, according to her, enumerates a series of senseless images and films – including Emin endlessly riding a horse and rubbing money against her vagina as well neon lightings which say '*My Cunt is Wet with Fear*' – Coco comes to the conclusion that modern-day art turned into 'some exclusive club that you can join if you've got more money than interesting things to communicate to the rest of human species'. Upon visiting the 2013 Art Basel in Miami, the world's largest art fair, the author's opinion[2] on modern day-art becomes even more straightforward. The canvases painted in one colour or the vision of a couple of empty banana boxes and some spotlights – just to mention a few examples – makes Coco conclude that 'it's probably "Blair Witch syndrome" where someone sees another person making a ton of money doing something that they themselves could have done and it makes them temporarily lose their mind' and a simple black square cost more than 'an entire third-world school'. It seems that there is an entire artistic movement built on provokingly simple and/or shockingly explicit pornographic content, and cinema is no exception. Similar to Coco, I also felt 'crass and uncultured' when, following the screening of Lukas Moodysoon's *A Hole in My Heart* (*Ett hål i mitt hjärta* 2004) in a film club, my fellow cinemagoers started to praise the film for its brave images, excellent mise-en-scéne and honest portray of modern-day sexuality. The low-budget digital video production which includes several unsimulated sex scenes gave me one of my most shocking film experiences to date. It was not the film's impossible-to-follow narrative form, shaky-blurring-underlit images and very explicit imagery that left me with an open mouth but the *reaction* of critics who would discuss this 'masterpiece's artistic quality' for long hours afterwards. As a true exploitation-trash film fan and horror-cinephile, it is quite difficult to shock my senses with any kind of subversive spectacle. However, when I watched the masturbation scene with a toothbrush in *A Hole in My Heart*, I could not help but ask the spectacle's role/meaning in the narrative. Similar to Coco who did not get 'art', I could not wrap my head around the *meaning* and *artistic gesture* of this form of 'art' in cinema. In the post-screening roundtable discussion, cultural commentators compared *A Hole in My Heart* to Makavejev's and Pasolini's sexual poetry and oppositional cinema and called it an example of bourgeoise social order criticism. I have never had any trouble in piecing together narratives into a coherent form and seeing the connotative layer of/behind films, be that in the cinema of Buñuel, Pasolini, Makavejev or Lars Von Trier. In *A Hole in My Heart* however, I could not see any 'class struggle' or 'feminist criticism'. On the contrary.

Since the 2000s, there has been a growing tendency in global cinemas that aestheticises bodily violence on the audio-visual, narrative and thematic levels. Often called 'extreme cinema' (Horeck and Kendall 2011; Hobbs 2015; Frey 2016), New Extremism (Quandt 2011; Beugnet 2011), 'Feel-Bad Film' (Lübecker 2015), 'cinema du corps' (Palmer 2012), 'cinema brut' (Russell 2013) or 'extreme realism' (Williams 2009), this transnational trend was first associated with New French Extremity. Often calling forth the films of Catherine Breillat, Bruno Dumont, Philippe Grandrieux, Gaspar Noé, Michael Haneke, Ulrich Seidl or Lukas Moodysson, extreme cinemas engender visual, ethical and narrative controversies which all make the phenomenon an often-debated and questioned art form of cinema. It is no doubt that with their provocatively pornographic content (unsimulated sex), psychological cruelty (prolonged rapes) and hard-core violence (un-erotic images of sex), extreme cinemas form an active (political) dialogue between film and spectator and make us explore our own fears concerning violence and pain (Butler 2012: 29). Often deemed unwatchable and intolerable, this new category demands an ethical-affective response from the viewer, as well as prompting critical interrogation (Horeck and Kendall 2011: 8). Because of the ethical controversies and common tropes of horror cinema, Western scholarship has examined extreme films from the perspective of genre studies (Coulthard and Birks 2015; Frey 2016), spectatorship and ethics (Baker 2011; Horeck and Kendall 2011, 2012; Gronstad 2011; Butler 2012; Frey and Choi 2014), the corporeality of images (Palmer 2012; Beugnet 2012) and the institutional and extra-cinematic structure (Frey 2016; Hobbs 2018). All these investigations come down to the very debate of the representation of hard-core sex in extreme art cinema, the slippery slope between art and

INTRODUCTION   3

porn, and the very question why audiences watch such content. *Is extreme cinema art?*

Extreme Cinema = Art Cinema?

Throughout the years, art cinema has created its own conventions based on the opposition to Hollywood pulp fiction literature (Kovács 2007: 62). Overall, it has been argued that modern art films focus on the character's psychological motivation which explains the narrative's episodic structure, the lack of cause-and-effect logic as well as the viewer's temporal and spatial confusion (Bordwell 2012). Opposed to psychological complexity as the principal characteristics of art cinema, Kovács sees psychological description as irrelevant in modern narratives. He argues that in modern cinema, protagonists become abstract entities who have 'lost all (their) essential contacts to others, to the world, to the past, to the future or lost even the foundations of (their) personality' (Kovács 2007: 65). This then constructs delaying or entirely supressing solutions in the plot (Ibid., 99) and fragmentation (Ibid., 121). The viewer is 'provocatively faced with the fact that in order to understand the film, there is no need to look for reasons in the past, no need to try to expect causal chains of events extending into the future' (Kovács 2007: 63). If we follow the conventional academic approach to art cinema as a realm of psychologically motivated character-descriptions (see Bordwell 2008; King 2019; Buckland 2021) and categorise the extreme tendency in films as art, we find mentally disturbing, debauched and decadent individuals whose perversity functions as the narrative motor of the films. Perversity and art film[3] of course, as in Makavejev's *Sweet Movie* (1974), Stanley Kubrick's *A Clockwork Orange* (1972), Lanthimos' *Kynodontas* (2009) or Michael Haneke's *The Piano Teacher* (2002) – just to mention a few – are not mutually exclusive. The motivation behind the explicit depiction of perversity often serves as ideological criticism. The driving force of displaying sexual organs in such a violent and confusing way in *A Hole in My Heart*, however, remains confusing. The characters' psychological depiction (if there is any) collapses under the representation of their naked DV-embodiment.

Even more concerning is when, instead of individual psychology, scholarship looks at such characterisation as the representation of a collective-sociological Zeitgeist. While, as Lykidis (2020) demonstrated, such examination functions well in the case of Yorgos Lanthimos or Athina Rachel Tsangari, *A Hole in My Heart* poses an interpretational challenge for the viewer. Kovács's theory of abstract entities in modern cinema presupposes that the person's estrangement and the radical form of narrative

4 THE EXTREME CINEMA OF EASTERN EUROPE

go hand in hand. This argument could explain the radical elliptical narrative structure of *A Hole in My Heart*; that is, the characters' aimless sexual drifting in the film points toward the crisis they experience in the midst of neoliberal capitalism and disposability. Still, the episodic sequences that intercut between incomprehensible actions (a character vomiting into the mouth of the other and then squeezing dishwasher liquid into it) or the close-ups of vaginal reconstruction surgery, bring us back to the original question: what is the goal of portraying taboo-like imaginary in extreme cinema? Is there any connotative message behind such transgressive cinematic gestures?

Overlooking these questions, scholars have often identified art cinema with experimentation or realism. As King puts it, the goal of art film is 'commitment (…) to a greater immediate impression of realism or to a more expressive or distancing mode of presentation, although the latter is usually understood also to involve an engagement with issues of weight and substance' (King 2019: 45). If realism is that which 'foregrounds the author's specific unofficial and official market for artisanal objects' (Betz 2009: 12), we can speak about an institutional practice which propagates 'realistic' productions difficult to comprehend. In this case, seamless realism (Hayworth 2000) aims at erasing the idea of illusion by creating reality effect and frames the objective existence of human beings independent of their cultural and social background per se. In extreme cinema, however, this 'realism' includes explicit sexual imagery and indicates several overlapping points with pornography, and it often shows more analogy with exploitation cinema than (modern/post-modern) art films (see Hobbs 2018).

Michael Winterbottom's *9 songs* (2004) foregrounds a rock concert in Brixton and portrays at least eight sexual acts between the British scientist Matt (Kieran O'Brien) and the American tourist Lisa (Margo Stilley). Although the film has been heralded as 'the first [film] to scrutinise at length one couple's bedroom etiquette in a search for their identities' (Holden 2005), the lack of narrative cohesion, the openness of sexual plays and the amateur visual aesthetics of the film all push *9 Songs* towards exploitation. The conversations the characters have ('Fuck me', 'Come inside me', 'I think we will make love without using a condom') are almost always connected to sex and lack any kind of psychological depth which questions any goal of identity-searching in the film. Winterbottom attempts to overcome the insubstantial characterisation by intercutting sequences of Antarctica with the couple's love life. Matt's voice-over narration about the continent functions as an attempt to explain Winterbottom's goal to bring forth sequences of unsimulated sex. As the scientist puts it, with its topography

INTRODUCTION 5

and dynamics being the simplest on earth, the Antarctica is 'an exercise of reductionism'. Similar to sexual intercourse (as an animal instinct with the primary aim of biological procreation), the Antarctic is 'the memory of the planet', the beginning of all hi(story)'. Unfortunately, this metaphorical juxtaposition gets misplaced at the expense of sex and incoherent mise-en-scène. The diffused tonal variations, handheld cinematography, underlit, blurry images and the very lack of compositional aesthetics which cause cognitive discomfort, also work as reminders of exploitation filmmaking traditions. Consequently, as Ebert (2005) does, the objective/subjective realism of *9 Songs* can be questioned on many levels:

> [Winterbottom's film is] real, in the sense that the actors are actually doing what they seem to be doing, and real, in the sense that instead of the counterfeit moaning and panting of pornography, there is the silence of concentration and the occasional music of delight. Altogether, [the characters] go to nine concerts and hear nine songs, but this is not a concert film and the performers are mostly seen in long shot, over the heads of the crowd, which is indeed the way most of us see rock concerts. That works for realism, but it does the musicians no favors ... [Altogether] the film is fascinating, but as an experience it grows tedious; the concerts lack closeups, the sex lacks context, and Antarctica could use a few penguins. (Ebert 2005)

Others, like Kerner and Knepp (2016), discuss *9 Songs* as an 'unabashed erotic film eliciting arousal' (105) which, similar to a 'song (or poetry), needs only hints of a narrative through-line' (106). Unfortunately, with his rather subjective claims, Kerner universalises one's sensory experiences and spectatorial position. Yet, his (subjective) phenomenological approach might explain the spectatorial success of extreme cinema. Thanks to the very presence of sensual experience – that is, arousal – the author exonerates the lack of narrative and elements of precise aesthetic compositions. Rehlin (2004) states that, with its fearlessness and convention-breaking images, the film symbolises the decline of Western civilisation and works as an attack on the porn industry, yet he fails to explain *how* the film does that. In a similar vein, Catherine Breillat's *Romance* (Romance X, 1999) or *Anatomy of Hell* (Anatomie de l'enfer, 2004) both lack narrative cohesion and, instead of psychological layering, use transgressive images to shock the spectator. With its confusing story line, Clair Denis' *Trouble Every Day* (2001), as well as Philippe Grandrieux's *Sombre* (1998) and *New Life* (2002), also follows exploitation streams by giving up on causal plot development and character depth. The common ground of these examples is, on the one hand, the portrayal of explicit sex framed by handheld, shaky, blurring and underlit images and the lack of any psychological motivation on the other. Kovács's point that modern art cinema's characters become abstract entities presupposes a social-visual contextualisation which these productions' textuality dismiss. Hence, extreme cinema might become a key example of anthropocentric ideology which follows 'the process of projecting psychological depth onto characters' (Morrison 2021: 18). By doing so, scholarship often attempts to justify the place of extreme cinema in the realm of art by referencing the visual style or transgressive topics of well-known art directors.

On the other hand, when the portrayal of sexuality becomes contextualised and receives psychological-narrative drive, bodily realism seems to function grounded in art cinema. The explicit sexual imagery in Breillat's *Fat Girl*, Sacha Polak's *Hemel* (2012) or Ósima Nagisza's *In the Realm of the Senses* (Ai no korīda, 1976) all enhance narrative progression. In *Hemel*, the young girl's sexual odyssey is explained by Hemel's (Hanna Hoekstra) very motivation to receive the love she did not get in her childhood. Her confusing relationship with her father and his girlfriends, and Hemel's deliberate attempts to be loved both get a carefully composed narrative arc. Thanks to the psychological background that contextualises Hemel's behaviour and attitude towards men – her father did not want to have children and Hemel's mother committed suicide, Polak's film explains Hemel's preoccupation with her body and sexuality as proofs of her (loved) existence. Lars von Trier's provocative cinema also follows a carefully choreographed narrative structure. Although Kerner compares *9 Songs* to Trier's *Nymphomaniac* (2013) for its episodic form, the latter follows the sex-addict Joe (Stacy Martin/Charlotte Gainsbourg) for 35 years which gives the director enough space to build a multi-layered background for personal-psychological motivation. The Fibonacci-sequenced film form and intermedial-intertextual references of Trier, in contrast to Moodysson's DVCam, only add to the film's narrative cohesion. *In the Realm of the Senses* uses the colours of the *hinomaru* in its visual world to convey a metaphorical message (Nagib 2011: 186). Thus, as Krzywinska (2006) summarises,

> ... art films' co-option of hard-core sex – which continues a longstanding preoccupation with realism – is framed by aesthetic dexterity and psychological complexity so as to engage the intellect rather than, as is the case with most hard-core sexual representations, the body. (Krzywinska 2006: 227)

In the rare examples of extreme cinema, the directors foster the spectator's identification via carefully structured and contextualised narratives which, due to the cause-and-effect arc and the characters' psychological complexity, explain the use of explicit or even transgressive imagery. In the case of *9 Songs*, *Fuck Me* (Baise-moi, Virginie Despentes and Coralie

INTRODUCTION

Trinh Thi, 2000), *Twentynine Palms* (Bruno Dumont, 2003), *Sombre, New Life* and many other examples, the sudden explicit and shocking sequences are without any contextualisation and/or narrative role. What remains is sensual experience (mostly arousal by the male audience as Kernel's argument underlines it), which seems to be a form of new classification/categorisation of (extreme) films within the art canon.

Realism as a textual-narrative mode poses further questions. If the extreme is art, is *this indeed* (the) everyday reality we watch? Are the characters on screen representations and depictions of our real world? What does realism mean in and to extreme cinema? In the case of aesthetically motivated realism, the discourse must return to the Bazinian phenomenological-ontological, spatio-temporal realism and the camera's very function to read reality in a non-manipulative way and merge representation and reality. However, the blurry images and sudden camera movements which disorient the viewer in the selected examples outcast the very role of realism, that is, to capture the diegetic word in its whole objectivism. *New Life* depicts Eastern Europe as the exotic Other, a deserted, delipidated, timeless utopistic universe. *9 Songs* and *A Hole in My Heart* take place in an apartment that could be placed anywhere in the world. The diegetic space of the summer house in *Fat Girl* portrays a universal, upper-class family home. As the selected examples do not seem to fulfil any objective (location and storyworld) or subjective (psychological complexity) realism(s), the very categorisation of European extreme cinema as a modernist narrative wave can be questioned. Is European extremism art cinema or simple exploitation?

Extreme Cinema = Exploitation?

Realism – as the substantial essence of art film – has been also heralded as one of the cornerstones of exploitation cinema which, when emphasising reality, makes it even more difficult to draw an aesthetic-narrative line between art films (arthouse) and grindhouse (exploitation, camp, cult, paracinema, B-movies).

Most scholars argue that exploitation is a *style* (Waddell 2018) or institution/label (Roche 2015) which provides an oppositional vision to Hollywood as far as it cultivates taboo via the sexualisation or violation of corporeal beauty (Roche 2015; Waddell 2018: 21–2). In exploitation, sex and violence function as interconnected elements which engage with spectacles that confuse, disorient and shock the spectator, in this way generating sensationalism and profit (Weiner 2010: 51–2). Because of its focus on the commercial aspect, the capitalist mode of exploitation

8 THE EXTREME CINEMA OF EASTERN EUROPE

production overwrites aesthetic-narrative cohesion. The semantic trajectory of violence, sex, poor cinematography, bad sound and acting and flat characters (Roche 2015) foregrounds images of taboo, and the story is usually based on 'pieces of bodily sensationalism' (Waddell, 2018: 22). Due to anti-studio narratives, the story remains a cognitive challenge to comprehend. As Waddell puts it, exploitation films and examples that this style has influenced, are often 'feel bad movies' (Ibid., 22) for their incoherent narrative structure, lack of causality, and 'heightened and gritty verisimilitude' (Waddell 2018). As Baker emphasises:

> The relative lack of narrative immersion means that these films for their audiences always hover on the edge of being philosophical. There is a quality in many responses which verges on the level of wide-eyed disbelief that a film *dares* to do the things it does, leading to a 'what was *that* all about?' (Baker 2013: 234, emphasis original)

In contrast to Baker (2013) who, because of the incoherent plot and bad acting, highlights the anti-reality effect of exploitation cinema, Waddell accentuates the revelation aesthetic of exploitation film which challenges Hollywood by forgetting about the cut-away. Not only are violence and sex often portrayed in an explicit manner but thanks to the mise-en-scéne (handheld camera, genuine locations, non-professional actors, close-ups of sex/nudity and scenes of cruelty), even the technical implementation suggest pre-filmic reality (Waddell 2018: 185–6). Transgressive reality, as Carter (2010: 298) has it, is a key element to exploitation, for these films play 'on the audience's idea that the onscreen events were as close to reality as could be depicted outside of a documentary – truth, or at least the illusion of truth' (Ibid., 298). The aesthetic opposition of exploitation thus derives from the very same attitude of arthouse cinema to represent reality. The key difference between 'low' and 'high' culture is then the directors' profit-oriented approach to reality: art cinema aims to represent pro-filmic reality and taboo as devices for socio-political statements, while exploitation does the same for commercial motives (spectacle). This approach forgets about the industrial incentives of filmmaking or what Andrews (2013) calls 'the bad old story' that is, even an auteur must secure prestigious corporate distribution and compromise his/her vision for success. As demonstrated by Hawkins (2000) as well as Betz (2013), high culture (including post-war European art cinema) often trades on tropes that characterises low culture and paracinematic clusters. Whether Stanley Kubrick's *A Clockwork Orange* (1971), Roman Polanski's *The Tenant* (1976), Bernardo Bertolucci's *Last Tango in Paris* (1972) – not to mention the transgressive-provocative films of Peter Greenaway, Derek Jarman, Luis Buñuel, Jean-Luc Godard and the other European auteurs – all these

INTRODUCTION 9

filmmakers worked with exploitative-experimental images and advertisement that promised 'affect and something different' (Hawkins 2000: 23). These 'scenarios of excess', as Baker has it, call forth a search for logic which 'if found, shifts the film from pure body horror to the level of ideas' (Baker 2013: 235). It is then up to the enculturated moviegoer to decide upon the films' artistic value which puts the burden of cognitive perception and meaning-digging exclusively on the shoulders of the spectator. In case he/she does not understand the cultural crossovers of cinema and/or dismisses the film for any reason, directors (and the cultural discourse) often blame the viewer for his/her less sophisticated nature. As I emphasised elsewhere,

> accusing the spectator and criticizing her/his taste is always easier than facing the fact that the production has no deeper layer. More troubling is the fact that critics are informed by the frame of European art film and anti-Hollywood cinema to such an extent, that they desperately praise every film that features a long shot and/or a depressed protagonist in the leading role. This is how imbecile cinema gets boxed as art. (Batori 2017)

Does then extreme cinema, as Frey (2014) suggests, depend on the director's intention to produce 'something more sophisticated' than horror and the consumer's capability 'of rarefied taste to appreciate larger, deeper meanings beyond the obvious horror?' (157). Again, Frey's standpoint that extreme cinema depends on these two hermeneutic transformations relies on the old-school differentiation of 'highbrow' and 'lowbrow' cultures and it very easily (and sadly) assumes that the horror genre has less artistic worth. Furthermore, the approach to and definition of art cinema as an oppositional discourse to the 'lowbrow' builds on an anthropocentric ideology that, as Morrison (2021) has it, is based on the 'trinity of (character-centred) meaning, (dogmatic) critic, and (enculturated) viewer' (20). This critical approach to art cinema has

> a twofold ideological achievement: the disciplining-into-meaning of a form that would otherwise complicate anthropocentrism by showing character as an inadequate centre, and the disciplining into meaning-production of viewers who might otherwise come to critique an inexplicable and disordered world in which politics and identity are figured as contingencies. (Morrison 2021: 16–17)

In Morrison's reading, expressive realism re-creates the anthropocentric ideology that 'human character both *discovers* meaning and *is* meaning' (emphasis original, Ibid., 17). Consequently, 'in a kind of extended pathetic fallacy, the world becomes only a means of discovering a mythologised version of the human subject' (Ibid., 17). Instead of anxiously trying to explain art *into* a film or other artworks, it might be worth looking at the socio-historic and political Zeitgeist that has provided fertile ground for such extreme representations in art cinema. In this regard, commercial aspects cannot be overlooked. In the present-day neoliberal-consumerist age where VoD-s, social platforms, online video sharing portals, television and blockbuster films all fight for our attention, art cinema's only chance to compete with such a tsunami of visual entertainment is to present forbidden themes and shocking material. Extreme cinema is thus an economic phenomenon, a strategy that seeks alternative routes of circulation and distribution in the global system of capitalism (Herbert 2006). After all, as Wood has it,

> At the heart of every film – highbrow or low – is a promise of solace or excitement, one of the endless catalog of vicarious pleasures absent from ordinary life. The desire for escape or revelation which drew exploitation moviegoers into the grubby palaces of education and bottom-feeding vice are only less refined versions of the same desires felt by a 1930s shop girl attending an Astaire and Rogers musical, a '50s family of four slurping Cokes at the Miracle Mile drive-in, a '70s film student in a crowded classroom seeking vicarious flight from the encroaching responsibilities of adulthood. (Wood 1999: 11)

Sensation, shock and controversy have all worked well as marketing strategies throughout the history of cinema and one cannot blame film directors who, in the hope of commercial success, use a film form that mixes up horror, porn, snuff and exploitation. The question is why film critics and scholars praise and propagate such extremism in (art) cinema?

Similar to Coco who doesn't 'get' art, I think that critics often follow the dogmatic 'art' paradigm of niche film festivals and propagate these events' desperate attempt to sell art cinema in the blockbuster-driven market. After all, 'scandals can break, but much more often, make festivals' (Frey 2016: 67). Coco's statement that present-day art is often more about the market than talent and that it revolves around the very gesture to construe meaning into an artwork, has some valid points when compared to extreme art cinemas. The heated debate on Coco's articles on Reddit that questions the writer's competence in art demonstrates that scholarly debates seem to follow the dogmatic guides of valued festivals, niche exhibitions and well-known artists that dictate current trends. Instead of the explaining art *into* something, I suggest to take a step back and look at extreme cinema as a phenomenon that enumerates several quality films while it also embraces examples that would simply fit the exploitation (or even trash) label. Similar to Palmer (2006) and Hobbs (2018) who explain extreme art films as the hybridisation of lowbrow and highbrow traditions,

INTRODUCTION 11

I see the extreme tendency as a fusion of artistic traditions and grindhouse trends. In this postmodern marriage of art and exploitation of extreme cinemas, the latter often overwrites the former. Consequently, not all extreme films fit the label of narrative (art) cinema, nor can all European exploitation films be grouped as extreme films. This book sees the difference between exploitation-like art cinema (that I call 'wannabe art') and European art cinema in its very attitude and aim towards narrative causality and cohesion, as well as its justification and ethical responsibility for its mediated images. In other words, filmmakers must make their claim clear and understandable for the audience and justify the transgressive vision's presence in the syuzhet. Without such markers of intent, extreme films run the risk of being misunderstood, miscategorised and furtherly advertised as a distinct wave of art cinema.

Cinematic extremism has a very rich socio-political history and transgression on screen is nothing new. To me, extreme cinema is extreme *because the discourse* around it is *extreme*. In other words, I see extreme cinema as a discursive category (rather than a style, genre or a transnational wave) that dwells on the canonisation of journalists, critics, scholars, festival directors and filmmakers' own explanations and justifications for transgressive-shocking sequencing on screen. Extreme cinemas are extreme because the critical discourse (very often unconditionally) praise them. This raises a series of moral questions, not only about the responsibility of cultural commentators, but the contemporary value and highbrow categorisation of art.

Is Eastern *European* Cinema *European?*

When it comes to the scholarly debate on *European* extreme cinema, Eastern Europe often remains in the academic blind spot of any European cultural discourse. Although part of the European Union and the Schengen area, Eastern Europe does not seem to fit into the homogenous discourse with/on the West. It has been more than 30 years since the fall of the Berlin Wall, yet, as 'Western Europe's Other' (Gott and Herzog 2014), the region is still associated with clichéd forms of representation, corruption as well as aggression (see Iordanova 2003, 2011, 2013). Does the region belong to Europe (as its political positioning suggests), and/or should it be discussed as a semi-independent socio-cultural unit?

The rare examples of those scholarly debates on European extreme cinemas that mention directors from the post-socialist region, all focus on *A Serbian Film* or György Pálfi's 2006 film *Taxidermia* (see Frey 2016: 46, 73–5; Kerner and Knapp 2017). This limits the extreme film productions of a whole region to two films. Hobbs (2018) for instance argues that by investigating a series of under-explored films, his work offers a comprehensive image that overcomes historical and geographical restrictions and presents extreme cinema through a pan-*European* lens. Yet his transnational perspective overlooks Eastern European directors and cinema and, thus, limits his European analysis to France and Italy as well as the films of well-known European auteurs such as Michael Haneke and Lars von Trier. In the edited collection of Tanya Horeck and Tina Kendall, *The New Extremism in Cinema. From France to Europe*, only Michael Goddard (2013: 82–93) touches upon the region. Given the 17 chapters of the book, this absence clearly demonstrates the limited cultural and geographical lens of (European) scholarship. More worrying is that, by examining 'the primitivist clichés associated with Eastern Europe' (Ibid., 91) through the lens of Ulrich Seidl and Philippe Grandrieux, Goddard emphasises the (visual) confirmation of the region as the backward sibling on screen. Although his study very well outlines how the opposition of West and East becomes unstable in *Import/Export* (2007) and *La vie nouvelle* (2002), even the author himself acknowledges that 'these gestures of resistance may seem small in relation to the otherwise bleak environments' (Ibid., 90). Such examination, though fruitful in introducing the Western perspective and directorial gaze, omits to examine the region from within. That is, *how do Eastern European extreme directors see their own region*?

While there is no doubt that violence in (Western) films has increased over the past fifty years and films display 'more blood, violence, guns, and gore than ever before' (Markey and French 2014: 169), transgressive imagery has always been present in post-socialist Eastern European cinemas. In other words: post-1989 Eastern European cinema has always been extreme. This is one of the main reasons that prompted me to dig deeper in the origins of visceral practice and violent sexualised forms of representations on (Eastern) European screen.

As far as I can recall, my first memories of the region's cinema are connected to suppressed and raped women on screen. The numerous torture porn narratives provided such discomfort that after a while, I did not even want to watch Eastern European art films. I somehow came to the conclusion that the narrative key to (and limited success of) Eastern European art cinema resides in the way it recycles the very story of post-socialist poverty, rape and testosterone-brimmed masculinity. The slow cinema style, mixed up with pro-filmic miserabilism, sexism and the display of a region that lags centuries behind from its Western counterpart, only added to my visionary receipt of the 'Eastern European art film'. Since my personal experience is radically different from the stereotyped representations of

INTRODUCTION   13

the region, the images of oppressed bodies on Eastern screen inevitably made me look at the socio-political processes that are common in and peculiar of the region. Why does post-socialist Eastern European art cinema aestheticise violence and where does the representation as a backward region stem from?

I am aware that Eastern Europe is not a homogeneous entity but a historically, linguistically, socially, culturally and geographically diverse territory. As such, any categorisation that unites the post-socialist countries under the same label is in danger of being reductive. Hence, the book accounts for the region's socialist legacy and the transition to democracy as historio-political milestones which connect the once-socialist countries of Europe. Within the book, 'Eastern Europe' references the post-socialist countries in Europe that during socialism had a similar politico-economic and social structure based on the Marxist-Leninist dogma of egalitarianism and later went through the capitalist transition. The several decades-long cultural, military and economic oppression of the Soviet Union is discussed as a form of colonisation. Conversely, the post-1989 transition period and the post-2004 neoliberal epoch are analysed as forms of capitalist re- and post-colonisation.

Eastern Extreme: A Post-Socialist, (Post-)Colonialist Reaction

It is important to note that, while the present book touches upon tropes of Western European extreme cinema, it is to frame the discourse of extremity and the transgressive *representation of genders* in Eastern European films. Hence, the post colonial theoretical perspective – the main approach of the book – aims to add to the understanding of stylistic, historical and socio-logical processes which frame extreme representation in the region. I am aware that, as Hall (2003) argues, colonised societies were not colonised in the same ways, and postcolonial societies are not postcolonial in the same way. Still, the (post-)colonial examination can be a helpful approach to highlighting the centrality of 'patterns of global politics and power in the early modern and modern worlds' (Ibid., 3), while shifting focus from the 'supraregional colonial enterprise' to locally experienced ways of colonial situations (van Dommelen 2012: 398). Although the examination of Soviet occupation over Eastern European socialist countries in a colonial context is rather risky – the insignificant question of race (Bhabha 1984), together with the Soviet Union's varying degree of economic, cultural and political influence in different parts of the Eastern area (Mazierksa et al. 2014: 7–8) do not distinctly recall global colonialisation processes – the Soviet

Union's lengthy influence and control over its satellite countries provides a fruitful context to examine the subjected-dominant dichotomy and its psychological and cultural aftermath in Eastern Europe.

While the disciplinary mechanisms of the Soviet (colonising) power by means of political legislation, military influence and economic exploitation have been widely discussed in scholarship, less attention has been given to the analysis of gender and identity in occupied Eastern European socialist countries. For this reason, the present book focuses on the body as an instrument of the colonial rule since, as argued throughout, the origins of extreme violence on the contemporary Eastern European screen can be found and traced back to the socio-corporeal oppression of women during the decades-long totalitarian rule.

Colonialism does, of course, not only denote political and economic characteristics but various forms of social, cultural and psychological oppression. In a similar vein to Bosworth and Flavin's (2007) standpoint that the symbiosis of colonialism and culture has been widely overlooked in scholarship, in his work *Colonialism and Culture* (1992), Nicholas Dirk emphasises the importance of studying culture in colonised societies for, as he states,

> Although colonial conquest was predicated on the power of superior arms, military organization, political power, and economic wealth, it was also based on a complexly related variety of cultural technologies. Colonialism not only has had cultural effects that have too often been either ignored or displaced into the inexorable logics of modernization and word capitalism, it was itself a cultural project of control … culture was what colonialism was all about. (Dirks 1992: 3)

Dirks understands colonialism as a cultural project and culture as a colonial formation whose linkage helps to 'realize cultural intervention and influence were antidotes to the brutality of domination' (Ibid., 4–5). In this context, culture acts as a trope of violation, which also recalls Scott's approach to (authoritarian) history as a gender-biased structure (Scott 1999, 2010).

Connecting the two, my approach to understanding violence on screen rests on the examination of cultural colonialist (and later post-and self-colonialist) gender structures. In this manner, forms of colonial representation become a key factor. As Dirk highlights, in order to classify an authoritarian form of control, representation in the colonial context was and is violent, for torture becomes a weapon of terror through the culture of colonialism: 'Brute torture on the body of the colonised was not the same as the public exhibition of a colonised body, but these two moments of colonial powers shared in more than they differed' (Dirks 2000: 5).

INTRODUCTION   15

Colonialism, in this sense, deprives the colonised of their (cultural) identity – including his/her language, national education, living environment and corporeality – and calls forth a new, forced identity dictated by the central political power (Panikkar 2003). Kirsten Holst Petersen and Anna Rutherford (1986) for instance, coin the term 'double colonisation' to describe the way women simultaneously experience the oppression of colonialism (and colonialist representation) and patriarchy. In a colonial discourse, they state, women's representation is subjected to patriarchal values. The gendered nature of colonisation and the socially structured violence against women trigger a series of psychological patterns 'which include self-hatred, sense of inferiority, helplessness and despair, mutual distrust and hostility, and psychological distress and madness' (Moane 1999: 20). This 'internalized oppression', as Moane has it, is strongly connected to questions of body, sexuality and nation. The term is analogous to Alexander Kiossev's (2011) concept of self-colonisation as a theory for cultures that succumbed to the West European cultural power without being conquered militarily. These states stand under foreign cultural supremacy and voluntarily enter the colonial structure and become 'extra-colonial periphery' (Ibid.). As Kiossev summarises this process, while these nations absorbed the values of the centre,

> ... they imported something else: the ... parodical image of themselves ... They were compelled to internalize these embarrassing images precisely as they were coming from their source of recognition and were charged with its authority. All this fostered a controversial nation-building process: one that borrowed models hand in hand with resistance against the models. Such borrowings were meant to Europeanize yet at the same time they stood in the way of actual cultural emancipation as they never failed to recycle the secondary, submissive, and opaque role of small peripheral nations on the world scene, thus failing to acknowledge their sovereignty, authenticity, and autonomy. (Kiossev 2011)

Tlostanova (2017) calls this process 'the postsocialist drama' in which the initial euphoria to return to Europe has soon shifted to 'discovering [the] secondary status, the more traditionally subaltern fate of the non-European Soviet ex-colonies' (5). The progressivist paradigm to always keep a sufficient lag between Eastern European countries and Western Europe, together with the socialist and pre-socialist memory of the Eastern nations and the trust in neoliberal capitalism as a form of legitimate modernity all doomed the region 'to the next twenty-five years of stagnation, catching up and forever emerging (Tlostanova 2017: 7). The Western media interpretations of Eastern European countries often broadcast sensational, violent and poverty-ridden images of the region, something now exacerbated by the brutal imagery of the Russian-Ukrainian war. These negative descriptions leave the region in a postcolonial, post-imperial, post-socialist and secondary Eurocentric position. At the same time, as will be discussed in Chapter 6, the self-perception of the region seems to preserve a sense of inferiority which gets manifested in Eastern Europe's own visual downgrading self-portrayal. This cultural discrepancy between East and West seems to be a profitable construction in cinemas for, as Ognjanovic puts it, West buys

> … imperfect, 'authentic' local product[s] believing that some humble 'savages' make [them], without realising that these products are industrial products designed for a niche market. At the same time, consumers – for example, in big festivals – buy allegedly 'authentic' films that fit into their presumed notions of a 'local style'. (emphasis in original, Ognjanovic: 2015: 82)

Post-Colonialist Sexuality: Eastern European Supererogation

In the development of becoming fully European, sexuality becomes a key component (Navickaité 2015: 123). Regarded as 'too individualistic and bourgeois' (Heitlinger 1996: 88); issues of sexuality, sexual assault, personal autonomy and self-determination became non-issues in the socialist public discourse (Buckley 1989). Although the amount of sexual violence against women shows similar figures to the West – in 1966, about 1.7% of all criminal convictions were results of rape, with 85% of these acts being considered assaulted rape[4] (Morrison 2018: 124) – sexual abuse remained a highly considered taboo. As Brzozowska highlights, 'most of the state socialist regimes had a very conservative, puritanical attitude to sexual matters, very close to that of the Catholic and Orthodox Churches' (2015: 694). In this ideological context, the common understanding of art was to serve the official ideology of the state. Topics that would promote imperialistic artistic manifestations and/or go against the interest of society were closely monitored and banned (Kiss 2018: 235–7). Such content was pornography, the critique of authorities and politics, talk about dissidents and any other subjects[5] that were termed 'bourgeoise' (Schrober 2009: 52).

The lack of emancipation and gender equality – the attributes of Western civilisation – and the representation of the region as aggressive, violent and un-civilised territory, together with the current waves of postcolonial nationalisms put the Eastern European Other even more backwards. Anikó Imre (2002) also sees the sexual violation of women as a result of the recurring national failure to be European. That is, the malfunction to belong to (West) Europe registers in the sexual identity of

INTRODUCTION   17

Eastern European men as a form of emasculation (74) which evokes sexual essentialism and traditional forms of masculinity. Women, on the other hand, have seemingly accepted their suppressed role and the masculine viewpoint, and have learned to conform to traditional sexual roles:

> ... the woman protagonist, beautiful, often racialized, ravenously sexual but at the same time submissive and nurturing, victimized and idealized, embodies the male intellectual's attempt to both represent and anchor his slipping masculine identity in the female body. The symbolic emasculation that intellectuals had suffered as a result of a long history of inferiority to the real Europe, exacerbated by Soviet colonization and co-optation by the communist state, required representation and compensation in the realm of gender. (Imre 2008: 276)

In this socialist socio-political context,[6] women developed supererogation, a sense of self-sacrifice (Miroiu 1996). Michaela Miroiu analyses the old Romanian legend of the Arges monastery which tells the story of the renovation of a convent whose walls collapse after each day of building. In his dream, Manole, the master of the builders is told that the construction will be unsuccessful unless one of the sisters or wives of the builders gets walled in. Fearing his own and his men's life, Manole decides to build in his wife Ana, who is forced to die within painful circumstances and whose restless crying, according to the legend, can still be heard around the monastery.[7]

Building on the interpretation of Mircea Eliade (1970) who states that Ana did not die but remained alive within the walls, Miroiu draws a parallel between the patriarchal society of socialist Romania and women's position within it:

> While in the Western world women struggled to assert themselves as individuals, as powerful and creative people, as different and able to create specific values, we experienced out self-creation in the walls of monuments built for the glory of a totalitarian megalomaniac power ... Behind this ... "reality" the real intention was: to be forced. Forced to live in a definite place ... forced to marry and to have at least four children, forced to work, forced to enrol in ideological courses ... forced to glorify the "supermaster." ... Our consent and our free choice were out of the question. (Miroiu 1996: 138–9)

Supererogation, a peculiar behaviour developed by women during the socialist era turned into duty, which generated a 'necrophiliac ideology' (Ibid., 40) governed by the lack of self-expression, respect, dignity, self-individuation and an overall colonised, subjected identity. As I argue, rape and women's physical abuse, which were strongly considered taboos in the socialist discourse became metaphors of supererogation, that is, a reaction to the loss of control over one's body and actions. If, as many Western theorists agree, the nation is projected as a female and the state a masculine structure (see Patterman 1996; Yuval-Davis 1998), the torture and rape of female bodies on the socialist screen functions as an oppressive act that aims to punish and suppress women's bodies.

The extreme representations of gender structures on screen can be a metaphor of the weakening of post-transition patriarchal structures. Questions arise why the extreme trend in Eastern Europe dwells on rape and why filmmakers employ graphic content that, by the sexual exploitation of women, strengthen orientalist constructions on the region? Is sexual brutality on screen a response to the global stream of extreme cinema or, do we find very region-specific features in these visual texts?

The book argues that subversive representations of the body on the Eastern European screen can be viewed as a post-socialist gesture of self-punishment. This is to say that, with the death of the socialist father figure (Andreescu 2011), slave narratives (Juhász 2012) describe a process of collective mourning whereby the European, post-socialist nations re-articulate their role in the building of socialism and punish themselves for their passivity in the past. In enacting such a masochistic process of national mourning, the extreme films often lack verbal interaction – the protagonists of the films are mute or incapable of expressing themselves. Using their bodies as channels for communication that are ultimately destroyed, the narratives portray authoritarian games that, by de-coding the allegorical language of the film, reveal a commentary on the recent socio-historical processes of the region and its conception of statehood. The self-Orientalist, self-colonialist approach on screen which presents Eastern Europe as a dangerous, third-world territory, also reveals a nation identifying itself as suppressed entity. The transgressive cinema of Eastern Europe is a reflection of the oppressive socio-cultural and political set-up of the Soviet Union as former coloniser, but at the same time, the region references the new, neoliberal colonising structure in similarly violent metaphors and allegories on screen. As with every post colonial society, getting rid of the trauma of the colonial wound often recalls the decades-long experience of colonial rule (see Tlostanova 2017: 16). Sexual violence, brutal depictions of rape and corporeal punishment in Eastern European art cinema are constitutive of the ideological set-up of the socialist era, while these visual-textual gestures reflect on the sudden 1989 capitalist transformation that, by working along the formula of corporeal self-punishment and victimhood, show striking similarities to the socialist identities on screen. Consequently, the reconstruction of the formal public domain and the (re-)birth of the patriarchal civil society in post-1989

INTRODUCTION   19

Eastern Europe encoded new dimensions of inferiority and domesticity (Watson 1993a) and gave birth to an explicit cinema whose sharp representation of rape and other forms of sexual assault became a code of the self-colonised and victimised self-presentation.

About This Book

Analysing all forms of explicit screen violence on Eastern European screen would go beyond the scope of this book. Because of the extremely large number of films that feature extreme bodily violence and various forms of erotic-aggressive spectacle, such a detailed discourse would be an impossible task to carry out. From the works of Walerian Borowczyk to Miroslav Slaboshpytskyi's *Tribe* (*Plemya*, 2014), Pintilie's *Touch Me Not* (2018) and the more recent *The Next 365 Days* (Bialowas and Mandes, 2022), my ever-growing list of Eastern European extreme films (up to the point of writing) includes 1,336 examples. In the light of this, one of the biggest challenges was to select films from such an extremely rich catalogue.

Rather than opting for country-by-country descriptions, I decided to investigate past and current trends in Eastern European extreme cinema. Films have been chosen on the basis of thematic intersections, reflections on socio-historical processes and their state of recognition in scholarship. I have chosen to discuss the mix of well-known films and possibly unfamiliar cinematic examples, so that any reader has clear points of reference.

The book mainly focuses on forms of rape on screen. It is not only my personal trauma that triggered this choice of topic, but the nauseating magnitude of sexual violence against females on the Eastern European screen. I see rape on screen as a symbolic gesture associated with cultural, economic, historical, political and social processes. Therefore, the book negotiates female corporeality, torture and other transgressive acts in the context of the socialist period, post-socialist/transition epoch and post-2004 neoliberalism. Because I see the female body on screen as representative of the nation, extremism is discussed as illustrative of the region's fractured self-perception and self-presentation.

This book's interdisciplinary approach draws on feminist theory, cultural geography and history, gender studies, trauma theory, discourse analysis and further sources within and outside film theory. Because I see cultural history in relation to social power – what Shohat and Stam (1994) described as polycentric multiculturalism – the main methodological base of Eastern European extreme cinema is, as described above, postcolonial theory.

Chapter 1 focuses on the films of the Yugoslav Black Wave, with special attention given to Dusan Makavejev's *WR: Mysteries of the Organism* and *Sweet Movie*. Makavejev's self-critique of political modernism is based on the aesthetic excess of obscene sensual pleasures which made him one of the most provocative authors of the Eastern European screen. Chapters 2 to 6 focus on the period of transition. The end of this epoch is marked by the acquisition of most post-socialist members states to the European Union in 2004.

Chapter 2 explores the extreme cinema of the transition period (1991–2004) and the changing perception of gender roles within the new, capitalist economic system. Drawing on the theory of emasculation and feminisation of trauma, this section investigates the continued maleocracy and explicit and violent imagery of female suppression in what I call the 'cinema of castration'. The analysis of the continued aesthetic and thematic characteristic of explicit brutality in the selected examples (*The Conjugal Bed, Pleasant Days, She-Shaman*) is framed within a postcolonial (post-socialist) and neo-colonial (accession to the European Union) reading. Chapter 3 focuses on animal torture in global cinemas (*Japón, The Cove, I Stand Alone, Carné*) and the possible connotative layer of animal death on screen. The discussion is followed by animal cruelty on the Eastern European screen and its symbolic role as representative of the colonising historical reality and female body. As argued within this chapter, the material and figurative animal-imagery is strongly linked to femininity in the region's cinema. While focusing on *Somnambulance, Angel Exit* and *Alone* as selected examples from this corpus, animality is discussed as a discourse that foregrounds foreign aggression and Eastern European victimisation.

The heated debate on the difference of extreme cinema and exploitation in scholarship prompted me to set up the category of 'wannabe art' and 'extreme cinema'. 'Wannabe art', as shown in Chapter 4 through the examination of Breillat's *Anatomy of Hell*, uses elements of (s)exploitation (as well as trash when it comes to filmic form) and a non-narrative structure whose cinematic codes are built on pure sexual spectacle. In contrast, extreme cinema in my reading encompasses examples from the art cinema canon that, while mixing (s)exploitation and other grindhouse elements with modern art narration, communicate a comprehensible as well as connotative narrative. Chapter 4 discusses this distinction further when focusing on Želimir Žilnik's *Marble Ass* and Alexo Petkov's *Baklava* as examples of 'wannabe art' of the region. It is important to mention that I by no means aim to judge the value of any film. I do not agree with the distinction of 'low' vs 'high' forms of art and, as a

INTRODUCTION   21

grindhouse film-fan and scholar, I genuinely enjoy consuming all forms of cinemas. The book only aims to raise awareness of *how* and *why* the superficial praise of all films that employ explicit imagery holds dangers.

Chapter 5 is dedicated to the sexual (national) body of contemporary Serbian cinema. Although *A Serbian Film* and *The Life and Death of a Porno Gang* have been examined by Western scholarship, they have not been theorised from within, that is from an Eastern European perspective. Therefore, the new Serbian cinema is discussed through the lenses of the Balkan's cinematic heritage and regional historio-social processes. This chapter also focuses on the films' pseudo-snuff approach to ideological criticism.

Finally, Chapter 6 focuses on female subjugation and oppression as reflections of the neoliberal age. It analyses the 'double form of neoliberal subjugation' in *Slovenian Girl*, *Bibliothèque Pascal*, *Touchless* and *Ryna*. This part of the book discusses the role of emasculated, impotent male figures who, while being colonised by Western powers themselves, suppress their female relatives via various forms of bodily exploitation.

With no major book on Eastern European extreme cinemas currently available on the market, this monograph, no doubt, is imperfect. It cannot possibly include all the films and literature it would desire. As a point of departure, however, its intention is to shape understanding of Eastern European (extreme) cinemas and be an entrant for further investigations.

CHAPTER 1

The Cradle of Eastern Extremism: Sexual Oppression and the Yugoslav Black Wave

Despite the harsh socialist censorship, the Eastern European modernist waves often called forth subversive topics and experimental aesthetics that did not follow the Zhdanovist dogmas. The new waves in cinemas that emerged in the 1960s in (Eastern) Europe – including the Czechoslovak, Hungarian, or Polish New Wave – all had tendencies that criticised the alienated side of the individual and her/his ideological oppression through the stark representation of bodies. One of the most outstanding cinemas of rebellion in this case is the Yugoslav Black Cinema. As a trend within the Yugoslav New Film (*novi film*, 1961–72), Black Cinema promoted stylistic experimentation and the expression of contemporary themes that crossed censorship (Goulding 2002: 66–7). These films 'touched the raw nerves of the Yugoslav collective constitution' (Schrober 2009: 52) by featuring rape, prostitution, ethnic and religious conflicts and torture on screen, while harshly criticising the country's socialist leadership. The reason for choosing the body as metaphoric device, as Schrober notes, was that

> In state-socialist societies … the private sector and privacy were regarded by the authorities with general suspicion and were subjected to repression, control and even destruction … It was precisely because of this general suspicion hanging over anything 'private' that the focus of some of the protagonists of the Black Cinema on love, sexuality, intimacy and sensuality had such a politically explosive force. (Schober 2009: 51)

Black Wave filmmakers were, however, not anti-communists (Sudar 2014). Many of them were influenced by the Praxis philosophers of Zagreb and Belgrade who criticised dialectical materialism, the country's market-oriented reforms and authoritarian framework and called for creating Marxism (Dragovic-Soso 2002: 23–8). The young generation of Black Wave filmmakers thus simply confronted the orthodox tendencies of the Yugoslav state by producing a ruthless critique on contemporary reality, while aiming for a better socialism (DeCuir 2010: 88–9). Because the

THE CRADLE OF EASTERN EXTREMISM   23

government promoted Partisan action movies, these highly controversial –
and often experimental – films were often censored and banned (Vucetic
2018: 75).[1] For instance, Lazar Stojanović's *Plastic Jesus* (*Plastični Isus*,
1971) resulted in the director being put in jail. According to authorities, the film propagated anarchic, anarcho-liberal and anti-communist
discourse (Kunicki et al. 2018: 271). The movie remained banned until
1990 (Mortimer 2009). Stojanović's graduation film portrays a Croatian
filmmaker whose everyday actions – that include running in full-frontal
nudity on the streets of Belgrade and numerous explicit sexual scenes –
are intercut with archival footage of anti-communist Chetniks, Yugoslav
partisans and Nazi soldiers. The deeply layered metaphoric form of *Plastic
Jesus* criticises personal freedom, the ethnic tension among South-Slavs
and the personal cult of Josip Broz Tito (Levi 2009). In his nondialectical
strategy, Stojanović equates Tito and Hitler and communism and fascism
by incorporating documentary footages of the advancement of Yugoslav
partisan forces and the German army in the World War II that coexist
within the larger antihierarchical narrative. In one of the numerous associate montage sequences, Stojanović uses archival footage of Tito's speech
in which he calls forth the 1968 events in France and Czechoslovakia
and argues that socialism cannot be built without a man. In the next
scene, the main protagonist, Tom (Tomislav Gotovac) gets arrested for
his counter-revolutionary activities, and he is forced to get rid of his long
hair and beard. The images of his shaving by a policeman are cross-cut
with sequences of marching Nazi soldiers and later with archival footages
of the Soviet forces' occupation of Berlin and the defeat of Hitler. The
Kuleshovian structure that Stojanović uses to stress the similarities of
ideologies and dictatorships and the dichotomy of black and white and
coloured images that juxtapose past and present within the same sequence,
call forth Tom's absolute subjected position within an oppressive political
structure that does not allow sexual, nor political freedom and aim at
bodily alternation to communicate the message of repression.

   Besides images of torture, sexuality and (gang) rape were reappearing
motifs in the Yugoslav cinema of the 1960s and 1970s (Vuković 2019).
In Miroslav Mika Antić's *Breakfast with the Devil* (*Doručak sa đavolom*,
1971), a peasant woman gets raped by a pro-Stalinist man in the attic; in
Živojin Pavlović's *Red Wheat* (*Rdeče klasje*, 1970), a state official rapes a
mother who sacrifices herself for her virgin daughter; in Bate Čengić's *The
Role of My Family in the World Revolution* (*Uloga moje porodice u svjetskoj
revoluciji*, 1971), a mother is sexually assaulted by communist intruders;
and in Krsto Papić's *Handcuffs* (*Lisice*, 1969), the virgin, young and obedient bride is brutally raped by a local politician. This list is, of course, not

24 THE EXTREME CINEMA OF EASTERN EUROPE

exclusive as out of the 286 Yugoslav films between 1961 and 1972, approximately 15% feature rape (Vuković 2018). The common point in most of these productions is sacrifice through rape. In *Breakfast with the Devil*, the female protagonist obediently surrenders to the will of the communist man who collects the wheat in the village; in *Red Wheat*, a mother protects her daughter by sacrificing her own body as sexual object. In *The Role of My Family in the World Revolution*, the rape of the mother happens during the confiscation of parts of the family's house. After her rape, the young bride in *Handcuffs* prays to God for forgiveness and punishment. Later, the celebrating males attack her for dishonouring her husband and kill the young woman. Rape in these films thus stands as an allegory for physical and ideological abuse (Vuković 2018) that supresses the female body and so the nation via political power.

This connotative message is further accentuated via images of prolonged mass rapes in socialist cinema. In Drašković's *Horoscope* (*Horoskop*, 1969), the kiosk-girl's rape by the local gang happens in the barren, deserted landscape; in Miloš Radivojević's *Crazy World of Ours* (*Bube u glavi*, 1970), the woman's rape is framed in the middle of a forest; in Evald Schorm's *The Seventh Day, the Eighth Night* (*Den sedmý – osmá noc*, 1969) the act is shown in the woods, while in Živojin Živojin's *The Return* (*Povratak*, 1966), the young girl's abuse is represented on the street. The transgressive imagery in these films is strongly linked to the national landscape that gets marked by female mass rape (Vuković 2018). The scenes of abuse and their realistic staging – the wobbling, high-angle handheld camera takes that capture the acts in long shots – share a similar visual aesthetic and allegorical connotation. In *Horoscope*, the rape of Milka (Milena Dravic) is accompanied by the diegetic sound of clashing rocks. The young girl gets trapped in the circle of half-naked men who, as predators, pass her body around, while they tear her clothes. The action is devoid of any spoken words. Instead of verbal language, Drašković accentuates the extreme nature of the act through various camera angles and a rhythmic montage that illustrate Milka's trapped position. Thanks to the fast-paced editing, this sequence enumerates various frames from long shots to extreme close ups of the girl's naked thighs and breasts. After she has given up fighting, the camera focuses on Milka's crying close-up and the naked backs of the men around her. This realistic staging gives the transgressive act a documentary-like atmosphere and, besides channelling an absolute spectatorial alignment, it invokes the metaphor of the eradication of the body of the nation. In the three-minute-long mass rape scene of *Crazy World of Ours*, the representation of the abuse shows a striking resemblance to *Horoscope*. Although the staging is different – the violence happens

THE CRADLE OF EASTERN EXTREMISM   25

in a forest – Radivojević does not use any spoken words in the scene. What is more, in order to contrast the transgressive imagery with the peacefulness of the nature, the director mutes the scene to the idealistic, calmed sounds of birds chirping. In this way, the unflinching, shocking act in these films gets embedded into silence. On the one hand, silence represents the muteness of the female body and its incapability to take any stance of resistance[2] during rape. On the other, silence is strongly linked to the nation's grief and trauma. The allegorical device of supererogation is visually contextualised within a transgressive visual imagery that, with prolonged sequences of rape, silence and realistic mise-en-scéne, implicitly invoke the trauma of the nation.

Sexual Supererogation and Extreme Eroticism: The Case of Dušan Makavejev

Dušan Makavejev – one of the most prominent figures of socialist Eastern European extreme cinema – also uses explicit sexuality and associative montage sequences as tools for political criticism (Testa 1990). Influenced by the psychoanalytic theories of Wilhelm Reich (1897–1957), his obsessive themes are a 'craving for individual spiritual freedom channelled through tragic efforts to break sexual frustration, which is caused by the political totalitarianism of an oppressive social system' (Stojanović 2014: 79). Wilhelm Reich, one of Sigmund Freud's favourite students, tried to reconcile psychoanalysis with Marxism (Sudar 2014: 46). He argued that *orgastic potency* – the ability to lose the self in an uninhibited orgasm by releasing the emotions from the muscles – is key to one's health (Corrington 2003). After his migration to the United States, Reich started to experiment with orgone accumulators. These human-sized wooden boxes, as he stated, concentrate the orgone – units of cosmic energy – that heal one's body and energise the nervous system by means of producing microscopic orgone units in the cabinet. The Orgone Energy Accumulators – together with his books – were then destroyed when Reich got into conflict with the Food and Drug Administration (FDA), who filed for an injunction to stop the circulation of his books and orgone boxes (Corrington 2003). In 1956, Reich got arrested for violating the injunction and was imprisoned for two years where he eventually died of heart failure. Reich – a controversial psychoanalyst who was expelled from the International Psychoanalytic Association (IPA), the German Communist Party and was constantly accused of scientific charlatanism – was an advocator of a sexual revolution that would erase the authoritarian ideology by enduring sexual relationships (King 1992: 87). He argued that taboos on childhood sexuality that are embedded within the patriarchal family's authoritarian structure are ideological weapons that serve to reinforce the authoritarian political structures of class society (MacBean 1972: 3). In other words, in his theory the suppression of sexuality would lead to the individual's internalised sexual repression. Liberating people and society thus meant reaching free sexuality and 'unmitigated satisfaction of mature genital sexuality' (Ibid., 4.)

As a Marxist thinker living and working within the confines of an oppressive regime, Makavejev – an outsider himself – used the Reichian framework to convey a harsh criticism on the Yugoslav regime (Mortimer 2009). A common theme in his films is the sexual repression of men who get liberated by sexually unconstrained women through sexual contact (Sudar 2014: 47).

In *WR: Mysteries of the Organism* (*W.R. – Misterije organizma* 1971), he uses the Reichian ideas of sexual freedom and bioenergy to channel liberatory change. The film is divided into two sections: the first documentary part deals with the work of Reich in a direct cinema approach to his life, and ideas on orgone energy. Makavejev connects sexual frustration and violence by sequences of the poet Tuli Kupferberg who mimics masturbation with his gun on the streets of New York. These images are then intercut with orgasmic sequences and the Fugs' song 'Kill for Peace'. In a later episode, artist Betty Dodson discusses her drawings about masturbation, while in the next scene, Nancy Godfrey makes a plaster cast of a man's erect penis. Makavejev also features the bisexual Jackie Curtis walking in New York with his partner and gives us an insight into the editing process of the underground hard-core pornography magazine *Screw*. Thanks to the associative montage technique, all these sequences are intercut with archival footage that brings them a deeper, connotative level throughout the film. The dissolves and inserts which are separated from scenes of sexual intercourse 'provide a structural filmic equivalent to Reich's belief that we live in an age of incomplete sexuality, in which sex has become subservient to politics, institutionalism, and dogma' (Goulding 1990: 232). For instance, the images of Buckley's erect penis are intercut with the idealised portrayal of Stalin in Chiaureli's socialist-realist propaganda film, *The Vow* (*Klyatva*, 1946) in which he announces reaching the first stage of communism. The juxtaposition equates Stalin with a frozen phallus and, as Golding puts it, 'emphasizes the frozen nature of the revolution under Stalinist centralized, hierarchical dogmatism' (Ibid., 233). Following the speech of Stalin, Makavejev cuts to a Nazi psychiatric ward with a patient who constantly pounds his head against the wall. This segment is accompanied by the non-diegetic music of the Communist hymn and is followed

Figure 1.1 Tuli Kupferberg in *WR: Mysteries of the Organism*. Yugoslavia: Neoplanta Film, 1971.

by Tuli Kupferberg's masturbation with a gun (Figure 1.1). This long associative montage sequence brings oppressive associations with fascism, communism, US militarism and authoritarian institutes (Ibid., 233), which is further stressed by the frontal portrayal of Stalin, the patient in the psychiatric yard, and Jackie Curtis and Tuli Kupferbeg's slow-motion close ups as they look straight into the camera. These associative shots – together with Buckley's erect penis that is captured in an extreme close up – create a tableau of sexual freedom while they also convey the message of sexual – and political – oppression that, according to Makavejev, go hand in hand. Stalin thus becomes a phallic signifier (Synder 1994: 166), a symbol of oppressive patriarchy that connects these sequences. This is further stressed by the lack of orgasm on screen. While *WR* is brimming with erotic spectacle, the fulfilment of one's desire – and so personal liberation – is missing from the images. The sexual revolution, as the film illustrates, is doomed to fail for its repressive tactics of ideology cannot bring freedom.

The second part of the film puts the viewer in a fictional world within Yugoslavia where the young revolutionary Milena (Milena Dravić) preaches the ideas of Reichian sexual freedom to people. This sequence of the film opens with her stepping in Reich's Orgone Energy Accumulator while pronouncing that 'communism without free love is a wake in a graveyard'. This is the main message of *WR: Mysteries of the Organism* (as the title itself accentuates – W. R., alias Wilhelm Reich and World Revolution): Milena's mission is to spread the gospel of sexual freedom within the communist bloc. Ironically, when she falls in love with the Russian ice-skating champion, Vladimir Ilyich (Ivica Vidović) who rejects any kind of sexuality and intimacy, Milena's main aim becomes to seduce the man. After long philosophical and political talks – that include socialist clichés, allusions to 1968 and Yugoslavia's own path towards socialism – she finally manages to have intercourse with the ice-skater for which she must pay with her own life. In the final scenes, Milena's head, covered in blood lying on the autopsy table, announces that even now – after she has been decapitated by Vladimir Ilyich – she is not ashamed of her Communist past, thus conveying Makavejev's message of reforming existing socialism into a non-repressive establishment.

The very explicit sexual scenes of *WR: Mysteries of the Organism* function as an anti-establishment and anti-totalitarian gospel against the Yugoslav oppression and the lack of individual freedom. Milena converts the Reichian sexual politics into political cant (Goulding 1990: 145) which is presented via the juxtaposition of archive footage and the fictional diegetic layer of the film. Besides the harsh criticism of ideologies, the transgressive imagery of psychiatric treatments, the series of close-ups of genitals and explicit sexual scenes were factors that prevented the film from domestic distribution. Although *WR: Mysteries of the Organism* was never officially banned, it remained on the shelves up until the system change (Mortimer 2009).

With its transgressive tone, Makavejev's next film, *Sweet Movie* (1974) goes even further in terms of extremity. The film portrays the sexual odyssey of a young beauty queen (Carole Laure) who wins the title of Miss Canada for her outstanding hymen. Her prize is to marry the billionaire American, Aristoteles Aplanalpe aka Mr Kapital (John Vernon), but their marriage soon falls apart. The tycoon's family guard, Jeremiah Muscle (Roy Callender) takes her away and forces the woman to masturbate on him. Later, the bodybuilder packs her in a suitcase that he sends to Paris. Here, Miss Canada meets the Latin singer El Macho who wins her over with Spanish love songs and sequined eyelids. Their sexual intercourse at the Eiffel Tower gets interrupted by nuns who scare the pair into penis captivus. After her shock and humiliation, Miss Canada gets adopted into the Milky Way Commune led by Otto Muehl who – recalling the ideas of Reich – believes that freedom can be achieved by playing with others' genitalia, food and body excretions. Regressed to a foetal position after the

THE CRADLE OF EASTERN EXTREMISM   29

penis captivus incident, Miss Canada acts as a newborn. In the Milky Way community, she sleeps in a crib and is breastfed by an older black woman. It is here where she witnesses the commune's hysterical play with urine, faeces, vomit and flesh. As a reference to consumer capitalism and human metabolism that prevail over Makavejev's idea of society, Miss Canada's journey ends with a TV commercial to sell candy. Covered with liquid chocolate, she slowly reaches orgasm but gets suffocated by the chocolate.

The second narrative line of the film concentrates on Anna Planeta (Anna Prucnal) who captains a large boat called 'Survival' in the canals of Amsterdam. The ship has a large paper mâché figurehead of Marx at its prow and a large sugar-bed in its cargo hold that all attract the young Russian sailor Potemkin (Luv Balkunin) who, after boarding the ship, starts a relationship with Anna. Eventually, Anna stabs him to death after their sexual encounter in the sugar bed. The story ends with the arrest of the revolutionary woman and the resuscitation of the sailor as well as the four children that Anna has seduced (and probably murdered) earlier. *Sweet Movie* thus wraps up the film with the possibility of rebirth.

To this day, with its obscene, taboo-breaking topics and aesthetics, Makavejev's film deeply divides its audience. After its debut in the West in 1975, contemporary film critics acknowledged that it is 'one of the most challenging, shocking and provocative films of recent years' that, however, is impossible to comprehend (Ebert 1975) for it '(…) leads nowhere' (Canby 1975) as it is not a film, but 'porn' (see Houston and Kinder 1979: 563–4) and a 'social disease' (Cocks 1975). Despite its controversial reception in the 1970s, recent reviews appraise the courage and the outstanding collage aesthetics of *Sweet Movie*. Often called a 'masterpiece' (Kasdovasili 2019), and an 'artistically earnest, politically savvy film' (Sterritt 2007) by film scholars, film critics still condemn *Sweet Movie* for its overly graphic sexuality that hinders its political aims (Taylor 2004). Smalley identifies the film as an 'undeniable freak show (…) for those with strong stomachs: just be prepared for a cavalcade of unsimulated urine, puke, feces, mother's milk, and pedophilia' (Smalley 2013). Null goes ever further when drawing a parallel between Makavejev and Charles Manson (Null 2001), arguing that *Sweet Movie* degenerates into something the infamous cult leader might have produced.

Without doubt, most of the controversial responses allude to the infamous Milky Way scene in which Otto Muehl's[3] commune engages in rituals of vomiting, pissing and urinating on each other (Figure 1.2). The episode portrays Miss Canada in an infant stage as she is breastfed by a chubby Afro-American woman. First, the young woman is depicted in a regressive position lying in a cradle with her eyes and mouth open as she

Figure 1.2 Milky Way in *Sweet Movie*, V. M. Productions, 1974.

is being showered with lettuce leaves. While glancing into the abyss, her adoptive mother wets her lips with her own saliva. Thanks to the super close-ups, Miss Canada's inexpressive facial gestures get special emphasis. In the next shot, Makavejev uses the same zoom-in structure to focus on the lips of the once beauty-queen. In the breastfeeding scene whose establishing long shot portrays Miss Canada and the bare breasts of the Afro-American woman in juxtaposition, we arrive to the super close up of the beauty queen as she is sucking the nipples of the black woman. With her emotionless eyes, Miss Canada looks straight into the camera during the whole act, thus calling the spectator to identify with her and endure the scene. In the next sequence, Miss Canada is portrayed as a young child who witnesses the infamous feast scene from a passive position. The taboo-brimmed Milky Way section features members of the commune eating from each other's' mouth and then vomiting and urinating on the table. Later, they poop on plates that they serve to their fellow members and sing the German national anthem, while moving into a cheerful dance. These chaotic acts are intercut with the baby Miss Canada's exploration of male sexuality. The young woman's face is juxtaposed next to a man's legs who puts his false penis on the table and cuts the huge chunk of meat with a cleaver (Figure 1.3). He then throws pieces of it on his fellows. A woman tries to feed Miss Canada with a portion from the false phallus, but the beauty queen rejects it and throws the remaining chunks away that are then gnawed upon by people. Instead, she dips into the man's pocket

Figure 1.3 Chaos in *Sweet Movie*, France: V. M. Productions, 1974.

and takes his real phallus out of it. While the so-far depicted sequences were filmed in a documentary-like, cinéma verité mode – with handheld camera, often blurry images and rhythmic cuts giving an all-encompassing image of the vulgar acts – Miss Canada's encounter with the man's penis has an identical filmic structure with the previous breastfeeding scene. In contrast to the hysterical atmosphere and abrupt filmic structure of the feast sequence, the penis-sequence is filmed in a fixed, zoom-in shot. Accompanied by soft music, Miss Canada slowly strokes the phallus and rubs it against her cheeks. Similar to the framing of Momma Communa's breast, the beauty queen is now depicted in an extreme close-up as she carefully fondles a man's flaccid penis and touches it against her crying face. Opposite to the breastfeeding scene where she took on the role of an infant, in the penis-sequence she expresses some activity and psychological growth. Even though her movements and expressions are minimal, she now steps into an older, baby-like stage. Interestingly, her advancement in age is signalled through male and female organs of copulation. The identical filmic structure that frames her with the breast of a woman and then a penis – and which create an aesthetic contrast to the documentary-like sequences of transgression – signals an ideological rupture in the movie. Despite Otto Muehl's belief that the play with body excretions, food and genitalia would bring freedom, in Miss Canada's case, it brings about (sexual) repression and bodily sacrifice. While the commune mimics childbirth by forcing a member to relieve himself and then covers the man's body his own defecation, the young woman remains in the embrace of a sofa. Shivering and with her hands cramped, she slowly turns her face into the chair. After the 'childbirth', the others embark upon a naked crowd-dance, during which Miss Canada remains excluded and starts crying in the corner. That is, while the commune experiences freedom via performing vulgar acts, the beauty queen remains in an isolated viewing position, and she goes through stages of repression via her encounters with organs of copulations. The aesthetic contrast between the cinéma verité-like sequences and the fixed camera position that captures her, only exacerbate this conflicting dynamic. For Miss Canada, there is no liberation throughout sexual acts. She is oppressed by eroticism that, as a metaphor of commodity in the film, puts her in a repressed position. Her journey as a subjected individual in the capitalist age ends with her masturbation for a commercial in a vat of chocolate where she eventually drowns, thus 'swallowing capitalist ideology to the point of drowning in it' (Hamblin 2014: 39). For Makavejev, capitalism signals the unlimited accumulation of goods – sugar, chocolate, drinks and free sexuality – that, however, turn the main protagonist's body into a commodity (Ibid., 39). In contrast to the members of the community that regress to infancy as an act of political liberation to discard all cultural imprinting (Houston and Kinder 1979: 553), Miss Canada is constantly molested by 'free sexuality' – by the golden penis of her husband, then by Jeremiah Muscle and El Macho and eventually by the commune – rendering her escape from consumer capitalism impossible. The faith of individuals in *Sweet Movie* – be that the commune, Anna Planeta or Miss Canada – is already determined by ideologies. This message is accentuated by archive documentary materials that are intercut with the film's surrealistic sequences. The feast scene, for example, is interrupted by Nazi archival footage of baby gymnastics which does not serve as a controversial comparison between the Fascist and contemporary, Western eroticism (Testa 1990), but highlights one's determined role within any absolutistic ideological framework. Later in the film, when Miss Canada slowly sinks into the bath of chocolate, Makavejev suddenly cuts to a German documentary footage of Nazis discovering the Katyn graves. The black and white images of the exhumation of corpses recall the inhuman nature of mankind – over 20,000 Poles were murdered in Katyn, which, to this day is regarded as the greatest crime committed by Russians against Polish citizens (Mazierska 2014) – and positions one's body as a tool of Nazism, Stalinism and consumer capitalism. The very message of *Sweet Movie* – that is, all bodies are sacrificed on the altar of Ideologies – is communicated by deaths. Miss Canada and Anna Planeta are also interlinked by the representation of corpses: the beauty queen

THE CRADLE OF EASTERN EXTREMISM   33

eventually becomes a corpse, while Anna is producing corpses by murdering his seduced victims (Cavell 1979: 320).

Following his orgasm, the Russian sailor is stabbed by Anna Planeta in the sugar bed so that Potemkin's blood mixes with sugar and creates a thick paste. On his death bed, the man links himself to Vakulinchuk, the martyred sailor in Sergei Eisenstein's *Battleship Potemkin*, while his frozen death mask resembles the corpses of Katyn (Goulding 1990). Similar to Milena in *WR*, Anna's lover becomes a revolutionary martyr who, in contrast to Vakulinchuk, dies naked after his orgasm.

The four pubescent boys that Anna seduces with candy and her semi-naked striptease also die in the film. In the long seduction scene Anna strokes the face of the boys with her stockings that she then ties around the children's neck while she slowly gets rid of her lacy lingerie. She unzips the fly of one of the young boys and almost sits on the boy's face with her uncovered genitalia. After her erotic dance that is cross-cut with background images of Lev Trotsky, Stalin, Marlon Brando and Jesus, she whispers to the boy – 'You can fuck me if you are lucky, Mister Sugar' – and pulls the bunk's curtain across, thus ending the scene. Makavejev's critique of idolatry is evident in this episode. Recalling the Hollywood star Marlon Brando alongside idols of Communism and religion, he openly passes strictures on (repressive) ideologies. Still, such an explicit portrayal of child molestation poses ethical questions and the very boundaries of art and parabolic filmic language. As Stanley Covell has it, the episode raises severe moral difficulties:

> We recognize our complicity in finding in a world of corpses a world whose common coin of relationship is seduction, and we recognize our complicity as seducer and as seduced. But is this lesson sufficient justification for subjecting these young boys to this treatment? … She really is taking off her stocking for this boy; really placing her naked leg over his shoulder, her pubic hair tufting beyond the edges of the strip of fabric hanging loosely down her front; she really is unzipping his fly... (Covell 1979: 320)

Despite the ethical concern of representing child abuse, several scholars justify Makavejev's choice to feature young boys as sexualised objects by arguing that these children have

> ...already been seduced over and over and more intractably than any way in which this nice lady will affect them in providing them and herself for the camera. The artist knows this not in a spirit which would say that a little more seduction won't hurt but knows it out of a conviction that the process of going through these gestures- with friendly preparation 'and with explicit delimitations, for the comprehensible purpose of producing the communication in these matters for a film-is, on the contrary, potentially therapeutic'. (Ibid., 321)

34   THE EXTREME CINEMA OF EASTERN EUROPE

Covell's concerning statement that the boys might have benefited from the scene as a remedial exercise, questions the fundamental objective of art, that is, how far can one go to provoke the spectator? In defence of the scene, Houston and Kinder (1979) also argue that the metaphoric sequence 'displays the potential positive value of child sexuality (as Makavejev) ... exposes Anna as one who exploits [the boys] because she, herself, is the victim of a perverted revolution' (558). Houston and Kinder understand the scene as an attack on the failure of the revolution and Tsarist orthodoxy that considered child sexuality a moral breakdown. They argue that, instead of exploitative pornography, in the context of Reichian sexual politics that fostered children's sexual impulses, *Sweet Movie* can be read as a 'dangerous sweetness of art' (550). Corresponding to this statement, Mortimer (2008) recalls Sir Owen O'Malley's motto in regard to the Katyn massacres of the film – 'Let us think of these things and speak of them never' – that, she argues, also alludes to the unspoken reality of child abuse as a 'repressed and dirty secret' present in our societies. The question is why the communication of this political message had to include child actors and why the filmmaker did not consider animating the scene? Referencing to contemporary Serbian cinema, Kuzma argues that the film 'highlights the weak points of Balkan cinema, where it is often but a crumbling facade of meaningless sex and violence that covers up the blatant lack of meaning' (Kuzma 2012). Indeed, the scene of child abuse – together with images of coprophilia and emetophilia – might go too far in its provocative imaginary and the very message of the sequence disappears behind its shock-aesthetics. Beyond doubt, the erotic, shocking montage-sequences provoke the viewers into impassivity so much so that, 'while watching the film, we may feel stupid, ridiculous, confused, perverted or counterrevolutionary' (Houston and Kinder 1979). Yet, as Stanley Cavell puts it:

> What is the meaning of revulsion? If rotting corpses make us want to vomit, why at the same time do live bodies insisting on their vitality? But the members of the commune themselves display images of revulsion, as if to vomit up the snakes and swords and fire the world forces down our throats. (Cavell, 1979: 316)

In Sarah Hamblin's view, disgust 'signals an alternative engagement with negative feeling as a mode of communist self-critique, one that at the same time complicates the radical potential of desire' (Hamblin 2014: 30). The liberating ideals of a new humanist Marxism, such as self-emancipation that is embodied by (sexual) desire, get disrupted by images of disgust that hinder the communication of an objective revolutionary politics (Ibid., 30). In this way, the problematic representation of revolutionary

THE CRADLE OF EASTERN EXTREMISM   35

thoughts 'operates as a means of "nonarticulation", in line with the politics of radical self-emancipation that preclude a didactic cinema aimed at teaching the audience the truth of revolution ... As such, disgust produces a vexed aesthetics that at once expresses both the possibilities and the limits of revolutionary cinema' (Ibid., 30). Indeed, the shock aesthetics of the film, including harrowing scenes of child abuse, mutilation and transgressive sexual sequences, might hinder the very aim of the film: to attract attention to convey the failure of ideologies. Makavejev chose a rather provocative leitmotif to shake viewers into a new consciousness and, as Hamblin outlines, the extreme imaginary eventually achieves the opposite of what the Yugoslav director aimed for. Testa (1990) even questions whether *Sweet Movie* was an art film: 'Makavejev transgressed the "decorum" of the art film ... He moves toward the possibilities of a transgressive cinema that serves a concept of therapy, not art, one in which hilarity and outrage, juxtapositions of horror and erotic delight become favourite strategies' (238). Testa explain the 'tactics of transgression against taste, art and sexual codes' (Ibid., 239) by recalling the anti-art Belgrade Surrealist School whose objective was to confront Stalinism and leftist fascism by placing special emphasis on the body, psyche and their therapeutic liberation from ideological repression. Jonathan Owen (2014: 4) also adds that cultural openness as well as the 'the potential revolutionary weapon of humour' that characterised Serbian Surrealism, are also present in Makavejev's works. As such, *Sweet Movie* follows the surrealist doctrine of the Belgrade School. Makavejev's surrealist oeuvre has been underlined by several scholars,[4] who emphasise the impact of Rene Clair's, Salvador Dalí's, and Luis Buñuel's[5] films on the Yugoslav filmmaker. There is an undeniable connection between the symbolic and parabolic political modernism of the 1960s and 1970s and Makavejev's surrealistic oeuvre and avantgarde technique of interconnecting different realities within the same filmic framework (Kovács 2007: 376). Still, as Kovács outlines, Makavejev's provocation differs from Godard's self-reflexive, discontinued narratives and political cinema as 'instead of withholding the aesthetic attractiveness of his film, he stuffs it with the most vulgar, excessive, even disgusting, motives of sexuality, which political modernist countercinema attacked and tried to avoid' (Ibid., 381). While the main characteristics of the *nouvelle vague* – cinéma verité style, reflexivity, parody, radical discontinuity and genre parody – are present in *Sweet Movie*, Makavejev's obscene imagery disconnects it from the modernist anticinema movement of the 1960s and 1970s. Although the surrealistic stance of the film – the collage-technique, the abstract visionary that blurs vision, imagination and reality (and works with the lack of narrative cohesion), and topics of human nature – cannot be denied, 'Makavejev's exploration of sexuality ... proves more complex than certain sexual-liberationist strands of Surrealism ..., even if [he] ultimately mines the same terrain of psychic drives and desires that the Surrealists first artistically investigated' (Owen 2014: 10). As outlined by Testa (1990),

> ... Makavejev does not really succeed in combining Surrealism and intellectual montage ... The montage that Makavejev attempts is underdeveloped: he tries to juxtapose materials while also leaving the materials assembled intact ... What he rather grandly terms his "meta-montage" and described operationally in his lectures fails to function either rhythmically (in Eisenstein's sense of a montage of the images' internal compositions) or textually ... The problem with *Sweet Movie* as a montage film is that its transgressions are not relentless enough, so that the system of "meta-montage" never becomes the engine of outrage. (243–4)

In contrast to examples of early surrealist films – such as *Entr'acte* (Rene Clair, 1924), or Louis Buñuel's *Chien Andalou* (1929) and *L'Age d'Or* (1930) – Makavejev uses sexuality as the very core of his ritualistic aesthetic which, as Kovács notes, 'makes his film part of the same obscene media business that abuses human beings for the sake of eroticised seduction, whether with the goal of promoting consumer culture or critiquing it' (Kovács 2007: 380). Even though Makavejev's self-critique of political modernism is based on the cinematic experience of provocation and displeasure, the aesthetic excess of obscene sensual pleasures in his films create a controversial, multi-layered textuality which gets overwritten by – and often mistaken for – provocation for its own sake. For this reason, the film's surrealistic view of sexuality and its metaphorical use to convey messages on social, cultural and political orders, have often been dismissed, while many critics have named the director a charlatan and pornographer (see Testa 1990: 229).[6] *Sweet Movie* eventually ruined Makavejev's career and forced the Yugoslav filmmaker into commercial filmmaking (Bergan 2019). The film was banned in several countries while in other cinemas, vertical as well as horizontal black-out bars covered genital areas in the screened version (Goulding 1994), which ultimately erased Makavejev's ritualistic aesthetic of extreme displeasure and his message of demolishing ideologies in order to gain freedom.

CHAPTER 2

The Political Transition and the Extreme: Cinema of Castration

While each of the Eastern European countries have experienced their own version of post-socialist transition, there are several political, social as well as ideological changes that are relatively common in the region. The political transition from a bloc-wide, monolithic system into a market-based economic structure brought about as many positive affects as it did disadvantages. While many celebrated the post-1989 turn and the political freedom that accompanied it, the privatised economy and political democratisation came with a shock-therapy which resulted in massive unemployment, widespread insecurity, the reduction of the welfare system and severe societal conflicts (Outwhaite and Ray 2005). By 1994, the GDP of former socialist countries shrunk to almost 60% of the 1989 level (Minagawa 2013a). Together with the economic reorganisation in the region and high inflation rates, the living standards started to decline (Anachkova 1995). Thanks to factory closures and mass layoffs, social insecurity became one of the hallmarks of the new Zeitgeist. Unemployment, which was virtually unknown for decades, started to increase and, with high-rocketing consumer prices, many families started to struggle with daily life. These sudden changes introduced uncertainty, insecurity and great tensions in Eastern European societies. The 'transition recession' (Outwhaite and Ray 2005: 165) resulted in a universal social disorder, depression, growing suicide rate and the rise of criminality.

Beyond doubt, the accession of the Czech Republic, Estonia, Hungary, Latvia, Lithuania, Poland, Slovakia, and Slovenia to the European Union in 2004 is a crucial turning point in the socio-political changes of the region. Despite the high hopes and enthusiasm of the population, the accession has soon created anti-EU voices and disappointment (Balázs et al. 2014). The prompt ascendancy of neoliberal ideology centred on privatisation, macroeconomic stabilisation, the liberalisation of domestic prices and the construction of new markets resulted in a severe decline in economic output (Dale and Fabry 2018). As Kattel puts it, the recession that East

European countries experienced in the 1990s was 'worse than the Great Depression in the United States and World War II in Western Europe' (2010: 52). The massive inflow of foreign direct investment (FDI), the rise of cross-border loans, exchange rate depreciation (Appel and Orenstein 2016) and the region's incapability to answer the crisis resulted in an estimated 20–25% decline in GDP and 50% decline of agricultural production (Berend and Bugaric 2015) which led to mass unemployment (Cámara 1997) and a severe social crisis. The economic crash included declining living standards; growing suicide rates (Minagawa 2013b); gender, race and labour force status inequalities (Heyns 2005); migration to the West from the Eastern European region (Okólski 1998); and the rise of human trafficking (Surtees 2008). While Eastern European countries believed that Western neoliberal paradigms had to be adopted in order to achieve higher wages and so financial security and better life standards (Cámara 1997), most countries did not anticipate the price they had to pay for neoliberal reforms and the European Union membership. Their absolute dependence on the IMF, World Bank and the European Union[1] enabled western business leaders and policymakers to exploit the region for its 'low wages, high productivity and simple taxes' (Dale and Fabry 2018) and contributed to anomic decades in the region. As Dale and Fabry put it,

> ... the logic of transformation was not simply to liberate the countries of the region from the shackles of communism or to unleash entrepreneurial talent ... but to open up the economies of the region to the exigencies of global capital, while restructuring and bolstering the power of domestic elites. The outcome has been growing disillusionment, and public discontent with simplistic attempts to install a market economy and Western-style democracy ... The capitalist triumphalism of the early 1990s has everywhere given way to the dystopian realities of an authoritarian, restrictive and reactionary mode of neoliberal capitalism. (Ibid., 248)

In the late 1990s, the European Union pressed Eastern European countries to continue liberalisation in order to fulfil the Copenhagen Criteria – the political and economic conditions for joining the EU. Thus, although neoliberal explanations failed to provide answers for the growing instability and disillusion in the region, it pushed market fundamentalism to its limits (Dale and Fabry 2018). The two projects – the Single Market and monetary union – that aimed to consolidate the neoliberal structure in the post-socialist region, forced governments to seek financial assistance from the IMF, which led to the accumulation of foreign debt and left Eastern European economies in an especially vulnerable position. The transition thus resulted in the exploitation of the Eastern European region (Dale and Hardy 2011) by 'Western supra-powers' (Hall 2011: 707).

THE POLITICAL TRANSITION AND THE EXTREME   39

The sudden shift to a privatised studio system in the film industries of the region also had a deep impact on filmmaking methods. The competition of foreign films and the loss of state support created a deep structural crisis (Hames and Portuges 2006). The lack of censorship also fundamentally changed the attitude of several directors and resulted in major modifications in the role of film as political device. A crucial point is that, although the socialist authorities precluded any liberal discourse on the failures of the regime, the prohibition of open criticism served as a substrate for parabolic speech that gave birth to several outstanding artistic productions. After 1989 however,

> ... it was no longer the artists' subversive and audacious task to promulgate the goals of democracy, [and as a result,] film-making lost something of its earlier fantastic power and opportunity to be the leading art that it had been during those years. It became something more common, closer to entertainment ... Political struggle is no longer the privilege of the artistic endeavour. Something has been achieved, but something has also been lost. The exceptional role of film in the 1960s and 1970s worldwide is no longer prevalent. (Bíró, quoted in Portuges 2010: 99).

The fact that there was no longer need for connotative language and no demand for oppositional artistic activity, resulted in the re-articulation of the duty of the filmmaker and the role of the narratives themselves, which eventually led to several directors leaving the industry. Whereas for some, the lack of political censorship meant the loss of their artistic drive, the system change also opened up the discourse of long-embedded socio-political taboos. Such topics were homosexuality, prostitution, child molestation and various forms of sexual abuse. In the post-1989 corpus, (sexual) violence, psychological as well as physical torture, and raw images of bodily exploitation became common motifs. As this chapter illustrates, the stylistic violence in the Eastern European cinematic corpus of the transition (1990–2004) orientates toward the commodification of women as well as the emasculated position of men in the region by displaying the vulnerable body within the new and harsh economic structure. The system change, and sudden privatisation, and the accession to the European Union brought about a deep social crisis and deepened the region's Othered position.

A Gendered Transition

The 1989 political transitions had a deep impact on gender politics. With the demise of the quota system, women lost representation in the public sphere (Krizsán and Roggeband 2018).[2] In the private realm, the insecure structure of existing social policies (abortion rights, health care, maternity leave) only deepened the gender gap. Yet, the socio-economic change enabled females to establish women's organisations, which gave way to growing networking and cooperation between associations (Zacijek-Calasanti 1995). Also, with the exception of Poland, all of the post-socialist countries have now abandoned the strict pronatalist policies that ban abortion (Levine and Staiger 2004). While the more liberal legislation aimed at controlling the population within the severe economic crisis, it also granted freedom to women with regard to their bodies and decisions. As a result, Eastern Europe shifted from being Europe's highest-fertility region to its lowest one within only a decade (Sobotka et al. 2011). The highly anomic social system and the steep rise of suicide also contributed to the 'demographic catastrophe in the 1990s' (Minagawa 2013b: 1037). As Minagawa outlines, between 1989 and 2006, males displayed four times higher suicide rates than females (Ibid., 1044–5), which also demonstrates the sudden tendency of emasculation in the region. While socialist hypermasculinity framed the ideal man as 'a worker, a hero, and soldier who sacrifices his life for communism' (Hallama 2021: 210) and capitalist competition promised 'to … restore familial and societal harmony by allowing men to reassert their masculine authority as breadwinners' (Ghodsee 2021: 17), the post-1989 promises were not achieved. Without a stable income, many men lost their heroic position as the financial head of household. The feeling of loss of masculinity resulted in alcoholism, depression and physical violence that all became common phenomena in the post-system change period.

While it is no doubt that the sudden socio-economic change affected both genders, the transition to liberal capitalism clearly gave way to the rise of masculinism (Watson 1993). As Watson stresses, civil society and the institutionalisation of hierarchy – together with the patriarchal structure of the market economy – empowered men and masculinity. As the rates of female participation in the new democratic parliaments were low, men played a key role in shaping the new public sphere. Since the question of women's rights and representation were secondary to the process of democratisation and the establishment of a stable political and economic hierarchy, gender inequality remained a secondary issue.

The feminisation of unemployment, together with gendered wage differentials (Racioppi and O'Sullivan 2009), discriminatory hiring practices and the scarcity of women in labour unions re-invoked an 'antiwomen dash' in ideological discourses (Moghadam 1992: 24). Women's position as nurturant mothers in the socialist system identified them as collaborators of the socialist ideology and they were suddenly put out to accusations of having destroyed the traditional national values, national character and ethno-nation (Verdery 1996: 68). Paradoxically, gender equality has often been seen as a threat to national values (Krizsán and Roggeband 2018) as many feared that women would give up childbearing and their other domestic roles. What was born this way can be identified as a battle against women who, whether as socialist collaborators and/or anti-nationalist rebels, annihilated the cohesion of the nation. It is no wonder, then, that human procreation and questions of reproduction turned out to be the focus of heated public debate (Gal 1994). The discourse on pronatalist policies in the region became a tool for legitimating power by providing 'new, more radical ... definitions of woman as *exclusively* grounded in domesticity' (emphasis original, Watson 1993: 75).

The sudden liberalism also allowed the freedom for one to associate with the traditional feminine and masculine identity, one liberated from socialist ideology (Ibid., 73). As Watson (1993a) outlines, the creation of liberal democracy rests on traditional gender definitions which, in this case, expresses the desire of Eastern Europeans to be 'normal' (473) and return to traditional family roles. The re-birth of Catholicism in the region succeeded in filling the ideological gap that was left after socialism, but it also favoured conservative gender models. The reinforced religious dogmas were oriented toward the family apparatus and 'stressed women's "natural role" as mothers and housewives, endowed with specifically female personality characteristics (obedient, emotional, modest, accommodating)' (emphasis original, Jogan 1995: 235). As Jouzeliuniene and Kanopiene described in 1995, 'women are still not treated as individuals free in their choices and behavior, but as instruments in the state's various pursuits. The old socialist slogan: "a woman-worker in production" was being changed to: "woman-mother in the family"' (emphasis original, 1995: 163).

In Imre's (2001) view, Eastern European women have faced hardship when associating themselves with feminism for 'they have perfectly internalized the guilt and the shame of the colonized, transferred to them by men whose colonised masculinities are permanently insecure'. On the other hand, the rights of Eastern European women were evaporated for it was believed by liberal feminism that equality and emancipation must be fought for through activism (Ghodsee 2021). Also, the association of Western feminism with the imposition of neoliberal capitalism only contributed to patriarchal order and nationalist hypermasculinity. The failure to import liberal feminism in Eastern Europe was due to what Ghodsee (2021) calls the import of Western 'feminism-by-design' which

> attempted to erase the history of progressive state socialist policies for women in the region by claiming that it was illegitimate because ordinary women had not

advocated for their own rights ... Second, and more important, the importation of Western liberal feminism to Eastern Europe discursively created a predetermined category of expected losers in the new capitalist economy. Western liberal feminism emerged in conflict with capitalism, but also very much a part of capitalism ... [This model] encouraged projects to protect women from market discrimination and thereby discursively legitimating that discrimination'. (20–1)

In this way, the post-transition period has only stabilised the male-centred economic and social structure. Bystydzienski demonstrates the proliferation of sexist patterns as well as domestic abuse in Poland by highlighting that the majority of women in prison were sentenced for homicide for killing their abusive partner. As he describes, 'when the issue is raised with officials in the criminal justice system, the stereotypical reply is that "men only hit women when women provoke them" and that "usually women who need to be disciplined are hit by men" (emphasis original, Bystydzienski 1995: 198). Sexual harassment against females became a wide phenomenon and, because the law[3] did not protect them and crime policy was not a central political concern during the first years of transition (see Šelih 2012: 11), they became an even more vulnerable social group. For instance, writing in 1993, Lesnicka draws the following image of Poland:

> Available statistics indicate an increase in the occurrence of rape from 1,660 reported in 1989 to 1,840 cases in 1990. According to Polish law, rapists can have up to ten years in jail. Yet, in 1990, 40.0 percent of convicted rapists faced between one or two years in jail; only 5.0 percent received more than three years. Short sentences might be consistent with many Polish judges' convictions that rape is a result of "men's nature". (Lesnicka, quoted by Zacijek-Calasanti, 1995: 188)

The continued maleocracy not only brought about the re-emergence of the ideology of domesticity, but it also established a new inferior-superior structure by the commodification of women into sexual objects (Zacijek-Calasanti 1995). With the proliferation of pornographic magazines, sex shops and porn videos – merchandises that were all taboos in socialist newspapers – the market economy introduced women's bodies as commodities. The sudden market change in Eastern Europe and the elimination of censorship on pornography contributed to the proliferation of peep shops, brothels and sex-by-phone services. For unemployed women in desperate financial need, the porn business opened up new opportunities of earning a living and served as a compensation for occupational failure (Lobodzińska 1995). The international sex trade,[4] and trafficking of Eastern European women and children to the West offered a way out of poverty for families in need. The media's Westernised images of

THE POLITICAL TRANSITION AND THE EXTREME   43

independent women only exacerbated the frustration of Eastern European women who, in their subordinated gender status at home and in a low socio-economic position in society, saw an escape through trafficking (Morawska 2007). Following the lifting of international travel restrictions, the first commercial sex labourers were trafficked from Eastern Europe to its Western counterpart and Turkey (Gülçür and İlkkaracan 2002). Thanks to its unprotected, or poorly supervised borders and the region's geographic proximity to West European countries, Eastern Europe became the number one market for sexual trafficking. In 1995, it was estimated that the vast majority of those being trafficked from the region were women (around 90%) under the age of 25 (IMO 1995), out of which about 25% were transported for sexual exploitation (Mahmoud and Trebesch 2010). Eastern European women in the West were being forced to do '3D jobs (difficult, dirty, dangerous) which locals often rejected (Ibid., 177). In 2007 it was estimated that about 350,000–500,000 persons were being trafficked in and out of Eastern Europe annually, which made Eastern Europe the continent's centre of female trafficking (Morawska 2007). The current demand for female companions from the region is constantly rising. The reason, as Anca Parvulescu (2011) notes, is that Eastern European women

> passed through the "real-existing socialist" experiment [and] have nonetheless come out as traditional women, who cook, clean, and smile. Matrimonial agencies promise they would be "grateful." They are often referred to as "model-looking," a euphemism that describes the fact that their bodies do not carry (yet) traces of what Europeans dread under the name of "McDonaldization." Within the global market of women, they are also white and therefore can pass for European wives. They can reproduce white children in a Europe worried about the birth rate among its "native" population. They raise these children dutifully, disseminating the motherly love that, it is argued, has become scant in the Western world in the wake of second-wave feminism. Eastern Europe is a fresh reservoir of love. (emphasis original, 205–6)

It seems that, as Parvulescu argues, Eastern European women became desirable commodities for capitalist Western Europe – the only 'value' the post-socialist region could offer. The transitional epoch set up a new colonialist structure in which the Western imperial practice of trafficking exploits the Eastern region (Brown 2010). This class-based system of abuse that includes low wages, incarceration, slavery, rape and systematic humiliation, divided Europe into a re-colonised–re-coloniser structure. As Others, Eastern European women and men have remained outsiders of the Eurocentric establishment. To this day, they often remain invisible within Western societies (Brown 2010). What Brown does not recognise is that the post-1989 East-West (forced) migration also served as a new business opportunity for government authorities – politicians, law enforcement officials, state functionaries – to build prosperous trafficking networks (Surtees 2008). As such, Eastern European women were doubly exploited, by the colonising Western power and their own 'Third World' country. This 'double form of neoliberalist subjugation' (Batori 2020), as we will see in Chapter 6, created a structure of absolute dependence and vulnerability. Sold, humiliated and tricked into prostitution, many women fell victim to the male-centred business system that, especially in the period of transition, collaborated with local entrepreneurs, politicians and police, as well as oligarchs. Women were thus betrayed by the "protective" structure of their own countries as well as by the Western imperium.

Emasculated Cinemas

The films of the system change clearly reflect upon the change in gender relations. As Mazierska (2010) demonstrates, the traditional heroism which populated Polish and Czech socialist realist film gave way to defeated, disoriented or unfulfilled men. Disorientation is a key element in Kalmár's analysis too, who introduces the concept of the labyrinth as an aesthetic device which illustrates space confinement and the disorientation of male characters in Hungarian cinema (Kalmár 2017). He argues that the labyrinth acts as a metaphor for 'the brave new world of consumerist capitalism in Eastern Europe' (17) in which the films' pre-filmic space disorients the male characters and so the spectators as well. Lithuanian cinema presents 'violent anti-heroic post-Soviet masculinity incarnated in gross and abject screen male bodies' (Tereskinas 2011: 64), Serbia's 'local urban cinema' portrays the crisis of masculinity through domestic and criminal violence (Kronja 2006:18) and Bosnian war films foreground 'hypertropic masculinity' (Harper 2017: 77). Of course, one cannot overlook the rise of patriotic-patriarchal nationalisms in the region. It is not surprising that, thanks to the Balkan wars, the post-Yugoslav screen has given way to the stereotypical representation of the 'Balkan wild man [who] is a slave of his irrational passions, violent, drunk, misogynist, unable to control his violent impulses, and – as the ultimate consequence – (is) arsonist, rapist and murderer' (Pavicic 2010: 45). The representation of Eastern European men as testosterone-filled, violent characters on screen owes to the postcolonial crisis of masculinity in the region. Imre (2002: 74–5) describes this phenomenon as the result of socialist oppression as well as the post-system change inferiority to West Europe which led to Eastern European's feeling of shame to be fully European. As she accentuates, sexual essentialism in film functions 'as attempts to naturalise certain desirable masculinities', something which 'requires a compensatory

THE POLITICAL TRANSITION AND THE EXTREME   45

infliction of sexual violation on the internal colonised: on women and other national minorities'. In the light of this, it is less surprising that post-1989 films in Eastern Europe gave way to the exploitation of the nation through the subjugated representation of women[5] on the screen of the new capitalist order.[6] The proliferation of rape narratives – such as Erdőss Pál's *Last Seen Wearing a Blue Skirt* (*Gyilkos kedv*, 1997), Calin Peter Netzer's *Maria* (2003), Margineanu's *Somewhere in the East* (*Undeva in est*, 1991) and Stere Gulea's *State of Things* (1995), to mention just a few – all point toward the crisis. Prostitution, human trafficking, alcoholism and violence also became subject matters on screen (Iordanova 2003). These films of transition which I call 'cinema of castration', often feature masochistic tendencies where women get punished for their 'transgressive strive for independence' (Stojanova 2006: 99). Supererogation in these films functions as a continued aesthetic and thematic feature. However, in contrast to socialist cinema which relegated sexual assault, brutality and transgressive gestures to the offscreen space, the post-1989 cinema of castration foregrounds explicit imagery of brutality.

As a key film of the cinema of castration, Mircea Daneliuc's *The Conjugal Bed* (*Patul Conjugal*, 1993) is an allegorical representation of the post-system change 'panorama of [a] moral and cultural junkyard' (Pethő 2011: 405). The film evolves around the movie theatre manager Vasile (Georghe Dinica), who struggles to maintain the cinema and support his family. He desperately needs money for his wife's abortion as raising three children would be an impossible task in the period of socio-economic transition. He eventually decides to keep and later sell the child to the West. Daneliuc's film depicts a depressive, corrupt, hopeless present, with unemployment, privatisation and prostitution as the only solutions for women to survive. Vasile's wife has nostalgic feelings towards the socialist years where, as she argues, they had fixed jobs and decent salaries. She even raises money for a Ceaușescu-statue. His husband, Vasile, expresses his disappointment in capitalism which 'sells the country to France' and make citizens leave Romania. In the end, Daneliuc anticipates the future (set in 2006) of Vasile's son who is mentally handicapped and walks through the city's abandoned, dilapidated streets. In Danieluc's vision, the official language of the country is French, the prefabricated buildings of Bucharest are all empty and are surrounded by the signs of foreign investors that build new, Western shops in the heart of the city where Vasile's ex-lover (now sex-worker) is looking for clients.

The Conjugal Bed summarises the position of Eastern Europe amid the socialist-capitalist transition and depicts the process of the post-1989 emasculation and re-colonisation through the figure of Vasile. In the first half of the film, the head of the cinema loses all his power over his work and family life. The movie theatre has no visitors anymore, his salary gets stolen from his office, his wife is awaiting an unwanted child and his love Stela starts working as a porn actress and sex worker. The influence of Western power slowly overshadows his pre-capitalist position in the social structure. In the midst of the re-colonisation process, capitalism re-contextualises his life. While Stela and Vasile are kissing in the cinema, the sequences of the Ceaușescu trial on the screen get interrupted by Kodak advertisements and a statue's swinging figure which all give the scene an ironic tone. In this sarcastic scene, the naked Stela runs behind the screen and, assuming that it is his love's shadow that is swinging behind the canvas, Vasile climbs the ladder to reach her figure. He tries to cut a whole for his penis in the screen so that he can reach the swaying woman's vagina and thus can penetrate it through the screen. It is only the last sequence of *The Conjugal Bed* where Daneliuc reveals the mysterious figure behind the canvas. At the meeting of the new democratic party in the cinema, the movie screen falls down toward the crowd, thus showing Vasile's hanging body. The man is tied to a swinging statue of a woman whose missing genitals are joined with the rope around Vasile's neck. This symbolic connection points toward the post-1989 emasculation process and one's metaphoric connection to the past as well as colonised future. In the film, capitalism re-contextualises history via interrupting the Ceaușescu trial with Western advertisements on the screen, thus overwriting and replacing the images of the past with the future economic structure of the nation. In the new set-up, the nation undergoes a severe crisis and the symbol of the new world – the castrated female statue – eradicates Vasile's existence. It is not only the man who loses his reputation, wealth and his very role as the head of the family, but his wife too whose unwanted pregnancy serves as the focus point of the film's narrative. Motherhood becomes the symbol of the nation, a process of re-birth which eventually fails. At the peak of his emasculation process, Vasile decides to commit suicide by hanging himself from the female statue, thus connecting himself to the lost nation whose symbolic umbilical cord (rope) suffocates him (Figure 2.1). Past (Vasile) and future (statue) thus create an infertile oneness in which, as an ultimate abortion, the product of the socialist days and the transition (emasculated man) bonds himself with the already damaged statue.

The film's most disturbing scene conveys a similar message. As the true believer of the socialist system, Carolina (Coca Bloos), Vasile's wife sells his husband's closely guarded Ceaușescu book on the future of Romania. Raved with fury, the man first tries to strangle her with the same rope he later uses for his suicide. In the next shot, he stabs his wife in her

Figure 2.1 Connected to the past: *The Conjugal Bed*, Romania: Alpha Films International, 1993.

pregnant belly several times and jabs a nail into the skull of the screaming woman. The excruciating close-ups of the oozing blood that spurs out of the head and belly of Carolina give the sequence a visceral blow (Figure 2.2). This subversive tone gets further emphasised in the next shot where Vasile grabs a pincer to move around the nail in his wife's skull. The scene 'could be described as an encyclopaedia of domestic violence and contains scenes which could be compared to the violence in Tarantino's movies' (Iordanova 2001). As an ultimate step to the loss of masculine carnality, the scene's hard-core explicitness of torture acts as a metaphoric bridge between socialism and capitalism. Vasile is incapable of bearing the burden posed by the inheritance of the socialist system and, as the symbol of the Ceaușescu regime, he punishes his wife and unborn child for the sudden crisis. The mental, physical and verbal abuse he imposes on Carolina illustrate his frustration and anger towards the new sociopolitical establishment. His slow process to emasculation eventually ends with his suicide. The death of Vasile – the socialist father figure – also references the upcoming subjected position of the nation. In the film, the streets of Bucharest are brimmed with German marks and dollars, Stela shoots pornography in French, the Romanian currency has no value anymore and – without Western money – the young sex worker stops going out with Vasile. Set in 2006, the film's last shot foresees an ideologically inscribed Romania: Stela still works as a sex worker, Vasile's son is handicapped, the landscape of Bucharest is ruined and the national language of

Figure 2.2 Torture by emasculation: *The Conjugal Bed*. Romania: Alpha Films International, 1993.

the country is French. The extreme tone of *The Conjugal Bed* thus serves as an allegory for national manhood and mirrors the burden of the sudden colonisation-emasculation process which eradicates the previous leading position of male characters.

Interestingly, as in the case of *The Conjugal Bed*, lost/violated motherhood becomes a symbol of the new era. As mentioned earlier, the end of the strict pronatalist policies and the continuous structure of maleocracy-patriarchy resulted in an anti-women dash which, on the one hand, made women responsible for eradicating the cohesion of the nation by abortions, independence and a higher self-awareness which helped them to reckon their subjugated position. On the other hand, the new capitalist system – with the proliferation of pornographic magazines, films as well as prostitution – womanhood has been turned into commodity. Together with the process of emasculation[7] and re-colonisation process, it is less surprising that Eastern Europe's symbolic castration led to transgressive violence on screen, with the focus shifting to female bodies and motherhood.

Rape, Colonisation, Motherhood: *Pleasant Days*

Kornél Mundruczó's *Pleasant Days* (*Szép napok*, 2002) is one of the emblematic films of this new socio-cultural phenomenon. The story revolves around Péter (Polgár Tamás) who returns from prison to his native town to reunite with his sister Mária (Wéber Kata) and start a new

THE POLITICAL TRANSITION AND THE EXTREME 49

life there. He soon learns that his sister's friend, Maya (Tóth Orsi) sold her newborn baby to Mária who pronounces the child to be her own. Although Péter knows the truth, his attention shifts towards the easy-going Maya with whom he soon falls in love. When the woman wants to take her child back, Péter finds himself torn between Mária and his new love. Uncapable of taking control over Maya, he brutally rapes her and flees the country.

Pleasant Days exhibits constant violence against women to such a degree that brutality against the female body becomes the film's narrative motor. Maya gets constantly beaten up, pushed, undressed and humiliated by the story's male characters who sexually exploit and pass her around in the town. Her subjected position gets emphasised by the frequent display of her naked or partially naked body which dominates the visual sphere of the film. First, it is the scene of childbirth which showcases her half-naked, agitated body in labour. Placed on the floor of a noisy laundromat, Maya's close-up mirrors agony and suffering as she delivers her son in complete silence. The lack of dialogue, the cinéma verité style and the underlit, fluorescent room, together with Maya's excessive bleeding and the new-born's pure spectacle as he lies covered with blood and the umbilical cord on the dark gaze tiles, all provoke an extreme discomfort in the viewer. The hard-core explicitness of the film's opening scene gets constantly repeated by Maya's uncomfortable sexual acts and encounters with the film's male protagonists. The un-erotic images of intercourse with her lover, the middle-aged, married János (Horváth Lajos Ottó) who supports Maya's living in exchange for sex, often turn into sado-masochistic games which offer prolonged glimpses of the woman's suffering body. In one of the scenes, Maya is depicted in a fixed camera position as she is put in breast and neck bondage by János. Mundruczó's unusual, off-centre composition structure displays the woman's breasts in close-ups so that the frame excludes János and, instead of his figure or body parts, he captures the dull, empty background of the office where the scene takes place (Figure 2.3). By focusing on Maya's sexual organs, this carefully composed, fragmented close-up structure and the very act of the sado-masochistic tone of the sequence objectify the woman's very existence. The images of her physically restrained position and insensible facial expression suggest a submission indifferent to Maya's social situation.

The commodification of the young woman's body begins when she sells her child for 3,000 euros. From this point on, her femininity is formed in a process of ritualised, sexual, colonised subjugation. Not only is she utterly humiliated at the hands of János, but all the other male protagonists of the film, including the father of her child as well as Péter, exhibit violence against her. The more independent she becomes (she leaves János and

Figure 2.3 Un-erotic images in *Pleasant Days*. Hungary: Mafilm, 2002.

decides to take her son back), the more heightened the repetitive hitting, pushing and snapping become in the narrative.

When examining violence in arthouse cinema, Celik Rappas (2016) explains the aesthetics of brutality with the contemporary economic structure which, based on commodification, capitalises the human body. As he states, the representation of the body's mental and physical decay and vulnerability 'provide a commentary on the violent disposability of bodies as well as their adaptability under post-Fordist econom[ies] obsessed with efficiency, competition and risk-taking' (677). Contemporary films of aesthetic violence illustrate the limits and disposability of the human body while showcasing the violent nature and effect of the neoliberal corporeal regime. Extreme films thus not only 'capitalize on bodily violation', but 'represent how neoliberal capital shapes, changes and invades the body' (Ibid., 677). As *Pleasant Days* indicates, the sexual brutality and corporeal violence originate from the loss of masculinity in the neoliberal age: Péter and Ákos (Réthelyi András), Péter's best friend, are both unemployed and live from pick-and-shovel work or steal cars which János later sells in the West. Without a roof, Ákos lives in a decaying, old trailer and Péter stays with his sister while waiting for his passport so he can emigrate. Maya enjoys the economic support of her lover, while Mária's living is financed by her boyfriend who works in Germany. Without concrete goals and a promising way of living, the characters drift as objects of neoliberalism, while they dream to leave Hungary for the prosperous West. To balance their emasculated position, the male characters constantly wrestle with each other and/or are depicted half-naked in the film. As Kalmár (2017) describes them, they are 'betrayed, outcast and unloved, men who grow angry, frustrated and confused ... outside the reach of the human (moral) order' (6). Because they do not have any more tools left to demonstrate power, nor can they change the course of their lives, these male characters let off their frustration via violent physical force.

The dramatic culmination of this is Maya's rape. With its four minutes, the longest – and most disturbing – scene of the film is set on an empty parking lot at dawn and occurs in one observational take reminiscent of cinéma verité style.[8] Starting from an extreme long shot, the handheld camera slowly moves in into Péter's over-the-shoulder shot and circles around the figures (Figure 2.4). As if making a clinical inventory of the contents, the high-angle camera is constantly on the move to document on Maya's naked, skinny body and her fight against Péter. Enhanced by natural lighting, on-location filming and the avoidance of optical work and special effects, the tactile quality of the sequences plunges the spectator into close proximity with Maya's suffering. The kinetic, nauseating camerawork which focuses on her violated body during and after the rape is encoded in empathic alignment with Maya's suffering.

This 'in-the-body-ness' (Nicodemo 2012: 33) which places the viewer in the shoes of the film's protagonists without a subjective point-of-view shot, enables the spectator to contemplate Maya's excruciating agony with detailed dispassion. The difficult-to-stomach content pushes the viewer's boundaries to a limit, to such an extent that the socio-political allegory of the scene (and the film as well) might get lost on the audience. This is

Figure 2.4 Clinical inventory in *Pleasant Days*. Hungary: Mafilm, 2002.

demonstrated by the reviews on the film's IMDb page.[9] Users highlighted the film's 'nudity, violence and profanity' which generate an 'incomplete', 'weak', 'shallow' and 'sketchy' narrative. Most of the reviews comment on the shock effect of the film: one of the users notes that the 'frequent sexual episodes and constant reference to genital parts … are written into the script either to shock or to suggest that the characters have sex constantly on their minds'. Another one adds that 'if the director's intention was to shock … he definitely failed, unless he thinks that in the era of hardcore porn and Hollywood B-movies nudity and superfluous violence are shocking'. Interestingly, while these reviews criticise the film's exploitative textuality, scholars appraised Mundruczó's film as that of a 'promising newcomer in terms of an innovative representation of the body and gender issues' (Stőhr 2016: 140), and appreciated its honesty (Bakács 2003), 'frank realism, upfront sexuality and grim humor' (Stratton 2022). Mundruczó himself expressed that his intention was to mirror the 'pressure of society' (Mundruczó in Horecky 2002) on a bodily level and to highlight the corporeal nature of the film, which are manifested through brutality. Although, as he adds 'one can see much more brutal things on the evening news' (Mundruczó in Formanek 2008).

Festival Triumph = Body, Commodity and Self-exotism

The critical acclaim and Mundruczó's statement raise several questions about post-socialist Hungary and in a broader sense (Eastern European) art cinema. Reading *Pleasant Days* as an artwork that 'evokes culturally specific bodily experiences' (Stőhr 2016: 140) presupposes that the exchange of children, deprivation, petty crime and the mistreatment of females are everyday practices in Hungary. As Strausz emphasises,

> Mundruczó … exoticizes (the) recognizably Eastern European setting and refrains from emphasizing the ways his images contribute to audiovisual processes of marginalisation. Subsequently, these gestures are awarded in the cultural centres of high art, such as Cannes … The distant othering function that is recognizable in these awarded gestures becomes very clear, and his films seems to play upon this set of cultural expectations. In this context, his films reflect a strong postcolonial critical success to raise awareness about the ways these cultural-geopolitical enunciations contribute to the production of Eastern Europe as the Other. (Strausz 2006: 159)

The often-exploitative spectacle which erupts without narrative or psychological motivation and depicts a 'deviant grid of human relations' (Batori 2018: 174), suggests that some of the episodic sequences are about the turning of profit through the commercial exhibition of taboo.

The confusing depiction of the siblings in the film and Maya's enforced scenes of nudity are all indicative of this gesture. Mária and Péter bath and wrestle naked together, the sister washes the genitals of her brother, and they almost kiss in some of the scenes. The representations of 'deteriorating, aberrant domestic gender relations' (Strausz 2016: 159) not only probe the relationship between ethics and the position of protagonists/ spectators but, as they do not contribute to the narrative arc of the film, they only seem to be placed within the film's textual sphere to stir up controversy – and make profit. In another scene, Maya is seen showering with another female whom she asks to express her opinion about her 'cunt' (*pina*). While touching Maya's vagina, her friend notes that her 'pussy' (*punci*) is completely normal. These genitally explicit images only serve the elliptic and fragmented narrative structure of the film and strengthen the film's exploitation stance.

On the one hand, *Pleasant Days* can be read as a metaphor which seeks to illustrate the identity crises, the burdens of patriarchal society, and the characters' material, mental and spiritual deprivation through the symbolic representation of the body (Stőhr 2016). Critics of extreme cinema often come to a similar conclusion when arguing that pornographic features, sexual arousal, or rape, as in the case of Catherine Breillat's or Noé Gaspar's films, displace sex into critical thought (Bordun 2017). Similar to the sexual violence against the teenager Anaïs (Anaïs Reboux) in the last scene case of *Fat Girl* (*À ma sœur!* 2001) and that of Alex's in the nine-minute sequence of *Irreversible* (*Irréversible*, 2002), Maya's rape excludes the explicit portrayal of pornographic elements from the frame. The long takes, shaking camera work, diegetic sound, and the close-ups of the female characters in these films highlight the suppressed, paralyzed position of the violated. The documentary-like images thus demonstrate the 'presence of sexuality under patriarchy' (Bordun 2017: 134) and, instead of pure sexism, serve a deeper directorial goal. In *Fat Girl*, the subjugated position of women is clearly communicated in the twenty-minute seduction scene of Elena (Roxane Mesquida) who gets blackmailed into sexual intercourse. As a fifteen-year-old teenager, the young girl has no experience with men. When she is told that anal sex does not count with virgin girls and adds that he has to look for other girls if Elena is not willing to have sex with him, the patriarchal structure and the oppressor-oppressed structure gets stressed. In *Irreversible*, Noé uses handheld camera work and underlit scenes to set up the "the syndrome of the West" – sexual exploitation and violence – as the characters put it in the film's establishing shot. In both films, the portrayal of naked bodies serves to convey a deeper message about contemporary social-gender sets. Although it has been argued that, in case of *Irreversible*, 'there is little narrative or compositional motivation for showing this kind of cruelty in its actual duration' (Gronstad 2004: 202), the brutality in the rape scene serves as a crucial element in the narrative's cause-and-effect chain for it explains Marcus's similarly brutal physical violence as a response. In the case of *Fat Girl*, Elena's pure spectacle of her genitals has little or no arousal effect at all. Her motionless, pale body reflects her virgin vulnerability that is about to be destroyed. In the case of *Pleasant Days*, the violent manipulation of Maya's body in the post-1989, neoliberal setting and her son's objectification via Western currency point towards a colonising set-up in which Maya gets punished for trying to stand on her own feet and fight for her child. The rape scenes in these films thus use the body as a metaphoric device to draw attention to the neoliberal disposability of the body. Wannabe-art and art cinema thus fuse to create absolute awareness.

The Patriarchal Gaze and Sexuality: *She-Shaman*

The very same phenomenon of the juxtaposition of neoliberal disposability and the extreme can be witnessed with Andrzej Żuławski's *She-Shaman* (*Szamanka*, 1996). The film recounts the troubled love story of a Polish architecture student, 'The Italian' (Iwona Petry) and an anthropology doctoral student, Michał (Bogusław Linda) who accidentally meet on the streets of Warsaw. In need of accommodation, Michał agrees to rent a room to the young girl and their first encounter ends in a violent sex scene. Although the Italian has a boyfriend and Michał is engaged to Anna (Agnieszka Wagner), the newly-met couple cannot surmount their mutual attraction, and they start an aggressive-obsessive sexual relationship. In the meantime, Michał becomes obsessed with the examination of the newly discovered 2,000 year-old well-conserved shaman whose body was found surrounded by mushrooms. In the laboratory Michał and his colleagues consume the drug. Michał has a vivid hallucination in which the shaman awakes and tells him that his skull was fractured by a woman who wanted to capture his magic power. Upon his return to their love next, Michał breaks up with the Italian who eventually crushes the back of his skull and eats his brain.

Wherever screened, Żuławski's film still stirs up controversy. Because of its very explicit sexual content, Polish authorities limited the theatrical screenings of *She-Shaman* and the film had a very uncomfortable aftermath. The director himself described his film as being 'without masks', intending to portray the violence, grim social realism and power structures in post-communist Poland (Goddard 2014; Ostrowska 2017: 136).

THE POLITICAL TRANSITION AND THE EXTREME   55

Żuławski argued to represent the 'rest of the communist system', the backwardness of Poland and its petit bourgeoise (Żuławski 2012). Critics mainly concentrated on the chauvinist representation of the post-socialist Polish Zeitgeist whose symbol, Iwona Petry accused the director of emotionally abusing her during the shoot. The actress had a nervous breakdown and attempted suicide after the shooting (Janisse 2012). It is less surprising that after these events, critics accused the film of the inaccurate portrayal of Poland as well as its unethical stance which resulted in the overall reading of *She-Shaman* as a misogynist work. Some voices tried to draw attention to the feminist screenplay, but even these voices emphasised how Żuławski altered the original text and created his own cinematic vision (Goddard 2014; Goddard 2012: 305–9). Because of the various sexual games between two strangers, this vision has been compared to Bernardo Bertolucci's *Last Tango in Paris* (1972) and some critics dubbed *She-Shaman* 'Last Tango in Warsaw' (Haltof 2002: 123).

Yet, as Ostrowska points out, Żuławski's film produces an effect of disgust, rather than moral disdain (2017: 134). Critics labelled the film 'violent', 'brutal' (Jagdzinski 2007: 317–18), 'an art film about sex and sweat, one that seems to have emerged from the guts as opposed to intellectual game-playing, or in the bleakly absurd streets of mid-1990s post-Communist Poland' (Kipp 2011). Regarded by reviewers as 'the most peculiar movie' of all times and a 'uniquely vicious' and 'exhilaratingly grotesque' film, *She-Shaman* definitely poses challenges to the viewer (Pinkerton, 2014). Żuławski's genuinely shocking 'repetitive nightmare cycle' (Kipp 2011) simultaneously arouses and frustrates the demands of pornographic phantasy. Similar to Mundruczó's film, *She-Shaman* is brimming with unpleasant associations of violence, sex, power, domination and degradation that are all tied up along a confusing and ambiguous narrative chain. Indeed, *She-Shaman* is a controversial work, one that overflows with acts of violence that erupt without narrative or psychological motivation. The first sexual encounter between Michał and the Italian happens so suddenly and violently that the spectator barely has time to make sense of the scene. The two protagonists barely enter the room when Michał starts to zip off the Italian's jacket. He then cuts his finger, licks his blood and adds that the girl would be 'quite a honey' without her cap. In the next shot, the man unbuttons the sweater of the petrified girl, pulls up her shirt and puts the Italian's body in a half-lateral position on the bed. Shivering in a cramped position with her naked lower body, the half-naked Italian is then raped by Michał. Żuławski registers the girl's face and naked breasts as she helplessly grasps for air and cries. The man's fully dressed figure (his long black winter coat and scarf) overshadows the Italian's white body and puts her in a deeply subjugated and vulnerable position (Figure 2.5). This power mechanism is further stressed by the next over-the-shoulder shot which frames the girl's desperate facial expressions from Michał's point-of-view. In a prolonged sequence, Żuławski then cuts between the Italian's crying and then smiling face and Michał's excited close-up.

This enforced, deeply disturbing sexual encounter which 'is stripped of any placatory cultural camouflage of love or romance' (Ostrowska 2017: 133), not only provokes disgust but, since rape functions as the motor of *She-Shaman's* episodic syuzhet, it communicates a juxtaposition of rape and sexual intercourse. After their first sexual encounter, Żuławski cuts to the post-coital portrait of Michał and the Italian. As if the previous aggressive scene did not happen, their relaxed bodies face the camera and Michał puts his arms around the girl's legs. The two then discuss Michał's profession and the very fact that both of them are in a relationship. *She-Shaman* is replete with these kinds of sex scenes which technically constitute statutory rape and serious physical abuse, yet they are normalised throughout the film.

After the researchers find out that the shaman had 'female sperm' in his rectum, Michał anally rapes the Italian. Beyond doubt, this is one of the film's most disturbing scenes. The violent acoustic realm of the sequence – with the girl's scream and Michał's parallel explanation of why she has to undergo such an act, is further supported by the Italian's visually locked-up position. Her hands are kept down by the man's rear

Figure 2.5 Subjugated: *She-Shaman*. Poland: Canal+Polska, 1996.

THE POLITICAL TRANSITION AND THE EXTREME 57

grip who strongly grabs the girl's whole body. Their bodies are framed by the bathroom's shower pipe which, with its bracketing vertical line, hooks up the Italian's figure and gives the whole scene and even more suffocating atmosphere. Michał often requests oral sex and pushes the Italian's head aggressively downwards or feeds her violently and/or wants to exchange his new girlfriend for drugs. He even adds that the Italian is like 'a little machine' who only 'eats, sleeps and fucks'. Everything in *She-Shaman* is thus deeply corporeal, grounded in the intersection of pain, abuse and a series of incomprehensible acts which all portray the Italian's utter subjugation and humiliation at the hands of Michał, as well as the whole of society. In one of the scenes, the anthropologist asks the Italian to spit in his mouth. In another one, the Italian is seen vomiting on the train, then she is portrayed licking and hyperventilating over a glass display at the university museum. Later, she erupts in a voodoo dance at a university party and rubs raw meat into her vagina and eats cat food from a bowl on the floor. With her incomprehensible acts, the girl's deeply troubled figure resonates an internally colonised entity. Not only is she deprived of her subjectivity for not owning a name (Ostrowska 2017: 132), but she is constantly pushed, humiliated and raped by the men in the narrative. As a second-class citizen, the Italian's body gets objectified. For this reason, Żuławski constantly portrays the Italian naked while, interestingly, Michał almost always wears heavy black jacket or long clothes (even when committing his rapes). Also, the two lovers never kiss or have any conversation: the Italian is only seen eating, drinking, working in factories or/and undergoing physical abuse, while Michał is depicted in power positions: he does his research, goes out with his friends or seduces other women. Consequently, the Italian's suppressed figure only functions as a puppet in the narrative. The pornographic rape air of *She-Shaman* and its oblique and provocative terror and shock shots give the film a visceral blow. The use of female suppression thus functions as an organising element of the film. Violence in *She-Shaman* is tied to a normative form of masculinity that ultimately grounds chauvinist forms of violence. The main narrative line, the various rape scenes between the two protagonists, is surrounded with unconnected, shocking acts whose narrative and/ or psychological motivation remains foggy. The mental illness of the Italian or the reason/cause of her animal-like demeanour – she eats cat food and screams and vomits on the street, greases glasses with food and endures rape – remain unanswered. Instead, the Italian's body remains the site of intense affects and violent acts which clearly operate directly on the spectator's body and the senses. In the process of sensuous, affective articulation of female subjugation, *She-Shaman* forms a portrayal of

58   THE EXTREME CINEMA OF EASTERN EUROPE

post-socialist masculinity. The very identity of this emasculated canon is built on a superiority complex which registers sexual violence and physical abuse against women. Similar to *Peasant Days, She-Shaman* can be read as a metaphor of emasculation and the burdens of patriarchal society. Still, in contrast to Maya's representation in Mundruczó's film and the often objective, cinéma verité camera work, *She-Shaman* portrays the Italian through a very masculine gaze which strengthens Michał's and society's patriarchal perspective.

Reception and Rape: Recipe for Success

In Jan Jagdzinski's Lacanian reading of the film, *She-Shaman* develops a battle between two conceptualisations of the body that circumscribes the postmodern condition: the film juxtaposes the body of desire with biological drives and instincts whose common mediator is death. In contrast is the body of enjoyment/jouissance, Michał's figure embraces the body of sacrifice for his experiences are based on the transcendental plane of shamanism, that is, he chooses 'life in death' as opposed to 'death in life' (2007: 321). Through her very act of eating Michał, her materialised *object a*, the girl becomes a femme fatal and demands a place in the Symbolic order of Polish society that constantly rejected and ignored her. This 'radical feminine Act' (Ibid., 323) helps the Italian to find her jouissance and combat the patriarchal order. As Jagdzinski summarises:

> Not only is the signifier denied to her, the only signifier she is allowed to bare is one where she is like a man—a steel worker—or perhaps a member of the sex trade, a prostitute. Iwona in effect has no place except to be the Sadean woman, to act as a post femme fatale, as a destroyer of men. Why post? She is willing to commit a feminine act to steal back her jouissance. She survives through her instinctual body rather than being destroyed as in classic femme fatale narratives. She inverts her drives so that she can destroy/sacrifice her fantasmatic support—her perverted lover, Michael. But at what price? Having experienced the perversion of jouissance, all "ordinary" men seem to be a joke to her, unable to satisfy her drives. She knows nothing of desire, having been denied it, while Michael has no escape either, neither as a pervert nor priest. (Ibid., 327)

While Jagdzinski's psychoanalytical approach highlights significant points of the Italian's position in the transitional patriarchal Polish society, even the author himself admits that 'this discourse of sacrifice, however, is presented to us obliquely ... anamorphically throughout the narrative' (Ibid., 321). Although the Italian's animal-like body and behaviour can indeed be hysterical sites of rebellion against the symbolic order, Żuławski only demonstrates the girl's authority at the very end of the film, after which she is seen working as a sex worker on the streets of Warsaw. Thus, by eating Michał's brain, she only defeats her superior position for seconds. What is more, she descends even lower on the Polish patriarchal ladder by quitting her studies and deciding to do sex work in 'this dehumanized, materialistic word', as Michał puts it in one of his lectures. Further readings of the film are similarly problematic when trying to defend *She-Shaman's* 'undeniably sadomasochistic elements' (Deighan 2016). Deighan for instance states that she has 'no tolerance for anyone who views Żuławski as a misogynist', and that the fundamental problem with the film is its 'sheer unconventionality' and its criticism of Polish conservativism. Somehow controversially, she then emphasises that (anal) sex in the film 'is depicted as an unpleasant, but possibly pleasurable surprise for the Italian, it is difficult to make sense of her visceral, quite unconventional reactions to sex and orgasm' and the couple's first encounter 'feels like an assault [but] she doesn't push [Michał] away and he comments how wet she is'. Another author comes to a similar conclusion:

> There is no emotion in him, no passion, and she has done nothing to invite this transaction. She doesn't fight but stands there stunned in what nevertheless plays out like a rape scene. As he positions her on the bed, her expression betrays her sense of violation, but when his face contorts in that orgasmic moment when he is outside of himself, she smiles. (Janisse 2012: 157)

In a similar vein, Godard discusses violence and horror in the film as an intended attack on post-socialist Poland, 'an attack that the film certainly transforms and identifies but does not necessarily submit to any misogynist agenda' (Goddard 2014: 254), yet he fails to explain *how* the director does all that. Ostrowska's (2017: 137) more complex analysis discusses the appetite of the Italian. She sees *She-Shaman* as a political allegory that subverts hegemonic ideology by the Italian cannibalistic act. This act of retribution mirrors 'all catastrophic changes pertaining to both individual and collective post-communist bodies' (Ibid., 137): that is, *She-Shaman* mirrors the post-socialist, perverse commodification of the female body.

The problem with these readings is twofold. First, as stated earlier, not only do they blur the difference between one's biological organism/ reaction to touch and sexual arousal (it is well-known that one can get raped even if he/she produces fluid), but they interconnect rape and art. In other words, these readings often identify rape as an artistic gesture, and they paradoxically defend the director's chauvinism as a legitimate artistic choice to express a feminist perspective. Unfortunately, these readings only focus on the act of cannibalism as retribution, whereas the largest part of the narrative handles the very oppression of the female body.

Second, these readings omit closer analysis of the narrative structure of the film. While I embrace the idea that sexual violence can, indeed, function as a tool of ideological-political and social criticism, the very lack of causality in *She-Shaman* only endangers such connotative readings. While *Pleasant Days* and *She-Shaman* both offer a portrayal of the post-socialist aegis of Eastern Europe, they also convey an (anti)aesthetic tabloid which only supports the colonised position of the region. *Pleasant Days* often promotes the naked body in highly exploitative ways which, with its throbbing, under-lit images, voyeuristic and disoriented handheld camera work, alternating off-centre composition which frame sexual organs, chaotic plot causality and awkward performances, strengthen the self-exoticist, sensationalist gesture of the filmmaker. *Szamanka*, as acknowledged by some, is driven by the 'frank exploration of the body, not by character or plot or even narrative, really' (Kipp 2011).

The attitude to include codes and elements of exploitation, horror, pornography, philosophy in extreme cinema has been widely discussed in scholarship (Beugnet 2007; Horeck and Kendall 2012). Some scholars accentuate the artistic value of transgressive images on screen and see them as a gesture to meet up with the Hollywoodian market (Quandt 2004) and the festival circuit. As Hagman (2007) sees it,

> festivals need a bit of controversy for the marketing purposes of signifying to the world that this is the place where bold decisions are still made and aesthetic risks still taken; it is meant also to connote that there is already a market in place, namely the international festival circuit, for the film that dares to be provocative and 'transgressive'. The irony is, of course, that this transgression is already anticipated, and to some extent constituted by, the market, thus serving to drain the word 'transgressive' of its very meaning. This, furthermore, carries the implication that cultural expression is not formed on the level of national film-industrial decisions but through transnational considerations of distributive potential. (34)

This 'affect economy' (Ibid., 36) not only leads to the hybridisation of lowbrow and highbrow cultures (Palmer 2006; Hobbs 2018) but prescribes sexually explicit images and shocking sequences as a recipe for economic success. Mundruczó's film won the 2022 Silver Leopard at the Locarno International Film Festival and was nominated at several other international film festivals which supports the above-described claims for transgression. The question, however, lies in the very distinction of art and pure exploitation. In *Pleasant Days*, the two merge into one another and create a unique example of exploitative art cinema.

It is no doubt that the most intriguing questions of extreme cinema concern its genericism and artistic value. As outlined in the previous

THE POLITICAL TRANSITION AND THE EXTREME   61

chapter, the blurry boundaries of allegorism, elliptical narrative and excessive visual style in Mundruczó's *Pleasant Days* and Żuławski's *She-Shaman* question the very positioning of the film as a production of art. In *Conjugal Bed*, the transgressive images convey a clear metaphoric message (the characters even break the fourth wall to communicate the gruesome nature of the socio-political transition). Makavejev's subversive sequences, however unethical they may be, provide ideological criticism and shock the spectator into political consciousness. Films like *She-Shaman* or *Pleasant Days*, however, put (Eastern European) art cinema on the path of extremism where the very motivations of displaying nudity, eroticism, pornographic fantasy, violent and extreme sexual acts become incomprehensible. The demand, as scholarship often emphasises, 'is placed on the spectator to assemble the images until they make sense' (Borgun 2017: 141) but without narrative momentum, the (embedded) socio-political critique of extreme cinema might easily get reduced to chauvinist manifestations.

While Mundruczó's film questions the objectivity of art in foregrounding disturbing and subversive sexual sequences, another post-1989 Eastern extreme wave goes even further in downplaying subversive and perverted images via the transgressive display of dead/live animals and the characters' interaction with them. The graphically explicit (often sexual) sequences and loose narrative structure of these examples suggest that the boundaries of sensationalism, connotative message, taboo and art are now merged into one another. Is there any artistic value in these productions or should we reduce them to simple gestures of (commercial) exploitation? The following chapters analyse the art/exploitation dichotomy. First, to frame the discussion, the analysis focuses on selected case studies of animal torture in Western European cinema. Through selected case studies, the chapters later introduce another wave of extreme tendency in post-1989 Eastern European cinema.

CHAPTER 3

Post-Socialist Animality: Towards an (Eastern European) Extreme Cinema

The representation of animal violence has accompanied the history of film since the birth of art cinema. Be that the Soviet avantgarde (Eisenstein's *Strike*, 1925), French Lyrical Realism (Jean Renoir's *The Rules of the Game*, 1939), European Modernisms (Jean-Luc Godard's *Weekend*, 1967; Ingmar Bergman's *Persona*, 1966; or Huszárik Zoltán's *Elégia / Elegy*, 1965), New Hollywood (Francis Ford Coppola's *Apocalypse Now* 1979), German New Wave (Rainer Werner Fassbinder's *In a Year of 13 Moons*, 1978) or Greek Weird Wave cinema, animality on screen has usually been interpreted as a legitimate artistic choice that heightens films' connotative value (see McMahon 2019; Lippit 2002: 119–39; Lawrence 2010: 63–87; Galt 2017: 7–29).[1]

Lippit's (2000) well-known semantical-ontological approach to cinema emphasises the animals' textuality on screen as a mediator without language. The material-figurative trope of the animetaphor, as he has it, 'brings to language something that is not part of language and remains within language as a foreign presence' (166). That is, because the animal is said to lack the capacity for language, its function in language can only appear as 'another expression, as a metaphor that originates elsewhere, is transferred from elsewhere' (166). This trope, however, can disrupt the rhetorical configurations of film language. Because there is no proper death in cinema (by freezing the frame or rewinding the scene, any animal can be resuscitated), the portrayal of animal death becomes 'an impossible spectacle' (Ibid., 12) which 'problematizes the figurative value of such representations' (2002: 13). Lippit demonstrates this through Eisenstein's metaphoric slaughterhouse scene in *Strike* (1924) and the scene of rabbit slaughter in Jean Renoir's *Rules of the Game* (1939) whose animals repel against metaphorisation:

> As a trope, Renoir's slaughter of rabbits, like Eisenstein's scene of slaughter, pierces the reconfigurative language of the expression "to die like a rabbit" by animating

POST-SOCIALIST ANIMALITY   63

the metaphor. It becomes, in *Rules of the Game*, a living, animate metaphor, an ani-metaphor. To die like a rabbit becomes animetaphorical, actual, in the biomechanical drives of the film world. (Lippit, 2002: 14)

For Lippit, the deaths of animals turn into anti-metaphors which, by ani-mating the metaphor, erase the very connotative link for the animal is itself a metaphor. Meat thus becomes a rhetorical trope that, as in the case of *In a Year of 13 Moons* or *Apocalypse Now*, demonstrates the meat-acquisition process and as such, draws attention to capitalist mass production and/or the never-circularity of savagery. Nicole Shukin (2009) also focuses on the capital that manifests the form of animals as fetishist currency and service-able flesh. In her materialist-cultural reading, animals stand at the intersection of power relations and ontological bioproduction that is, they signal 'a tangle of biopolitical relations within which the economic and symbolic capital of animal life can no longer be sorted into binary distinction' (7). Shukin contextualises the double form of rendering which reproduces and interprets 'an object in linguistic, painterly, musical, filmic, or other media' and the 'industrial boiling down and recycling of animal remains' (20). Rendering brings together arts (ideology and culture) and indus-try (economics and technology) to demonstrate the power of biological capital. This power can, as demonstrated by her through Maclean's double rendering of Canada's national symbol, the beaver, reinstate economic (material) and symbolic logics (fetish) of power. In this process, 'animal and capital are increasingly produced as a semiotic and material closed loop, ... in the nauseating recursivity of this logic, capital becomes animal, and animals becomes capital' (16). As argued below, (Eastern) European extreme cinemas utilise the representational rendering of death, dying and/or tortured animals as exploitative cultural signs to draw attention to capitalist mass-production in the region and paradoxically, to support the literal economy of such representations. That is, extreme cinemas sacrifice the dying/tortured image of animals on the altar of political–ideological criticism, while they also expropriate the spectacle for commercial/festival success. Somehow in a contradictory manner, they do obey, and do criti-cise the mechanisms of the capitalist-neoliberal Zeitgeist at the very same time. The paradoxical gesture can be clearly seen in Gaspar Noé's *Carne* (1991) that features the meticulous butchering and skinning of a horse at the start of the film which has deeply affected spectators. As the reviews on the film's IMDb page[2] demonstrate, viewers endorse watching the film for its shocking images. One reviewer adds that 'this isn't ... gore, it's real butchering. ... I recommend this movie to all those of you who want something to think about or simply watch something different of [sic] what you find in your average cinema'. Another reviewer also emphasises the butchering-effect in *Carne*: 'The most shocking to me is when they slaughter a horse .... It is a good watch but be warned, it challenges your senses'. Similar to these reviews, other comments also stress the shock value for which some categorise *Carne* as 'a very good film' and 'astonishing', one for which 'you have to have a stomach'. Following its premiere in Cannes where it won the top prize of the short film section, *Carne* has been generally praised by critics and audiences.

The film tells the story of a horse butcher whose wife leaves the man with their newborn daughter. On the day of the now young teenager's first menstruation, his father misinterprets the blood on the girl's skirt. Being certain that his daughter has been raped, he stabs an innocent worker and cripples him. Following the act, he gets imprisoned, loses his butcher's shop and apartment, and his mute daughter gets placed in a mental hospital. Upon the butcher's release, he starts working for 'the fat woman' in a pub-cafeteria he used to visit every day when he was a respected consumer. The woman ends up pregnant and, despite the ex-butcher's plan 'to fuck her ass so strongly that she will have a miscarriage', the two eventually stay together and move to another city. At the end of the film, the butcher visits his daughter in the asylum, but leaves frustrated as to how his life turned out this miserable way.

Carne renders the horse iconography as a connecting element to interlink the various timetables of the story and establish a linear cohesion in the narrative. The girl's upbringing is accompanied by her riding on her father's knees and then a horse machine in front of his shop. The motif of riding is intercut with the butcher's monotonous work. Whichever year Noé presents, the butcher is seen slicing horse meat in his shop. Consequently, *Carne* interconnects the very motif of the horse with the passage of time and circle of life, in this way to link the industrialised slaughtering of the animal and the life of the butcher. The horse meat references the impermanence of the family's monotonous-capitalist way of life which is further strengthened by Noé's chapter-like episodes and voice-over narration in the mise-en-scéne. Most importantly, the butcher's figure can be identified with the fate of the horse. It is no accident that, instead of featuring a slaughterhouse, Noé depicts the slaughter of *a single* horse. The two modes of violation ('No animal was harmed' versus 'All resemblances to persons living or deceased is purely coincidental') which, to paraphrase Lippit, 'are lined by the singularity ascribed to humanity and the multiplicity that is said to determine animality' (2002: 11), are reversed in *Carne*. Be that the horse, or the butcher, Noé only foregrounds individual entities to help the juxtaposition of the man and animal. As monotonous and inhuman as the production of horse meat is, so the butcher's life is repetitious and cruel. The explicit cruelty of the establishing shot is synchronised with the meat-production circle of *Carne*: thanks to the tactile camerawork, the characters only exist in the film through his touch. First, he carefully washes his daughter's legs and cuts horse meat after. Later, he is portrayed touching the body of his new girlfriend. The touch of the butcher has a destroying effect: his wife leaves him, his daughter becomes mute, his worker dies and the fate of his new girlfriend and child is already predictable. The very textual metaphor of touch, blood and meat in *Carne* thus creates a unity and a never-ending circle of decay and birth. This is even more prevalent in the sequel of the film, *I Stand Alone* (*Seul contre tous*, 1998). Noé's first feature film continues its story where *Carne* left off. The butcher now lives with his pregnant girlfriend and mother-in-law in Lille. When he is accused by his girlfriend of cheating on her, he bursts out in anger and beats up the woman. He then leaves the city and visits friends and ex-colleagues to ask for financial support or a job, but he gets constantly turned down. Without work and money, his last trip leads to his daughter whom he brutally murders in the very same hotel room she was conceived in. It soon turns out, that the whole sequence was an imagination and instead of murdering her child, the butcher embarks upon a sexual relationship with her. Noé closes the film with the butcher's voiceover narration in which he explains how happy he is that he can be with his daughter, and makes a philosophical statement that humanity and freedom do not exist, but (his) loves does.

I Stand Alone omits any mondo effect, but it operates with brutal and explicit visual images, such as a porn-sequence in a movie theatre or the very visceral scene of the daughter's killing, all of which contributed to the film being discussed under the aegis of New French Extremity (see Palmer 2015; West 2016). The brutal reality of horse butchering in the establishing shot of *Carne* returns in the systematic killing of the daughter so that Noé can create a whole circle of death and birth. The visceral sequences of *I Stand Alone* thus reflect the 'endless, brutalizing, dog-eat-dog war' (Palmer 2015: 61) within modern French society (West 2016: 48) for which *Carne*'s mondo sequence serves as an establishing metaphor. Without doubt, the horse-shock effect contributed to convey Noé's troublesome message on French bourgeois society and, as the positive reviews and critics illustrate, helped the film to be circulated at festivals and arthouse cinemas.

Haneke's films function along the same aesthetic-metaphoric realm. The fish tank in *The Seventh Continent* (*Der Siebente Continent* 1989) suggests a juxtaposition between the family's suffocating life and the enclosed living space of fishes. The prolonged sequence in which Haneke captures

66   THE EXTREME CINEMA OF EASTERN EUROPE

the grasping fishes on the floor, enhances the film with a metaphoric layer that explains why the family, sick of their capitalist routine, decide to commit suicide. In *Benny's Video* (1992), Haneke uses the killing of a pig to draw attention to the lack of interpersonal relationships in the capitalist age and the way digitisation annihilates the boundaries between diegetic and extradiegetic words. As Lawrence (2010) argues,

> Haneke presents the death of an animal not as part of an investigation of the lives of animals nor as part of a realist project but as part of an allegorical representation of bourgeois alienation from, and responsibility for, *human* others. The deaths of the animals in these films … exceed their metaphorical function as a result of the spectacle of their incontrovertible and material deaths. The relationship between the world in which these films circulate and the fictional worlds these films present is made more complicated by such moments, in which the spectator is confronted with the violence of the fictions' sudden shift into the real violence of an animal's death. (74)

Besides the connotative use, the authenticity of the narrative has been a key argument for justifying the portrayal of animal death on screen. It has been argued that in extreme cinema, animals function as a 'sufficient substitute for human actors' (Wiegand 2017: 257) and their slaughter can be identified as 'an insight into what real death might look like' (Wheatley 2011: 96–7). While we would dismiss someone's death on the cinema canvas as trickery, animals' real death is indisputable (Ibid., 97). The bullfighting in Kim Ki Duk's *Isle* (*Seom*, 2000), the death of the baby bird in Catherine Breillat's *Anatomy of Hell* (*Anatomie dr l'enfer*, 2004), the slaughter of the horse in Gaspar Noé's *Carne* (1991) or the decapitated chicken in *Hidden* (*Caché*, 2005) all foreground fictional worlds but rely on the indexical representation of documentary when it comes to animal slaughter. The sudden switch between the narrative and documentary space 'throw the spectator outside the diegesis of a film' (Jeung and Andrew 2008: 6) that is, the very textual switch itself creates confusion in the viewer. When confronted with taboo imagery, this shock effect might even be heightened for the viewer's impossibly passive position. Real death in extreme cinema can be thus used as an exploitative shock effect or 'shock entertainment' (Wiegand 2017: 258), a taboo experiment which goads viewers' curiosity and generates commercial/artistic success. It seems that the more bloody, documentary and gore-like animal death is portrayed, the more attention and economic prospect these films increase. But does this shock value produce cultural meaning, or does it remain at the pure level of economic exploitation?

When discussing *Strike*, Shukin and O'Brian (2015) evoke Eisenstein's method of 'the power of the pole-axe and the rifle to deliver [a] physical blow' (191) which aimed to convey a political message by means of cinematic affect. The montage of attraction in *Strike* – the famous sequence that intercuts the slaughter of cows and the rebellion of people – intended 'to strike the human out of the material' that is, to put screen textuality (passive spectatorship) into action. This cinematic affect, according to Shukin and O'Brian,

> abolishes the gap between image and action. In their affective immediacy, images should function not as representations that *mean* but as intensities that *move* bodies with an emotional-physical force. Slaughter appears to function as the raw image of this ideal simultaneity of image and action, cause and effect ... *Making feel* through techniques of cinematic affect is ultimately a project of *making humans*, a humanity that is realised and authenticated when spectators react with the appropriate feeling and action to the force of images. (Emphasis original, 191–4)

From a cognitive point of view, Torben Grodal also accentuates the shock-effect of Eisenstein's metaphor. He argues that, since the mental processing takes more time than verbal fiction, the understanding and interpreting of such metaphors in visual fiction becomes much more complicated for the brain and so for the spectator. In his account, 'art films may like experiments with metaphors because their viewers may prefer difficult processing tasks' (2016: 109), but he also adds that, because the very process in the brain to fuse pictorial and acoustic information takes longer, the spectator might remember the scene better. In other words, the processing effort might bring commercial success for the scene and might become part of a wider spectatorial discourse. Grodal emphasises that in order to avoid the confused interpretation to transcription, filmmakers must be aware of only representing the source domain (contexts and aspects) of a metaphor and thus leave the target domain (inner mental states or abstract mental models) invisible. This might be the reason why the cows in *Strike*, the slaughtered pig in *Benny's Video*, or the horse in *Carné* – which all follow the power of animal capital and try to interconnect the symbolic layer of the films with the extra-diegetic knowledge of the spectator – are well remembered among moviegoers. On the one hand, they only represent the source domain while they also use visual emphasis to activate the fusion of the pictorial and acoustic information.

In a paradoxical way, however, neither the slaughter of cows in the feature film *Strike* or the mass killing of dolphins in the documentary *The Cove* (Louie Psihoyos, 2009) resulted in the social change that the directors aspired to:

> Unlike the blow that unmistakably fells an animal, isn't the affective strike far more uncertain in its results despite the scientific rationality with which Eisenstein sought to determine its effects? *Strike* and *The Cove* inadvertently show that the relay

> between image, affect and action is far from assured, and that shadowing political cinema's ideal of their immediacy there is always the possibility of a disconnect, a failure. (Shukin and O'Brian 2015: 200–1)

Unsurprisingly then, other scholarly readings of cinematic animal death claim that the vulnerability of animals represents pure human control and domination (see McMahon 2019: 198; Lawrence 2010: 64–5).

Vivian Sobchack also calls death on screen the 'most effective cinematic signifier' (1984: 289) which, by contrasting the animate and inanimate, violates a visual taboo. She accentuates that when death is represented as real, 'when its signs are structured and inflected so as to function indexically ... the representation must find ways to justify violation' (1984: 291). In other words, the filmmaker must explain the reason of this cultural transgression and the use of an indexical sign in a symbolic representation and 'indicate that watching the event of death is not more important than preventing it' (294). Although Sobchack's ethical vision mainly concerns the embodied situation of the documentary filmmaker, she stresses that narrative representation also must comply with a set of ethical groundings to find cultural sanction. Often, these sanctions in fiction cinema deploy a colonial narrative. For instance, *Japón* (Carlos Reygadas, 2002) features an unsimulated scene of the shooting of a bird whose head is then torn off by hand and thrown in the sand. *Japón* centres upon a middle-aged painter who travels to an unknown valley in north Mexico to end his life. His suicidal plans soon vanish when he encounters Ascen (Magdalena Flores), an elderly indigenous woman who accommodates the painter at her isolated farmhouse in the Hidalgo mountains. Despite the lack of conversation, the monotonous everyday life there brings the two protagonists together and Ascen slowly resuscitates the man's sexuality that Reygadas emphasises via the man's subjective point-of views of staring at Ascen's sexual body parts. Before leaving, the painter asks the old woman to sleep with him and the former agrees. Despite her consent, the sexual encounter of the two remains the film's most upsetting sequence. Reygadas captures the shivering, naked body of the old woman as she tries to cover her breasts in a frozen, death-like corporeal figuration on the bed. Before the actual penetration, the painter moves her shaking body around to find the perfect pose for the act. During the sex, Ascen is framed in a close-up staring at the ceiling of her bedroom. Rather than a mutual intercourse, the scene calls forth images of rape. Following the act, Ascen loses everything: her nephew dismantles her home to take the stones of her barn somewhere else and the woman, who leaves with her nephew, dies in an unknown accident. The last scene of the film portrays Ascen on the railway tracks.

The corporeality of animals, including the decapitated bird or the three-minute-long copulating scene of horses, visualises man's superiority over animals, while also referencing man's sexual impulses (De Luca 2016: 223–5). Similar to the socialist extreme examples, Reygadas identifies nature with femininity which is overwritten by the presence of male characters who cause the downfall of the woman. Ascen's 'earth mother figure' and 'primitive, carnal spirituality' (Cramer 2016: 240) stand in strong contrast with her Westernised nephew and the white and civilised artistic-intellectual traveller (Ibid., 240) who both penetrate the very private realm of the indigenous woman. The painter thus represents a colonising historical reality which is further exemplified by the torture of birth in the beginning of the film. As representative of nature, the cruelty of this scene foreshadows the rape of the old woman and eventually, her death at the end of the film. That is, the man from the city destroys the untouched nature of the hinterland: first, he decapitates the bird and in the end, the death of the wilderness's symbolic figure, Ascen, closes the colonial narrative. With its recurring 360-degree pans, horizontal screen mobility and oscillating camera work, and magnified still close-ups of death – which De Luca names 'cinematic non-anthropocentrism' (De Luca 2016: 225) – the mise-en-scéne of *Japón* contributes to the authenticity of the story and heightens its realistic tone.

As we see, questions of reality, authenticity and the rhetorical role of animals are strongly interwoven. The very reason why the combination of authenticity and animal death might work as political device on screen and why extreme cinemas often follow a similar logic, is due to death's immense value to foreground certain taboos[3] and, in this way, cause a vertiginous effect. Unsurprisingly, the transition cinema of Eastern Europe follows a colonial (self)-representation which, on the one hand, is due to the region's historical construction as 'primitive, animalistic, and less human' (Galt 2017:10) and Eastern Europe's self-colonising metaphor to follow such stereotyped imagery. On the other hand, as we will see, the material and figurative animal-imagery is strongly linked to femininity in the region's cinema. Through animality, eastern European extreme cinema foregrounds the discourse of foreign aggression and Eastern European victimisation. In the selected examples, the figuration of animals is associated with the maternal deprivation of female protagonists; that is, directors utilise animality to translate the sexual objectification of women.[4] Within the post-socialist transition cinema of Eastern Europe,[5] the symbolic castration of the region which, as outlined in the previous chapter, got translated to the screen in the form of transgressive violence against females and motherhood, takes on another form that reflects upon the

70   THE EXTREME CINEMA OF EASTERN EUROPE

socio-economic and political changes via animal imagery. The death of livestock husbandry is strongly connected to the death of the nation as a neo-colonised,[6] subjugated entity.

Eastern European Animalities: Metaphors of Sexual Objectification

Set in 1944 on Estonia's seashore, Sulev Keedus's *Somnambulance* (*Somnambuul*, 2003) focuses on a father-daughter relationship in an abandoned village. While thousands leave their home country to escape the approaching frontline, the young and virgin girl Eetla (Katariina Unt) decides to stay with her father Gottfrid (Evald Aavik). The elderly man spends his days watching over the local lighthouse and taking care of his bewildered, confused daughter. Without his wife, Gottfrid's only joy is his obsession with ornithology. His stuffed birds cover the ceiling of their home, and the man constantly looks for other pieces to complete his Collection. While he is occupied with these daily activities, Eetla struggles to find a balance between fiction and reality. She repetitively recounts the story of her rape which, due to the mosaic-like narrative that mixes up elements of past and present as well as dreams and reality, becomes confusing to comprehend. The appearance of the local gynaecologist, Kasper (Ivo Uukkivi), only intensifies this hallucinatory context. In the belief that he wants to rape her, Eetla first stabs the man in the stomach (who then spends his days recovering at the farm). Following their unpleasant first encounter, Kasper and Eetla soon develop an intimate relationship. Suspecting that the young girl was not a virgin when they first slept together, the doctor calls her to account, upon which Eetla eventually recalls her rape by a mute Russian soldier. Unknown to the spectator whose child she carries at the end of the film, the pregnant Eetla sets fire to the lighthouse to kill herself and her unborn baby.

The narrative kern and recurring element of *Somnambulance* revolves around Eetla's unresolved rape. Caused by the traumatic nature of the event, the young girl is incapable of piecing together the act. Instead, she dwells into prolonged, lonely and confusing monologues in which she narrates memory-images of the event. These visual motifs consist of the rapist soldier's drowning-dying dog that could not swim and had to be shot (by Eetla) as well as the disappearance of the girl's mother who had an abortion and fled to Sweden and/or was murdered by soldiers. Also, the associative images include a fish penetrating the girl's vagina and tearing apart her intestines before leaving Eetla's body through her mouth. These narrative flashbacks are accompanied by Eetla's memories of dancing before the sexual violence. In the end, it becomes clear that these cloudy sequences all reference Eetla's rape by a mute soldier. It is almost half-way into the film that Keedus actually shows the real act. While Eetla narrates her vivid dream-like fantasy-images of penetrating fishes, she wraps her naked body into a white blanket and tells Kasper to 'look at' the happenings. In the next sequence, Eetla is portrayed in the same wrapped-up position as she enters the wooden shed of the toilet in a wide-angle shot in the barren snowy landscape. The sequence is then followed by the arrival of the soldier and his German shepherd. In this scene, the camera is strongly linked to the man's movements and his discovery of the family home. Thanks to the unbroken, mobile shot and lack of non-diegetic sound, the underlit scene attains an eery atmosphere. The dark tone of the images only gets outweighed by Eetla's sudden appearance in her white blanket wrapped around her shoulders which establishes a narrative-aesthetic bridge with the previous scene. The girl asks the man to leave but the mute soldier demands Eetla dance for him. After writing his message ('dance') on the wooden floor, he grasps and pushes the girl on the table. In the next low-angle shot, Eetla is seen hopelessly fighting, shouting and crying for Kasper who eventually appears in the background and knocks down the rapist.

Although Keedus avoids the display of sexual organs, the extreme violence of the scene – Eetla's body and hands in spasm; her screaming and hopeless fight – enhances the sequence with a visceral blow. This black and white contrast of the images and the still, observational presence of the camera that frames Eetla's desperate resistance, only exacerbate the suffocating atmosphere of the images. Interestingly, although in a slightly different set-up, the scene gets repeated at the end of the film. This time, the sexual encounter starts with mutual agreement and the soldier does not wear a uniform. Lying on a turned-up small handcraft boat, Eetla is represented in the same dress and position as in the previous rape scene. She tries to stop the man penetrating her, but her hopeless cry and desperate physical fight seem useless. The sustained focus on Eetla's rhythmically moving upper body and never-ending struggle undoubtedly challenges the viewer's boundaries. As if easing the tension of the scene, Keedus intercuts the images of rape with Gottfrid's arrival who, however, gets too late to the scene. As he approaches the cottage, Eetla hysterically runs out of the building into the barren landscape.

Eetla's rape starts a series of extreme acts in the narrative whose focus point lies on the already mentioned metaphor of birds. Gottfrid's obsession with the mating, eggs and taxidermy of lapwings and white-tailed eagles becomes the symbolic trajectory of femininity. The young girl is very often seen covered in feathers and/or feathering chickens. Given Eetla's barely covered body throughout the film, these symbols become even more visually outstanding. Just before the arrival or Russian soldiers, she is captured in a low-angle shot that emphasises her naked legs and a dead, white chicken in between them. Keedus focuses on the very act of feathering of the animal. The rhythmic interval of high-angle and low-angle shots is escorted by Eetla's diegetic narration as she recounts her childhood memories of her mother's rape. Similar to her own dream-like memories, Eetla's vague monologue does not uncover the real happenings. We only learn that her mother was lying in her wedding dress, covered by feathers and wore shoes that she got from Eetla's uncles from Sweden. According to Eetla's memories, she then only had the shoes on and when asked why she is naked, she answered that 'no one would understand'. Keedus fuses the feather-symbol of past and present and strengthens the painfulness of the memory via the tearing diegetic sound of the chicken's skin. From this point on in the narrative, Eetla's body references the victimised role, and she is often seen covered by feathers. Whether her rape or her miserable cry-outs that she often carries out naked, the girl's thin body is either framed by images of dead birds or feathers. The more the film progresses, the more Keedus captures her body in a flying bird-position as she spreads her arms in a low-angle shot at the top of the lighthouse and shouts that she does not want to be touched. In this way, *Somnambulance* turns the figuration of seagulls into symbols of repression. This suppression is strongly linked to Eetla's sexual assault and colonised position in the narrative.

Somnambulance depicts a heavily male-centred society, where every male character causes physical pain to the only female protagonist. Gottfrid beats up his daughter for her illogic monologues, Kasper – although first resistant towards Eetla – sexually assaults the young girl, while the mute soldier rapes her. Beyond doubt, the biggest trauma – and the narrative motor of the film – is Eetla's rape which speaks of the very colonial set-up of Keedus's film. Unable to communicate verbally, the mute Russian soldier's very weapon is his physical strength through which he can force himself upon the family. The sexual objectification of the daughter (as well as mother) thus positions Estonian women within an Oriental model of patriarchy. Unable to fight the invaders, Gottfrid passively witnesses his daughter's agony. Instead of active resistance, his only escape is taxidermy though which he can, at least symbolically, preserve and protect femininity in his territory. The more violence Eetla experiences, the more Gottfrid's absurd bird-universe falls apart.

At the peak of the film, the young girl masturbates under the army of hanging seagulls (Figure 3.1). While she recounts the story of her rape,

Figure 3.1 Femininity in *Somnambulance*. Estonia: F-Seitse, 2003.

she violently grasps her breast and squeezes her nipple. The camera slowly tracks her movement as she bends down to the gun in-between her legs. She puts the end of the weapon into her mouth but, instead of pulling the trigger, she starts riding on it. When she almost reaches orgasm, she fires off the gun, in this way to shoot the birds which frame her half-naked body and bizarre act. Under the falling down feathers – which slowly cover her shoulders – Eetla eventually collapses from crying. Later, she puts all the prepared, stuffed birds in her suitcase and gets rid of them one by one at the Estonian seaside. In the final scene of *Somnambulance*, Eetla's jumps off the lighthouse and is seen sinking in the water with dead seagulls. Together with all the birds as symbols of femininity, Eetla also disappears in the water. The girl is incapable of fighting the colonising, masculinist supremacy that slowly annihilates her body and soul. The film's resolution throws the national subject into the sea, thus uniting the symbols of femininity – Eetla, the stuffed seagulls – with mother nature.

Similar to *Somnambulance*, Vladimír Michálek's *Angel Exit* (*Andel Exit*, 2000) also connects the concept of lost femininity with images of dead or dying animals. The film follows the Prague-based drug dealers Mikeš (Jan Cechticky) and Kája (Klára Issová) who travel to Morocco to cook their last batch. Although Mike hesitates whether to continue with the meth business and thus leave behind his new love and neighbour Jana (Zuzana Stivínová), Kája convinces him that upon their final trip, Mikeš can finally leave the underworld. In Africa, Mikeš invents the 'Czech Jet', a new type of drug, but the couple gets threatened by the local mafia which

74 THE EXTREME CINEMA OF EASTERN EUROPE

urges them to return to Prague. Although Mikeš wants to leave behind his underworld lifestyle, their Czech dealer and his American friend threaten him, and he is compelled to continue cooking. In the meantime, Jana gets pregnant but due to complications, she must stay in hospital. Mikeš's life thus slowly falls apart and, in the end, he finds himself alone in Prague.

Based on Jáchym Topol's novel *Angel* (*Anděl*, 1995), Michálek's film builds on a series of impressions rather than following a causality-driven narrative. *Angel Exit* was shot on digital video which explains the handheld shakiness, rapid camera movements and often blurring images which all attempt to create a hallucinogenic visual flow. Due to audio-visual fuzziness, the images are often hard to decrypt, to the extent that the story becomes difficult to comprehend. The rapid cutting between the diegetic space of the film and hallucinatory images of eyeballs, abstract figures, cockroaches, and other insects disorient, confuse and nauseate the viewer. One such recurring motif is the trope of a dead child. The images of a graveyard and the lying statue of a newborn are both repetitive sequences which, similar to the episodic, often-non narrative elements in the film, suddenly encroach the syuzhet. Femininity and motherhood are key topics in *Angel Exit*. In the first sequences, Kája is constantly accompanied by a baby doll that she carries round with her. In the club of the American drug dealer in Prague, she shows the leg of the puppet to the foreigner while stating that 'this is all that is left of my baby'. She then adds that she wants to have a child with Mikeš who 'would be a great father'. In the next shot, Mikeš and Kája are seen in a drug-imposed delirium as they lie their heads against a crystal-like wall. Framed in a close-up upside-down, Kája tells Mike about her dream of facing tangled penises that then ejaculate on her. Like ovaries, the crystal-like background of this sequence enters the scene into a metaphoric trajectory (Figure 3.2). The textual context which resembes ovaries and gets even more emphasis through harsh lightning, connects the visual layer of the scene with Kája's wishes to become a mother. As ritual de-femininisation, the next scene shows Mikeš as he violently cuts Kája's long hair and then shaves her head in Morocco. Surrounded by foreigners who witness the process, the whole act is reminiscent of an exhibition, and it accentuates Kája's vulnerable and suppressed position. From this point on of the narrative, Kája is treated as an object: she is often pushed, snapped and humiliated by Mikeš and their boss. Her representation also changes. Opposite to her provocative leather-clothing and heavy make-up, after her head-shaving, she is portrayed in male clothes or long pullovers.

Following the meeting of the foreign drug-dealer, Kája thus slowly loses her feminity. In a similar vein, Jana is rushed to the hospital with heavy bleeding as she almost loses her child. *Angel Exit* thus clearly portrays the

Figure 3.2 Grasping perspectives: *Andel Exit*. Czech Republic: Buc-Film, 2000.

post-1989 colonisation process by the loss of the femininity which gets juxtaposed with the de-structurisation of the film's narrative and visual style.

This could be the reason why some critics – even though the film was nominated in seven categories at the 2000 Czech Golden Lion Award and eventually won the title of Best Editing – disregarded the film as 'countless chunks of indigestible psychedelia' which 'dies on the altar of so many chemical-reliant films: watching other people do drugs is dull' (McLennan 2003). The extreme zoom-ins into blurring images of eyes, insects, lights and non-figurative shots result in the breakdown of cinematic registers and enhance the film's experimental value. Brown (2015) emphasises the antihumanist, non-anthropocentric conception of what he calls 'key hole shots' which, thanks to digital video technique, pass through human bodies to suggest 'the insignificance of man through inhumanity' (66). In his view, this technical solution which blurs objective and subjective points of view and inner and outer sources by entering the human body as well as solid objects, leads to the breakdown in the differentiation of the fantastic and the real. In *Angel Exit*, the key hole shots create a continuum of human disposability. The super close-ups of Mikeš's eyes after which we enter his red eyeballs and, at the same time, take his point of view of seeing abstracts objects and movements, indicate his very vision as a trapped animal in the narrative.

The blurriness between Mikeš's disposable animal-existence and very actions is implied in the film's establishing shot. The opening credits show Prague during wintertime. The images are intercut with Christmas

76   THE EXTREME CINEMA OF EASTERN EUROPE

storefronts and ornaments, choking and thrashing carps as well as ambulances ringing their way through the crowded streets of the city. The prolonged glimpse of beheaded, bleeding fishes and the diegetic sound of tearing flash slowly oversound the Christmas songs of the street. The camera's spinning and twirling, and the rapid succession of low- and high-angle shots suggest an intradiegetic narration. As if the sequences were recorded from the dying carps' position, we witness in super close-ups how stray dogs eat the still moving and breathing heads of fishes. The sequence ends with the juxtaposition of bloody fish tanks and the sunset of Prague.

The scene draws a visual parallel between the orange-red sky and the bloody aquarium and it references Christmas time as a commodity-based event. At the same time, the mondo motif forecasts the faith of the characters in the film. In Morocco, Mikeš and Kája are incapable of replicating the drug they cooked as they cannot find the secret ingredient they used before. Kája accidently finds out that the mysterious material is their mixed blood that happened to get mixed with the original ingredients when they had a bloody fight in the kitchen. The recurring motif of blood, the colour of red and the images of suffocating fishes all create a metaphoric context. Just like the crops in the film, most of the protagonists die at the end. Kája and their Czech boss overdose, the local shop owner gets stabbed, and Jana seems to have a miscarriage when she is rushed heavily bleeding to the hospital.

The establishing shot and mondo trope thus serve as a contextual hinterland to the film, insofar as *Angel Exit* presents a harsh critique of capitalism and represents post-1989 Prague as a dangerous and claustrophobic place filled with crime, poverty, Western business and hopelessness. Children commit pretty thefts, men are alcoholic, the streets are filled with hysteria, blood and gangsters, and even the local Church gets robbed. In *Angel Exit*, the city is taken over by Western capital: the local shop owner's business is threatened by Australian and German groceries, and it is also a foreign drug lord who persuades Mikes and Kája to cook their last batch. The choking carps in the film's exposition and the film's key hole shots thus allude to the very position of the helpless and trapped protagonists: like fish in an aquarium, they drift in the corruption-laden and suffocating capitalist space of Prague. They follow and obey the Western capital which, however, comes at a price: their disposable bodies are used as capital in the neoliberal age. As commodities, their death becomes unavoidable. The clichéd representation of men dressed in leather jackets and sunglasses in wintertime, and their aggressive attitude towards women which gets manifested through their condescending tone and violent behaviour, all strengthen the very patriarchal set of *Angel Exit*. The male protagonists constantly consume vodka in the film, are accompanied by large dogs and

POST-SOCIALIST ANIMALITY

shout at everyone in their surroundings, all of which is proof of Eastern Europe's othering-self-exoticist attitude. Similar to *Somnambulance*, the extreme representation of violence, drug-addiction and the film's avantgarde-style all enhance the loss of femininity and as such, national values in the post-1989 Czech Republic.

Lucas Nola's *Alone* (*Sami*, 2001) also portrays a post-apocalyptic Eastern European setting and plays along the metaphor of motherhood which gets juxtaposed with dead or dying animals. The Croatian film recounts the story of a young man (Leon Lucev) who, under the influence of alcohol, accidently hits and murders a young boy. He later flees the scene and throws the child's body in a river. Following the tragic event, the man soon falls in love with a young woman – the mother of the deceased child as we later learn – who, as revenge, eventually stabs the man to death.

Nola's minimalist mosaic-narrative is difficult to comprehend. The film avoids any spoken words, and the only diegetic sound we hear is the audio tapes of birds and everyday actions that the main protagonist records. Whatever action he is doing, the man uses sound recordings to accompany his activities. He plays a track of frying meat when cooking omelettes and on his date with the mother, he puts his headphones on to listen to the chirping of birds. These incomprehensible gestures are accompanied by hard-to-understand acts which further complicate the narrative terrain. Most of these scenes correspond to the animal metaphors prevalent in the region's post-1989 extreme cinema traditions. Nola constantly foregrounds the images and sounds of birds and fishes as symbols of fertility and motherhood. After the scene of the accident, he cuts directly to a still image of flying seagulls and, to strengthen the connection of maternity and poultry, he uses the birds' diegetic sound in the soundtrack of the film. One of the strongest symbols in *Alone* is chicken feathers. In one of the scenes, Nola portrays the crying mother as she is feathering a chicken. The prolonged tracking shot plunges the viewer into close proximity with the animal and frames it in a high-angle shot head downwards over a plastic basin. With its purple-coloured splotches and lanugo, the shot of the chicken has a newborn appearance. The aesthetic parallelism between the child and the bird gets more explicit via the intercut of an associative montage sequence that features the mother's son. In the very next shot, however, the story jumps to another narrative line which centres on the relationship of the main protagonist and his girlfriend.

The blond girl whose role in the film remains somewhat foggy, is continuously portrayed in bizarre visual contexts. At the beginning of the film, she is captured in a rusty old bathtub filled with milk. Positioned in the middle of a dilapidated, unfurnished room, this grotesque representation gets even more confusing when the main protagonist throws a fish into the bathtub, and he starts taking polaroid pictures of the girl. He then sniffs the woman's used panties but, even though the girl spreads her legs out of the milk as a reaction and hint to intercourse, the man leaves the room. Instead of any sexual act, he tramples on the fish and quits the scene. Together with the carp, the chicken as symbol in this hard-to-understand sequence plays a crucial role. Following the passivity of the main protagonist, the girl's over-the-shoulder shot is intercut with the image of an angry white chicken which, suggesting the sexual frustration of the girlfriend, is ready to attack. It is when the man eventually falls in love with the mother of the murdered boy that Nola displays the feathering scene, and we return to the abandoned female protagonist. Following the portrayal of the crying mother figure, the director cuts to the blond girlfriend as she stands surprisingly in the middle of flying white feathers. In the next shot, she arrives home to her boyfriend who, having glimpsed the feathers on the woman's coat, gets aroused and rapes her. During the act, he rubs the feathers against his face and first inhales and then tastes and eats the eiderdowns. His robotic movements are intercut with the close-up of the girlfriend who puts her head on the dining table and while the man penetrates her from behind, she starts licking an unknown, blood-like fluid from the surface of the table (Figure 3.3). The rhythmic montage sequence alternates images of the woman's sliding tongue and the man's feather-covered face, which lends the love scene a grotesque and bizarre atmosphere. The cuts into (extreme) close-ups only exacerbate the

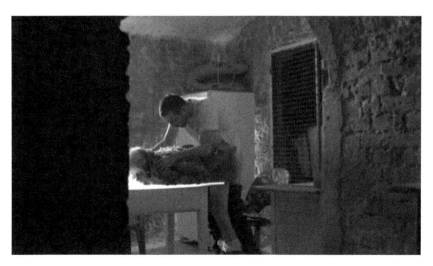

Figure 3.3 Feathers and femininity in *Alone*. Alka-Film Zagreb, 2001.

viewer's spatial disorientation and confusion and make the sequence difficult to comprehend. It is no surprise that some critics accused the director of an extreme eccentric approach and commented on his 'proclivity for poster-like and literal symbols' that makes his hermetic style difficult to understand (Kragic 2011). The lack of spatial-temporal coordinates, the utopistic, post-war ruined outer locations and the abstract inner places in the film, together with the one-word interactions between the characters and the bluish colouring of the film all create a loose narrative structure. The symbolic and often bizarre trajectory of *Alone* only adds to the dark tone and confusing storyline. Still, when looked at closer, Nola's visual metaphors have a dramaturgical role. Not only do the images of fish, milk, water and the crucifix have deeper meaning, but they also link the film's visuality to Christian iconography and iconology (Kragic 2011). The atonement of the male protagonist for the murder of the young child is mirrored via these symbols. The imaginary of the chicken and feathers enters the sequences into a metaphoric trajectory by connecting the man's penance with symbols of fertility and motherhood. After the accident, the man starts to remember his own loss, that is, losing his daughter in a car crash. These memory images signal the man's inner journey. As a reminder of motherhood, the feathers bestow his girlfriend with the mother's identity. The wild sexual scene thus represents a desperate and violent attempt to turn back time and return to motherhood. Despite the change in the girlfriend's iconography – she starts wearing a feathery winter jacket from this point on – the childless woman is incapable of fulfilling the wishes of the man. Before her suicide, she catches a glimpse of a mother who carries her baby in a stroller on the street. In the next shot, the child turns into a white chicken and the two leave the scene and move towards the man and the mother who happen to kiss at the end of the road. This symbolic sequence not only makes the girlfriend discover that her boyfriend is cheating on her but at the same time, she loses her symbolic imaginary of motherhood by letting the bird stroll away. In the end, she returns home and throws her ex-boyfriend's electronic audio-recorders into the bathtub, thus killing herself and the fish that swims in it.

In the selected examples, animal cruelty on screen has a deeper meaning. Without doubt, the torture of fish in *Angel Exit* or *Alone* or the shooting of birds in *Somnambulance* have a strong shock effect. The animal snuff-elements convey a stronger message of the hopeless state of post-1989 Eastern Europe. The very symbolic form of these films, together with their visual abstraction, unfocused colours and visual textures, the paucity of dialogue, handheld camera work and incoherent narratives, create a controversial – often uncomfortable – cinematic experience. Similar to the European pre-war avantgarde waves, they exploit the very medium of cinema to create a political standpoint. The minimalist-surreal trajectory of these films pushes the viewer's patience to the edge as she/he tries to put the symbolic puzzle together.

The connotative language of these films might be the heritage of the socialist filmmaking practices and their coded forms of criticism that have been inherited in the political transformation period. Their anti-establishment message, however, is well-defined: the post-1989 political changes and colonialism resulted in the loss of fertility and motherhood. For this reason, their narratives are open ended in indorsing a form of communicative action.

Angel Exit, *Alone* and *Somnambulance* all follow a metaphoric path to ideological criticism. Although the avantgarde form and animal torture on screen push the visual limits of cinema, the symbols represented in these examples have a clear dramaturgical function. Despite the loose narrative structure and lack of spatial-temporal coordinates, the representation of animals in the films creates a strong connection between the inner motivation of the characters and their current status. But are all examples of extremism part of such an allegorical trajectory?

While the realistic aesthetics of animal death has often been discussed as an authentic gesture 'of well-regarded "art" directors' (emphasis original, Wiegand 2017: 260), less scholarly attention has been paid to the exploitation-entertainment value of (animal) death in cinema. Are all animal deaths on screen used to redeem artistic-connotative value? Lippit's logic of disengagement from the animal and his overall generalisation become debatable, for in his view 'animals are seen only to make meaning for the cinema rather than for themselves' (Burt 2002: 51). This also flattens out the difference between an animal's killing or natural death on screen. As Burt puts it, animal imagery cannot be reduced to semiotics 'as if the animal is a sign easily interchangeable with other kinds if signs' (Ibid., 31) for each visual animal carries specific associations in relation to treatment and welfare, as well as cultural and social meaning (Ibid., 31). Furthermore, the danger of reducing animals to simple metaphorical signs in cinema presupposes the old-school differentiation between highbrow and lowbrow cinemas. These critical insights, as Hobbs (2016) emphasise, convert

> The instinctual, dismissive, and morally outraged response to animal snuff ... into a field in which death imagery might in some way enhance a level of aesthetic appreciation of formerly despised cultural objects, something increasingly common within the academic film study of marginal or neglected exploitation cinema, but virtually always present within the "high" minded critical engagements afforded Godard. (emphasis original, 67)

POST-SOCIALIST ANIMALITY

To this day, the very academic standpoint assumes that art cinema uses animal death/torture on screen as a political and self-reflexive gesture. As Kendall (2016) explains, the snuff movie conceit in extreme cinema mediates a series of anxieties about complicit witnessing and the ethical-affective dimensions of spectatorship in a global digital network culture. In doing so, the mondo trope puts our mediated relationship with real death into a new context, 'conferring affective intensity to the experience of viewing the suffering and demise of others' (Kendall 259). Other scholarly debates on (animal) death in cinema also accentuate authenticity as key to differentiate between rhetorical tropes and simple shock spectatorship (see Wiegand 2017: 256; Whetley 2011: 93–105; DeLuca 2016). Whetley (2011) argues that animal slaughter in extreme cinema offers 'an insight into what "real" death might look like' (emphasis original, 96–7), in this way substituting human death with animal torture. Authenticity is, however, a problematic term and approach for an animal is always going to be corrupted in the practice of becoming an image (Burt 2002). That is, be that shock entertainment and/or realistic aesthetics or nature documentary values, representation is always motivated and supervised by agency. Essentially, realism and realist aesthetics do not solely reference art cinema but are key to pseudosnuff and exploitation films whose amateurism foregrounds a realist mode of representation (Hobbs 2016). Some even argue that, opposed to Hollywood cinema that deals with carnal matters on an escapist level, exploitation addresses the sensual in a realistic form (see Wood 199: 173–4). Exploitation film 'is truly more cinematic ... because the viewer is made aware of the film's design, the methods of its construction' (Ibid., 36). Self-reflexion and realism which are key to art cinema aesthetics are very much present in exploitation. Consequently, not the mode of presentation (realist vs stylised), nor the political gesture of cinema seem to successfully draw the line between exploitation and art/extreme cinema. For this reason, I argue that animal death as well as subversive and explicit images in art/extreme cinema and exploitation must reflect upon their key narrative role: that is, to recall Sobchack (1984), they must mark an intent of the realist-raw representation in the story. Without such justification in representation, films can easily turn into non-narrative haptic experiments or examples of exploitation cinema.

CHAPTER 4

Eastern Extreme Cinema: (S)exploitation and Animal Death

Exploitation style, as outlined in the introduction, has often been discussed as a low-budget form of filmmaking (Wood 1999) which lacks narrative immersion (Baker 2013; Wood 1999), and focuses on taboo imagery such as graphic sex, bodily distress and destruction (Waddell 2018; Schaefer 1999). These explicit images follow what Waddell termed 'a narrative of threat' (2018: 35), that is, the plot and story are structured around the build-up, satisfaction and 'showbeating corporeality'. Although the classic three-act structure is often reversed and the narrative becomes secondary to taboo imagery in exploitation, the graphic content complements the narrative. Thus, very much alike extreme cinema, exploitation focuses on affect rather than narrative cohesion. Consequently, the common ground is the ideological platform of extremism which shows what mainstream cinema or traditional modern art cinema are not allowed to.

Breillat's *Anatomy of Hell* is a clear manifestation this taboo-breaking trend. The film starts in a gay club (right away with an image of male fellatio), where the main protagonist, a woman (Amira Casar) tries to commit suicide by cutting her wrist in a bathroom. Here she meets a homosexual man (Rocco Siffredi) who intervenes. The two start walking and suddenly, when the woman tells the man that she knows why he might have gone to the bathroom ('to get sucked like all men'), the man hits the woman. Some minutes later, the woman offers oral sex to the man. She then asks him to have a deal to 'look and watch her when she is unwatchable' for which she is willing to pay. The next day, the man arrives at her home and the two lovers start a four-day long philosophical-sexual journey.

It is already in the film's establishing shot that the incomprehensible cause-and-effect chain of the plot dismantles and, instead of a coherent stream of causality, the two characters embark on a series of unexpected sexual acts and (chauvinist) philosophical remarks. Since Breillat herself has in many interviews emphasised to be a true feminist, a list of confusing questions arise, such as: why would a girl who has been just beaten up, give oral sex to a (gay) strange man on the street? What is the narrative role and very objective of showing two gay men having sex right in the establishing shot of the film?

At the house of the woman, narrative comprehension becomes even more challenging. After she undresses, the woman lies naked on the bed and the two start a surreal conversation on female flesh; disgust and brutality; nothingness; offer and demand; and the female skin which 'stays lumpy like the neck of a plucked chicken' after shaving. In the midst of these parallel-like philosophical conversations, Breillat pans over the woman's naked body while her voiceover narration compares the 'black tufts and putrid hairiness' of the vagina with 'a just-hatched bird, still wet from the egg, so touching in its new-born weakness'. In the next shot, the film jumps to the French countryside and shows the detailed torture of a newborn bird that gets stepped on by a young boy. In the following sequence, the woman asks the man to look close at her vagina. He penetrates her with his hands and then tastes the female discharge.

In this above-described scene, Breillat does not present psychologically defined individuals, nor does she construct a canonical story. Causality, as the prime unifying principle of classical fabula and canonical spatial and temporal configurations (which all serve the construction of classical narration) is entirely terminated. The brutal torture of the bird or the super close-up of the woman's vagina both come as a surprise. Their representation and role in the plot are not justified, not even on a connotative level. The unity of time, space and action which aims to advance causal progression is broken and, instead of comprehensible and realistic and (even) compositional motivations, the spectator is faced with a series of shocking images. Not only do these unconnected sequences confuse the viewer's schemata, cues and hypothesis-framing, they also hinder the viewer's identification with the characters and the story. The spectator is thus left alone with his/her only recognisable motivation (in Bordwellian terms), that is, he/she must rely on her/his transtextual knowledge of the main actor, the famous Italian porn star Rocco. One reviewer on the film's IMDb page summarises the structure of *Anatomy of Hell* as follows:

> 1) beautiful, depressed, self-hating woman slit her wrists with razor 2) fantasy image of [the] same woman slit[ting] her throat 3) Rocco Siffredi's tumescent penis (okay, that wasn't so bad) 4) woman's mouth drip[ping] with sperm 5) image of boy throwing squashed baby bird on ground and stamping it to mush (it looked terribly real... where's PETA?!) 6) Outrageous comparison of Rocco's concept of female bits to smushed baby bird 7) full-on shot of female child displaying herself under a bush (perhaps they were made of wax to pass obscenity laws?) 8) boring scenes of woman

offering to pay gay man she is obsessed with to "watch her" 9) Rocco sticking finger up sad woman, then wiping her wetness on his hair (shades of Something About Mary?) 10) ridiculous pretentious French conversation about brutality and fragility 11) extended camera closeups of sad woman's bush 12) VERY CLOSE close up of Rocco sticking his hand inside her...(sic, jiffyxpop).[1]

As this quote demonstrates, the series of shock-images and lack of narrative cohesion give way to pure affect which is also key to (s)exploitation cinema. Because the narrative gaps do not get filled up, the chaotic plot of *Anatomy of Hell* might be considered a simple work which orchestrates the sensational. One can argue of course that Breillat uses a nonclassical narrative form (Bordwell 1985) or art-cinema (Buckland 2021) or modern cinema (Kovács 2008) narration which unites subjective and objective modes of storytelling. The episodic structure, the lack of deadline as temporal motivation, the focus on the characters rather than the story, the loosening of cause-and-effect chain in the plot, Breillat's abstraction, subjectivity and authorial reflexivity, and overall, the increased ambiguity[2] regarding the interpretation of *Anatomy of Hell*, all strengthen the film's modern style. Modern art films build on the characters' psychological description or the relationship between the protagonists and their environment (Kovács 2008) which justifies the lack of a linear plot. In case of Breillat's film however, the psychological description is substituted by pornographic, strictly bodily intrusions which hinders the spectator's 'conscious intellectual involvement in the plot construction', which is one of the main characteristics of the modern cinema movement (Ibid., 62). Even though Breillat adds that 'when sex has a soul, no matter how pornographic the image is, it is inhabited by humanity, and therefore it is no longer pornography' (Breillat in Maas 2019).[3] The very lack of character depth reduces her sequences to pure cinema of flesh. As Hester summarises:

> It is not only the pseudo-pornographic qualities of these vivid and striking visuals that is enhanced by their fragmented nature ... That is, despite representing the sexual organs in graphic details, these most explicit images stubbornly resist the viewer's initial attempts to make sense of them or to recognise them as familiar parts of the body. Factors such as an abundance of pubic hair, the sudden jarring cut to an extreme close-up, the sheer size of the image and the stripping away of any context-providing bodily landmarks all work to render this first genital close-up peculiarly ambiguous. (Hester, 2017: 53)

The foregrounding of obscene images without any narrative role might be the reason *Anatomy of Hell* has often been discussed under the aegis of pornography (see Ebert 2017:12–13; Russell 2004; Campbell 2014) and why it is still mentioned on so many porn sites.

When examined closer then, *Anatomy of Hell* enumerates all the characteristics of (s)exploitation cinema. Whether in the form of intertexts which suggest that the events in the film are based on real events and/or the film's aesthetic realm which mirrors documentary-like techniques, exploitation uses truth as a transgressive element (Carter 2010). *Anatomy of Hell* clearly plays with this marketing strategy when Breillat claims in an intertext that 'a film is an illusion, not reality-fiction or a happening. It is a true work of fiction' and that 'for the actress's most intimate scenes, a body double was used. It's not her body; it's an extension of a fictional character'. Yet, the body of the double is so much so real that one critic even added to nominate Pauline Hunt for the 'best supporting vagina of the year' (Lee 2004). Profilmic nudity does not differentiate between the body of the actress and her double. The very authenticity of the woman's naked body on screen does not even make the spectator question the fictional-documentary value of the sequences. The story is centred around revealing taboo images and its shock element is 'inseparable from the exhibition of bodily distress/destruction/seduction' (Waddell 2018: 22) which further strengthens its exploitation style. The gritty verisimilitude, both in the pre-filmic setting and the filming style, precisely documents the display of sexual organs. This style of directing does not leave much to the imagination.

Although Breillat's original objective was to represent sex from a non-pornographic point-of-view and 'show images that are not showable' (Breillat in Murphy 2005), even the title of the film[4] recalls the grindhouse realm. Exploitation titles suggest the 'depiction of graphically gory set pieces set within a contemporary ethos' (Waddell 2018), which Wood (1999) termed 'salivation-triggering words' (15). *Anatomy of Hell* suggests a journey into hell. This tagline tipoffs some shocking visual revelations (designed to shock the audience and thus bring profit the same way exploitation cinema does).

In an interview, Breillat herself admitted that without festivals, she and her films would not exist (Breillat in Maas 2019). She adds that she needs people to understand her films for 'cinema is so expensive' (Breillat in Richter 2015). The close-ups of sexual organs, or the scene where the man is offered a cup of water which hosts a bloody tampon of the woman, are only a few examples of Breillat's transgressive and profit-oriented approach. The paratextual context and marketing of the film only strengthen this view. The film's Canadian DVD cover, similar to other extreme cinema examples as Frey (2016) has demonstrated, employs sensationalist remarks. Quotations include Ballyhoo taglines (Hobbs 2018: 31–2), such as 'THAT'S ONE EFFED-UP FILM' and 'Going where no movie has gone before, whether mainstream or porn', while some words of the plot (boundaries, daring, sexuality, unshowable, unsharable, secrets) are emphasised with red and the 'Winner best film Philadelphia International Film Festival' with white. The front cover depicts the woman and the man half-naked in the bed which recalls the marketing of sex-themed art film.

To summarise, the three key characteristics of exploitation cinema – the use of shock as spectacle, the corporeal indiscretion as narrative motivation and the relationship between topicality and taboo (36) – all support that *Anatomy of Hell* better fits the exploitation label than art cinema. This is not to state that exploitation cinema is of less value and/or art films are of a higher cultural state. Exploitation films mirror a series of social anxieties and have often connected taboo imagery to communicate topical political problems. The verité-style horror of *Night of the Living Dead* or *The Last House on the Left* (Wes Craven, 1972) both presented violent narratives which, according to some scholars, questioned the way society deals with the consequences of the Vietnam War (see Waddell 2018:125–6; Towlson 2014: 104–30). The brutal torture and murder of the two teenage girls and the eventual bloody revenge of the parents in *The Last House on the Left* points to how blurry the dividing lines are between good and bad and that even good people can turn evil (Henry 2014: 41). These are only two well-known examples that demonstrate the rich oeuvre of exploitation cinema. My argument thus only aimed to highlight how critical debates often tend to confuse (s)exploitation for modern art cinema. The two are, of course, not mutually exclusive (see Hobbs 2018). The emphasis is more on the value and production of cultural meaning. The very often witnessed hypocrisy of filmmakers,[5] scholars and critics to frame all the works of recognised European auteurs as art cinema, points toward the capitalist mode of production (or the 'higher form of capital' to recall Beller's [1998] ideas on capitalist cinema). More troubling is that this approach has led to a new form of transgressive filmmaking and institution. Similar to porn cinema for male spectators, extreme cinema slowly rewrites and normalises one's relationship to transgressive, violent and often chauvinist acts. Consequently, the (artistic) institutionalisation of extreme cinema and the unconditional praise of prestigious directors (as we will see in the following sections), can easily become a hazardous cul-de-sac.

Eastern European Exploitation: *Marble Ass* and *Baklava*

In Eastern Europe, post-1989 exploitation cinema[6] often referenced the hardship of the system change. In this way, we can see a clear juxtaposition between the amateurish, Beta-film form and the profilmic reality of poverty and hopelessness. Želimir Žilnik's *Marble Ass*

(*Dupe od mramora*, 1995), the first film from the former Yugoslavia which openly discussed LGBTQ lives, is a clear example of this exploitation trend. The film follows two sex-worker transvestite friends, Merlin (Vjeran Miladinovic) and Sanela (Milja Milenkovic) in Belgrade. The friends soon welcome a visit by Johnny (Nenad Rackovic), Merlin's ex-boyfriend whose violent behaviour embitters their life. Having just returned from the Bosnian war, Johnny tries to make his living from petty theft and pool-tricks. He soon develops feelings towards Sanela, but the visit of Johnny's military girlfriend causes turmoil in their life. The man gets more and more violent with Merlin and Sanela. Because of his abusive behaviour, Sanela asks another friend to kill Johnny. Instead of a happy end, Jonny gets murdered, and Merlin goes on with her life as a sex worker on Belgrade's worn-out streets.

Marble Ass clearly aims for the exploitative quality of celluloid. The film's establishing shot features a naked massage sequence as Sanela puts some cream on Merlin's naked bum. The prolonged sequences of sex between Johnny and his military girlfriend as well as Sanela and his new bodybuilder fiancé all strengthen the grindhouse feeling of the film. The poorly constructed acts often lack any reasonable connection: the slow-motion kung-fu training of the characters at home; the inflations of condoms in the living room; or the sudden torture of a goat all strengthen the confusing and bizarre atmosphere of the film.

One of the most surprising and shocking scenes is the skinning of a goat that Johnny's military ex-girlfriend imported home (Figure 4.1). Lying on a couch with his back to the bathroom where the animal is tied to the wall, Johnny randomly starts shooting at the goat. His play of whether he can kill it without looking, gets interrupted by the visit of his girlfriend who laughs at Johnny's childish game. After a cut, we see the bathroom covered in blood. The woman stands above the half-beheaded goat and orders Johnny to skin the animal. Johnny then gets upset that the goat was not killed in a Muslim way but he finishes the job and prepares the animal. The very raw and explicit scenes of skinning and the diegetic tearing-sound of the skin get intercut with Merlin's hopeless search for 'Goaty'. Through a hole in the wall of the bathroom, Sanela and Merlin eventually get a glimpse of Johnny and the goat. They break down the bricks and climb into the room of the randomised slaughterhouse. Johnny is then portrayed in a wide shot with the head of the goat in his hands. Following the attack of the two transvestites, the man starts flinging around the skull of the animal to protect himself while his girlfriend points a gun at the two friends who, due to their heavy fall into the room, destroy the toilet tank. In the end, the absolute chaos turns into a scuffle.

Figure 4.1 'Goaty' in *Marble Ass*. Serbia: Radio B92, 1995.

This sequence first registers a tone of disgust in relation to the skinning of the goat which, after the interference of Sanela and Merlin, turns into a bizarre, hilarious and eventually violent act. With its immediate, shocking and commercially exciting characteristics, Žilnik enumerates all the key demarcations of exploitation. With no dramaturgical function in the narrative, these shocking elements only raise the commercial – and less the aesthetic – value of the film.

On the other hand, *Marble Ass* discusses several topics which, given the post-socialist, post-war years, can be deemed serious taboos. The handheld, documentary-like footage of the streets of Belgrade mirrors a poverty-stricken society where the only way out is to sell one's body. This dangerous business – the girls often get attacked and/or robbed – brings them wealth but not much respect. Sanela and Merlin dream of the West and aim for Italy 'where everybody has a car'. One of the clients even teaches Sanela of 'useful' English expressions she can use when interacting with Western clients. She concludes 'English is the most important language' for it can help the friends to flee to a wealthy country where they would gain money and respect. The process of Western colonisation is clearly referred to in *Marble Ass*. It is not only Sanela and Merlin who sell their bodies but so do all the other characters in the film: Merlin's middle-aged, ex-housewife

(S)EXPLOITATION AND ANIMAL DEATH 89

friend has to learn sex work to survive her divorce and Sanela's fiancé, albeit metaphorically, also sells his body at bodybuilding competitions. The bodily violation of humanity happens at every level of society. *Marble Ass* conveys a depressing message of the post-war, post-socialist Balkan reality where the only way to survive happens through the modification of the body.

Balkan Exploitation, Transvestitism and Political Cynicism

In a patriarchal set-up, the representation of two transvestites and their popularity among men in Belgrade become even greater taboos. Although in Tito's Yugoslavia sexual content was popular and the cultural establishment did not marginalise erotic imaginary (see Ibroscheva 2013: 76–7), transgender topics and homosexual content were untouchable subjects. In socialist member-countries, homosexuality was presented as 'a crime, a perversion ... an illness' (Fojtová and Sokolová 2013:109) and was thought of as a product of the Western capitalist establishment which is not compatible with socialist ideals (Szulc 2018: 71). Of course, there are significant differences in homosexuality-related prohibitions and laws within the Eastern bloc, ranging from the systematic persecution of homosexuals in Romania to relative tolerance in Hungary (see Szulc 2018: 61–86). The authorities' constant surveillance and harassment of homosexuals by police forces were however common practices in the whole region (see Szulc 2018: 61–86). The 1980s brought about some ease in legislations and thanks to gay movements in Poland, Slovenia, East Germany, Hungary and Czechoslovakia, these countries could manage to establish strong groups. The fall of the Pink Curtain – 'the homosexual version of the Iron Curtain' – has given way to a discursive development of same-sex issues in the region (Ibid., 85). The resurrection of Christian values in the post-Soviet bloc impeded acceptance and strengthened heteronormative discourses in the region. The homosexuality-religion dichotomy rested on homosexuality as an unnatural act and threat to family values (Hall 2015: 88). The newly inaugurated post-1989 national-ideological rhetoric and its focus on the preservation of traditional values favoured the scarcity of gay activism in mainstream media content. Although homosexually was officially removed from the list of diseases (Fojtová and Sokolová 2013: 43) the socialist legacy of homophobic structures remained dominant. It is one of the reasons Fojtová and Sokolová label the 1990s as the era of 'voluntary invisibility' on the part of homosexual activists (Ibid., 123). In the Balkans, the burden of Yugoslav wars only strengthened this invisibility. Because Bosnia, Croatia and Serbia identified the wars as a fight for an ethnically uniform and heteropatriarchal nation-state, alternative identities in the public space were highly discriminated against (Dumancic 2013: 59–62). As Dumancic stresses, 'in public forums, detractors of gay and lesbian rights often indignantly demand: "Did we fight the war for *them*?" (Emphasis original, Dumancic 2013: 61). The homophobic stance has been strengthened by the moral conservativism, male chauvinism and strong patriarchalism endemic to the Balkans (Ibid., 61). The still-prevalent encouragement of Orthodox Christianity and the Serbian Orthodox Church to condemn homosexuality in Serbia only supports this homophobic rhetoric (see Mikus 2015: 23–34).

In the light of this, *Marble Ass* cultivates the forbidden to cause offence to nationalist values by foregrounding the almost never-seen taboo imagery of transvestitism. With their heavy make-up, tight leather clothes, feminine movements and high voices, Sanela and Merlin go against the very typical representation of Balkan males on screen. In a similar vein, the representation of the war hero Johnny is inherently cynical. With his bare hairy chest and black leather jacket and sunglasses, his figure is supposed to stand for the testosterone-brimmed male archetype of the Balkans. At the same time however, he is incapable of murdering the goat or seducing Sanela, not to mention realising his wealthy business ideas in Belgrade. Johnny's manliness transforms into the sarcastic portrayal of a failed stereotype. *Marble Ass* thus turns old-school Balkan gender representations upside down. The reason Žilnik might have decided to use transvestitism to mock the strong Balkan patriarchy is likely the same as that for portraying the skinning of a goat or a sexual encounter in dough on the table: he aims for financial success. This is not to say that, as emphasised earlier, exploitation movies do not draw on the topical to make socio-political and/or allegorical statements, rather it is to suggest that, as Waddell has it (2018) 'any such motivation is expressed within a narrative that also maintains ulterior commercial motives: shock, spectacle, physical perversion' (43). The exploitation quality of the film is demonstrated by Žilnik's own webpage[7] which introduces the content of the film as follows:

> Merlyn has been pacifying the Balkans, turning tricks with countless Serbian guys. Merlyn is a lighting rod sheltering Belgrade, calming violent nighthawks, swanky big spenders, miserable loners and horny young studs, taking on the charge that would otherwise befall little girls, unprotected mothers and helpless old women. Combined with guns, this unbridled energy would eventually lead to bloodshed. Merlyn cools the boiling blood of violent Dinarides and enriches it with love. Johnny comes home to Belgrade, from the war. His motives are apparently similar, he also wants to cool the boiling blood, but he does it by letting it through the holes in the human body, which he makes with bullets or knives. This film is a treatise on the different methods of resolving conflicts, resorted to by Merlyn and Johnny.

We know that exploitation often involves material that the film eventually does not deliver (King 2019: 255). To mislead viewers, Žilnik's sensationalist expressions – violence, guns, bloodshed, boiling blood, horny – promise an entertaining, action-filled film experience but *Marble Ass* only delivers an incomprehensible story with undeveloped characters, unnatural dialogue, bad acting and never-ending continuity as well as sound errors. While guns indeed appear in the film twice – and so does a knife once – the only bloodshed happens when Johnny's girlfriend murders Goaty. Without psychological depth/motivation and a comprehensible cause-end-effect chain, *Marble Ass* only confuses, disorients and, with its amateur mise-en-scène and bizarre elements – sometimes shocks the viewer. Instead of 'helping some niche of free expression' (Žilnik 2022),[8] the Serbian director creates a derisive portrayal of Belgrade's (sexual) minority. One can argue, as Jelača (2016) does, that the film makes a statement 'about the way in which some bodies are too inappropriate to be interpellated into [the violent-normative] ethno-nationalist discourse' because they are 'literally too queer' (116). However, this statement highly overlooks the very cynical and superficial representation of the two sex workers. The world of Sanela and Merlin only revolves around sex, money and men, and the last thing that concerns the two transvestites is their very position within or outside the society. Another danger of Jelača's generalisation is that she identifies all Belgrade-based transvestites as sex workers and/or all sex workers as transvestites. Not only does such a reading overly simplify the diversity of the queer community and enhances a self-Balkanising standpoint, but as is often the case with academic texts concerning extreme films, it convulsively tries to categorise a paracinematic film experience as art cinema. This happens with Todorović too who analyses the film's establishing shot as follows:

> It is not a coincidence that the film begins with a long scene of transgender woman Sanela, while she lubricates her long and thin legs. In this film, her beautiful woman's body is emphasized a lot, and her femininity is not even doubted, especially if we consider that she notes how she visits doctors, meaning that she works on her body and identity, and how she is saving funds for sex reassignment surgery, with which she would end the painful period of her fake and hard life. (Todorović 2021)

Similar to Todorović, Juricic (2022) overlooks the director's exploitation strategy,[9] and he explains the skinning of Goaty as 'the metaphorical skinning of Johnny's masculine façade' (Ibid., 10) while adding that '... unlike the female characters in the self-balkanised films, Merlinka and Sanela are not the victims of men's rage and lust' (Ibid., 10). The above-mentioned readings, *inter alia*, seem to have skipped scenes from *Marble Ass*. At the peak of the movie, Johnny attacks Sanela with a knife, chains her neck, beats her up and later uses her head to hold up an apple that he tries to hit with a bow. In another scene, Merlinka is attacked and almost robbed at the street. At Sanela's wedding, both girls get seriously assaulted. To sum up, *Marble Ass* does directly what Juricic and Todorović deny: it uses a self-Balkanising exploitation strategy to attract moviegoers. The representation of a naked butt in the film's establishing shot or the bizarre scene where the protagonists fight over a beheaded goat in a ruined bathroom can be endowed with deeper meaning but without dramaturgical function; as we saw in *Anatomy of Hell*, they remain tools of spectacle.

It seems that Žilnik's self-Balkanising exploitation strategy has paid off. *Marble Ass* was screened at the Berlin Film Festival in 1995 and as best feature, won the Teddy award. Later, the film was presented at many other international festivals, including Toronto, Montreal, Moscow and San Francisco. In 2016, *Marble Ass* got selected to be screened at the 66th Berlin International Film Festival. Interestingly, as expected in a patriarchal-nationalist society, the international acclaim was not accompanied by domestic protests. Although at the premier, some people from the audience started throwing eggs on the crew and called the film a lie for misrepresenting Belgrade, 'nobody tried to censor [the film] … they said it was a bit extreme, but we had extreme films before' (Žilnik in Tot, 2020). As one of the main markers of exploitation cinema, extremity in this case not only refers to the shocking textual layer of films, but the very avantgarde form of production.

Exploitation, the Extreme and Moral Concern: *Baklava*

Alexo Petkov's *Baklava* (2007) foregrounds the very extreme on three different levels. The Bulgarian film, in working with orphanage children, questions the very ethics of representation by featuring underage characters in extreme situations which are then introduced in extremely confusing mise-en-scène. The story centres on the adventures of the newly re-united brothers Djore (Nikolay Yanchev) and Kotze (Hristo Herun). Having just returned to Bulgaria from a prolonged Euro-trip, the 26-year-old Djore sees a dream about a treasure that is buried at the Bulgarian seaside. The gift is the legacy of his dead grandmother who also shares with him the secret that he has a younger brother whom he must find in an orphanage, for the treasure can only be found with his assistance. This information calls Djore into action and starts a series of shocking events in the story.

Baklava operates with three main narratives lines which are constantly intercut with episodic, non-narrative – often blurry, dream-like – haptic sequences. The first plot line features the journey of Djore and Kotze who mainly drink, smoke and party on their way to the Bulgarian coast. The second focuses on an alcoholic father whose physical and verbal abuse drives his young daughter to suicide. The third line is a television show with corrupt politicians who discuss their vision about the future of Bulgaria. It is no doubt that Petkov aimed at the creation of a contemporary critical tabloid of Bulgaria's depressing and corrupt present/future and the three plot lines serve as three different perspectives to emphasise the state of difference between the socio-economic situation of the Balkans and the rest of Europe. The narrator's hypnotic voice-over at the start of the film enters the viewer in the world of the Balkan to 'forget about Europe'. Indeed, the tsunami of very explicit images of violence, prostitution, alcoholism, drug abuse and corruption throughout the movie give the least favourable account of Bulgaria – a country which had just joined the European Union in the year of the film's shooting.

Unfortunately, the director's message and intention to shake the viewer into political consciousness seemed to be greater than the film's ethical and even aesthetic content. Petkov did not veer away from recording children and teenagers in deeply disturbing situations which resulted in the banning of the film in Bulgaria. *Baklava* often features scenes where young boys smoke weed and drink alcohol. More disturbing is that in one scene, a group of young boys rape a teenage girl who, after the intercourse, lies naked on the bed with blood in between her legs. Although the very act of penetration is relegated to the offscreen space and the camera focuses on the boys' excited close-ups and rhythmic movements, Petkov shows the shocking outcome of the gang rape from different camera angles (Figure 4.2). First, the girl's wide-spread, naked legs and the blood in between her limbs on the bed are recorded in a low-angle shot. It is only a black quadrangle that censors the sight of her genitalia. In the next shot, the same scene gets repeated in a high-angle shot. Following that, Petkov focuses on the facial expression of the teenage girl whose inexpressive, empty eyes stare into the abyss.

The rape scene enumerates the semantic and syntactic components of pornography. During the act, the young girl is captured from the actual penetrator's over-the-shoulder shot while the other boys touch the girl's belly and breasts. The more they progress to fellatio, the more rapid the movements and the editing of the scene. In a rhythmic-intellectual montage sequence, we see how the boys' sperm lands on different objects in the room, including a telephone, a teddy bear and a small ceramic statue. Petkov then intercuts the drops of sperm with the moves of the girl as she puts her hands over her face, slowly closes her eyes and turns away from the handheld camera.

Figure 4.2 Shockumentary: Gang rape in *Baklava*, Bulgaria: Lost Vulgaros Productions, 2007.

The simulated pederasty provokes extreme discomfort in the viewer, especially because the scene features children and an underaged girl in an extremely literal, perverse and violated act which probes the very relationship between ethics and the position of protagonists. It is less surprising that the film was soon deemed inappropriate by authorities. The accusations included the promotion of child pornography, drug abuse, homosexuality and the employment of individuals under the age of 16. Petrov has fled to Canada, but he was trialled and sentenced in absentia. In 2009, an international arrest warrant was issued for the director, and it was only in April 2011 that the film could be released in movie theatres (Donev 2019: 65–6).

While *Baklava* was under siege by the Bulgarian government, Petkov published an open letter in defence of his film in which he stated that

> although, most of us cannot or just do not want to see the terrifying reality, the real life nightmare there is not a fiction. The film at some point might be entertaining, shocking or even might make people blush, but at least it shows what is really going on in Bulgaria – on the street, in our concrete apartments, at bus stations, on TV, at the overcrowded stadiums during pop folk concerts, at the bars, in the orphanages and children's care homes ... What is happening with the Bulgarian KIDS ON OUR STREETS is much more terrifying than what is shown in the movie. The extermination of all moral values makes us go away and search for happiness in temporary and easily gained spaces. (emphasis original, quoted by BHM, 2016)

Along with Petkov, the few critiques which are available in English also defend the film. Aretov argues that for the authorities 'the real problem was not the sex and violence but the portrayal of everyday reality in a Bulgarian orphanage' (Ibid., 80). In another essay on *Baklava*, Donev (2019) dissects the film as a 'passionate attempt ... to unmask the hypocrisy of a society that closes its eyes to numerous social problems ranging from violence against children in orphanages to the drastic inequality, poverty and depressing vulgarity in everyday life' (65). Born (2008) also states that the trailers contain 'quite explicit scenes', but the film 'does not contain anything that would be qualified as porn'. He then cites the open statement of the Bulgarian Union of Filmmakers: 'Are we out of our minds, for failing to see that it is not *Baklava* that is responsible for the unacceptable way of life here and now [in our country]?' (Ibid.). Another critic adds that after *Baklava*, he 'was not shocked or repulsed' and admits that 'the film featured some controversial scenes that could justify its R rating, but in no way was it more shocking than say Larry Clark's 1995 film *Kids, Thirteen* (2003) or the Polish movie *Swinki* (2003)' (sic, Georgi 2011). These critics also defended the extravagant textual style of *Baklava*. According to Popa (2010), the film is 'in fact a collage of semi-philosophical discussions, dark neighborhoods, funny characters, child's fantasies and bad dreams' (81). Aretov praises *Baklava* for its 'impersonal ethnicity' which is conveyed via its editing and the 'nature of the image' in the film. As he continues,

> Without any special cinematic qualities and being rather photographic, with many snap-shots and medium to close-ups, the image gives sometimes the impression that the director would only want us to "see" certain things, commissioning the public to complete the puzzles of the story. The effect is sometimes shocking and confusing in accordance with Petrov's intention of rendering the hard-hitting reality of a society found adrift. (Aretov 2010: 83)

Georgi (2011) calls the film a coming-of-age road movie with an almost documentary aesthetic and 'warm colors which give a surreal look to sunset, fields and mountains'. The circulation of the film at various international festivals seems to support the above-mentioned arguments which stand by the film's artistic quality and deep socio-political message.

Interesting enough, none of these scholars have commented on the exploitation style of *Baklava* or criticised the film's chaotic plot and mise-en-scéne. Thanks to the film's controversy and the scandal[10] around it, Petrov's film became 'the most wanted Bulgarian movie' (Aretov 2010) which generated the country's greatest success.

It seems that Petrov's intention to 'show what is really going on in Bulgaria' prompted scholars and critics to focus on the connotative language of the film and explain its metaphors and allegories. This phenomenon

96   THE EXTREME CINEMA OF EASTERN EUROPE

can be very often witnessed in the case of extreme cinema. The positive critiques of the film tend to overlook the very fact that it is not Petrov's social criticism which might disturb the spectator, but the very (exploitative) textual-narrative way this content and theme are conveyed. *Baklava* has a loose narrative structure to such an extent that the three main story lines become almost unidentifiable. The film's slow-motion, blurred images often turn black and white or blue and the handheld camera's rapid spinning and twirling only exacerbate the nauseating atmosphere. Due to the discombobulating cutaways, extreme zoom-ins, alternating off-centre compositions, changing colours, rapid editing and very subjective, unfocused camera work, the very object of looking becomes indiscernible. Petrov repeatedly brings in random scenes which have no connection to any of the three main plot lines. Such sequences, *inter alia*, include wrestling men and women, a rat climbing on people, someone urinating on the top of a table, images of parties, a burning chicken and documentary-like footage of people walking on the streets of Sofia. The only link between these random episodes is the recurring motif of sexually exploited women.

Following the brothers' reunion, the first trip of Kotze and Djore leads to a sex worker whom they later bring to a hotel room and tie to the bed. The little brother first touches the bum of the woman and primes the immobile girl with whiskey. Later, they spray a silver star on the belly of the sex worker and the two leave the room. The whole hotel scene is recorded in fast-motion so that the audio-visual style only adds to the uncomfortable tone of the sequence. *Baklava* then cuts to the narrative line of domestic abuse. The violent husband is shown watching a striptease-show and then wrestling. In the very next shot, Petrov showcases a party where the camera's subjective point-of-view records naked women's breasts getting sprinkled with vodka. The participants of the gang rape are then portrayed drinking, smoking, and dancing. Opposite to the fast-motion recording of the previous scene, the main part of the event is captured in still frames so that the succession of images create a story of progressive intoxication. The party sequence is then followed by the drunken husband who watches female wrestling on the television and demands his wife (whom he calls 'wench') to bring him more beer. After a very short return to the party, Petrov suddenly cuts to Kotze and a group of children looking at pornographic magazines and smoking. Following the images of naked women, we see two of the boys in a frontal, slow-motion shot kissing.

As these examples demonstrate, the identification of the very relation between the sequences is challenging. *Baklava* not only jumps between various random scenes, but it also uses a combination of diverse textual approaches which exacerbate the disorientation of the viewer. In this way, the identification with any of the protagonists becomes difficult – if not impossible. The lack of dialogue and narrative cohesion and the ever-changing slow-motion/fast-motion-blurry sequences cannot communicate the director's point-of-view in a convincing way. Petrov's very aim to draw attention to the hopeless socio-economic situation of Bulgaria and illustrate the 'extermination of all moral values' in the country is showcased in the very way that the director is opposed to. By featuring children in illegal situations and treating females as sexual objects/servants, *Baklava* only strengthens and encourages the misogynist, patriarchal and violent set-up that Petrov claimed he was opposed to.

Had it not been advertised as art cinema, *Baklava* could have easily remained on the home shelves of exploitation or trash film fans. Exploitation cinema has always been eager to work with the stereotype of the fetishised image of woman as sexual object (see Cook 1976:122–3) and, as Waddell (2018) has it:

> by making this objectification more apparent, even more honest (and thus less symbolic), the inherent voyeurism associated with watching 'exploitative' sex and violence is compromised. The spectator ... is engaging with an expectancy of sexual objectification and/or violent transgression when they pay to see these films. (Waddell 38)

Baklava's exploitative quality of treating taboo (pornography, prostitution, misogyny, rape, child porn) as contemporary inevitability might be the reason why the film generated such an upheaval in Bulgaria. The film clearly operates with the trinity of exploitation. Even the intertitle of the film – 'the film is a doucumentary (sic), based on actual events, dreams and other head trips' – mocks the style itself. Moreover, *Baklava* uses shock as spectacle: the bloody killing of a chicken and then another bird have no role in building a causal chain in the narrative. Together with the explicit portrayal of female bodies, drugs and the participation of children in both activities, these bloody scenes serve the sole aim of shocking the viewer. The corporeal indiscretion as narrative motivation and the relationships between topicality and taboo (Waddell 2018) as second and third elements of exploitation are also key approaches in 'the most wanted movie of Bulgaria'. Although the motivation to mirror the corrupt, misogynist nature of Bulgarian politicians and to provide an honest image of everyday life and hardship in the Balkan country can be spotted via the hilarious political television show in which participants talk contradictions and say empty promises to the public, the corporeal explicitness of the film overwrites any of these allegorical messages.

Marble Ass and *Baklava* both display physical perversity and demonstrate the sexual violation of the body/humanity. This spectacle, however, becomes a dangerous territory for it is 'posited and staged without the social or educational baggage that was once essential in avoiding legal difficulties [in classical exploitation cinema]. This also leads to a certain narrative ambiguity ... [that is] the relationship between subjectivity and objectivity/cause and effect/good and bad in is far less obvious than in Hollywood cinema' (Waddell 2018: 39). As this chapter has illustrated, one of the real dangers of extreme cinema is its very interpretation as an institution of art. While I do not doubt that *Anatomy of Hell, Marble Ass* and *Baklava* all possess artistic qualities and use a metaphor-laden textuality to embark on a politico-critical discourse, the connotative layer of the films (if there is one) gets dwarfed by the shock spectacle. As the next chapter will illustrate, in Eastern European extreme, *A Serbian Film* goes the farthest in this practice.

CHAPTER 5

Post-War Extremism:
Subversive Serbia

The wave of 'New Serbian Film' (Vojnov, quoted by Jelača 2016: 256) depicts a depressing and dark image of the post-war transitional reality by causing moral panic through graphic, visceral violence 'in order to address the brutality of post-conflict reality by sadistically objectifying those very weakest members of society as a means to ostensibly arrive at a wider critique of a system that breeds and perpetuates such violence' (Ibid., 256). Nikola Lezaic's *Tilva Ros* (2010), Stevan Filipovic's *Skinning/Šišanje* (2010), Srdan Spasojevic's *A Serbian Film/Srpski film* (2010), Mladen Ðordevic's *The Life and Death of a Porno Gang/Život i smrt porno bande* (2009) and Dejan Zecevic's *T.T. Syndrome/T.T. Sindrom* (2002) all seem to strengthen this new trend of national-extreme filmmaking. On the one hand, this turn can be understood as a political gesture which goes against the Western colonising[1] power by reflecting upon the global media broadcast of the war and Serbia's guilt in it. This criticism, however, rests on self-Balkanised narratives and aesthetics which, paradoxically, only strengthens the apprehension of the region as an uncivilised and wild third-world territory. The present chapter investigates this thematical contradiction by focusing on two films which, both in their self-reflexive narrative structure and thematic layer, bear close resemblance. *A Serbian Film*, through which 'new extremism ... found a way into the Balkans' (Jurković 2020: 721) and *The Life and Death of a Porno Gang* both rework the porn-snuff platform to criticise the (Serbian) society and raise socio-political questions about trauma, reality and national identity. Both productions deal with explicit taboo-breaking content which led to a deeply divided scholarly and critical response in film studies.

Similar to Jelača (2016), I argue that in the framework of trauma, 'it becomes impossible to separate into ethno-national entities the body of cinema that speaks to the same conflict(s)' and because many post-Yugoslav films are more transnational than ethno-national and refer to the

100 THE EXTREME CINEMA OF EASTERN EUROPE

Yugoslav cinematic tradition in an intertextual way (18–22), the chapter discusses examples from Bosnian, Croatian and Macedonian cinema.

Subversive Serbian Cinema

Tito's system in Yugoslavia was well-known for its contradictory nature. On the one hand, it was a one-party socialist state with strict central rules, while it was also a semi-capitalist country, the first in the Eastern bloc, to permit small-scale private enterprise. Although censorship was an existing practice, the country had no official censorship office and it allowed non-party members to criticise the system to certain extents (see Pamet 1999: 89–91). In the atmosphere of market-oriented economic policy and relative ideological freedom, the cultural establishment did not take a stance against erotic content in media (Ibroscheva 2013: 77). Compared to other socialist countries in the region, Yugoslavia showed much greater acceptance toward erotic imagery. The Yugoslav market promoted pornographic elements in newspapers, magazines and, less publicly, via videotapes. As we have seen in Chapter 1, the sexual discourse entailed emancipatory and progressive ideas on human sexuality and gave relative freedom to Black Wave filmmakers. The provocative visualisation of the female body and topics of sexuality on screen seemed to justify that the establishment was open to the idea of cultural transformation, and open to the West (Ibid., 94). Despite the 'omnipresent culture of misogyny, chauvinism and ethnonationalism' persistent in the region's socialist countries, this period brought about many positive actions for women's emancipation and equality (Petrovic 2018: 4; Lóránd 2018: 138–53). Yugoslavia was the first socialist country with a woman prime minister, Milka Planinć (1982–86) and women were granted higher political visibility and some additional rights, such as equitable pay distribution, maternity leave and subsidised childcare (Murtic 2015). Notwithstanding the significant strides forward, the ideological-cultural easing did not promote the dismissal of age-old patriarchal gender relations. Due to the labour surplus in Yugoslavia, women were not pressured to enter the labour force and their employment rate remained much lower than in other Eastern European countries (Bonfiglioli 2020). The gendered segregation of jobs and women's multiple obligations between family (reproduction) and society (production), similar to other socialist countries, created a 'working mother gender contract' (Ibid., 58) which hindered women's rights to control their bodies and time. In media, the patriarchal representation of females forecasted two images: the mother and the whore. As Matić (2015) puts it, 'while both images discreetly entered the media space, the latter, the image of the whore, soon became the norm' (94).

The political transition and the wars during the Yugoslav succession (1991–95) only exacerbated the subjugated position of women. The post-Yugoslav ethnonationalist propaganda saw the violent and conservative re-traditionalisation of gender roles (Petrovic 2018) and the re-emergence of the ideology of domesticity (Zacijek-Calasanti 1995). Religions also emphasised 'male authority in the family, in society, and even in heaven' (Jogan 1990: 45) and prompted women to focus on their family's private domain. Although the post-1989 socio-economic changes allowed women to establish women's organisations and form networking and political education, the sudden increase in women's employment and the closing of free day-care centres, together with women's commodification and violence against them, worsened women's social status and independence (see Zacijek-Calasanti 1995). As Ivanovic puts it, women were supposed to serve a threefold aim: biological preservation, cultural continuity and the maintenance of moral standards and traditional values (Ivanovic, quoted by Murtić 2015: 103–4).

With the return to domesticity, the nation-state concept of Balkan countries was a return to the most traditional and despotic values (Pavlović 1999), which recalled the age-old sexist patterns (Jogan 1995: 235). In these times of crisis, women's defence and survival strategy seemed to be the acceptance of their own subjugated position. This self-sacrifice meant a return to the domestic sphere which, as Papić (1999) puts it, 'actually helped the survival of the despotic nationalist system which had caused and provoked the very crisis which they had been trying to survive' (169). As accentuated by Simić (1999), the South Slav family – the kern of the domestic sphere – rests on the very understanding that family is a theoretically infinite development cycle which embraces more generations (including the dead). The strong attachment to parents, siblings, children and other relatives thus generates an 'extended childhood' with 'intense emotional and substantive reciprocity, family corpocracy and interpersonal dependence' (Ibid., 18). This reciprocal interdependency creates a sex-segregated, closed universe whose head, the father, makes the important decisions of the family unit. Interestingly, mothers gradually develop greater authority and through their 'parental duty, self-sacrifice and martyrdom' slowly exert power and influence within the family unit (Ibid., 21–4). Less surprisingly, this dichotomy between women's external-social and internal-family role (Mylonas 2003: 90) still provides one of the most prevalent themes of South Slav popular culture (Simić 1999: 28).

Family, Nation, Nationalism: The Route to Balkanism

As Ule and Rener (1996: 228–30) highlight, nationalism always handles historical regression in the form of the return of national legends, myths and the family. In its aggressive ethno-nationalist type in the Balkans, this has generated a masculinist, patriarchal discourse which, with its violent policies, eradicated the previously guaranteed social and civil rights of women (Papić 1999: 154). Ethnic nationalism, as outlined by Papić (1999), rests on a politics of gender difference in which women are mythologised as 'the Nation's deepest essence and instrumentalized as its producer' (155), thus recalling metaphors of the family and the homeland/nation as mother. As Ule and Rener (1996) put it, metaphors of nationalism express

> the infantile regression of the return to the mother's breast—it is the affirmation of the dual relationship between the mother and the (lost) son. In the conditions of postsocialist societies, such regression has an extra meaning—the stress is on the return of the lost son, who under the socialist "brotherhood and unity of the nations" lost his real mother and was developed instead by the socialist community, which turned out to be a cheating stepmother instead of a caring adoptive mother. This is also why the return is so sincere and so violent. (228–9)

The analogy between the patriarchal family and the new state created the narrative of the extended family where the father/president, or the Great Savior/Master/Leader/Father/Controller, as Papić (1999:165) has it, defends the newly built 'totally subjugated female nation' (Ibid., 165) and its essence of reproduction, women/homeland. In the upcoming wars, women's bodies became a symbolic territory to fight for (Petrović 2018: 2) while men constituted the brutal, often animalistic and barbarian force to build new nation states. Unless publicised as victims of the enemy or talked about in the context of bearing children for the nation, women were nearly invisible and absent from the public sphere (Papić 1999: 160). The extreme misogyny, as Milojević (2012: 63) puts it, 'manifested via narratives on the "good Serbian woman" who is either alive but silent and invisible or famous but no longer in existence (dead)':

> the nationalist abuse of women sheds light on the phenomenon of totalitarian ethnic nationhood as a naturalised fraternal order, in which women are doubly subjugated: as insiders they are colonised and instrumentalised in their "natural" function as "birth-machines"; and as outsiders they are reified into the targets of destruction mediated instruments of violence against other men's nations and cultural identity. The abuse of women and their bodies in the "pure" nation-building processes results in two interdependent forms of violence against highly restricted or no abortion for the insiders, and, in extreme (but consistent) cases, rape for the outsiders. (Emphasis original, Papić 1999: 155)

The rapes in the Yugoslav wars – especially Serbian soldiers' violation of Muslim women – have been examined from many angles, including the legal perspectives and social consequences of sexual assault as well as the victimisation of women (see Allen 1996; Boose 2002; Van Boeschoten 2003; Booth 2005). The number of rape cases is still unknown, but it ranges somewhere between 20,000 to 50,000 (Kennedy-Pipe and Stanley 2005: 73). The scale of sexual assault demonstrates that (mass) rape acted as an essential instrument of Balkan wars and only exacerbated women's position as sex-objects. This conscious tool served the purpose of ethnic cleansing, the deconstruction of culture, and genocide (Papić 1999), while it also functioned as a ritual male bonding of 'marking territory and desecrating the enemy man's "property"' (emphasis original, Kesić 1999: 193). Women's bodies became the symbolic battlefield of male war strategy (Papić 1999: 156), a way to demonstrate that women are indeed sex-subjects (Milojević 2012: 64).[2]

Anxieties about the family and nation are closely linked to anxieties about femininity and masculinity (Pavlović 1999). To this day women are still losing privileges in the post-communist, war-torn region of the Balkans. Tied to their land and (domestic) home, their identity became inseparable of the identity of the nation. Pavlović calls this process 'the domestication of women' which, as he argues, goes hand in hand with the creation hypermasculinity. The birth of 'Rambo-like characters [who] spring across national boundaries' exemplified the significance of the *Homo Balcanicus* in his leading role as the defender of the family and the nation (Pavlović 1999: 133). A common characteristic of the new man is his conception of woman as lower being. As Pavlović explains, 'In colloquial Croatian-Serbian the term for woman is *picka* (cunt). Women trapped in a male linguistic jargon is reduced to her sexual organ. Since the woman is only a cunt, *homo balcanicus* is not threatened by her' (1999: 133). Simić (1999) associates this machoistic behaviour with the dominance of mothers and moral-sexual double-standards in the region. He argues that this ecstatic behaviour of men usually takes place in public settings, and it maintains the illusion of total male dominance. The extravagant dramatisation of masculinity can be thus viewed as a counter-policy of men to overcome the domestic power of mothers. The patriarchal mindset is, however, embedded in a much broader socio-politic context. As Milojević (2012) explains, the rite of passage to turn boys into men and men into soldiers was a mandatory process in the former Yugoslavia and it blurred the difference between soldiers and civilians during the Balkan wars. When describing hegemonic, socially constructed masculinity in the post-Yugoslav territory and especially in Serbia, Milojević argues that because certain feelings are suppressed (such as 'feeling affectionate, loving, afraid, worried, sad, vulnerable, or helpless'), others, like being 'confident, aggravated, frustrated, cranky, impatient, irritated, angry and detached', are allowed to be expressed within society, and men are thus 'psychologically prepared to enact violence':

> Hegemonic masculinities ... are utilised to glorify and reward men's willingness to turn themselves and other men into violent objects ... A good Serbian man ... is a hero who fights for his people, refuses to negotiate and does not settle for less than victory. Two prerequisites are needed to become a Serbian hero: maleness and the skilled use of weapons. When it comes down to conflicts with 'others', all else is cowardly, naïve, inefficient or counterproductive. (Milojević 2012: 60–61)

The view of Balkan nations as 'evil, aggressive, barbaric and "naturally" violent' (Milojević 2012: 67) became a common template for Western nations and it has given birth to the 'wild man of the Balkans' stereotype (Jameson 2004). Hospitality, heavy drinking, destruction of property and other forms of physical violence – which Todorova (2006) famously named the process of Balkanisation, have been long associated with the Balkan atmosphere. This stereotype also served as a justification for Western nations to interfere in the wars and impose (military) power from outside (Jameson 2004). The Balkan as Europe's imaginary, violent Other has been famously played out, becoming the 'backward, the primitive, the barbarian' (Todorova 1997: 3) spectacle for the external gaze (see Bakić-Hayden 1995; Žižek, 1997; Bjelić 2003). Self-Balkanisation, the internalisation of the externally imposed stereotype, has been discussed by various scholars who classify the Balkan as the Other of the progressive West (Bakić-Hayden 1995; Todorova, 1997). In this view, the identity construction of Balkanisation is based on a binary othering of 'us' (the Balkan) versus 'them' (West) and helps the region to appear as a mysterious, exotic Orient and sell this image to Western audiences.[3] The phenomenon, however, seems to be much more complex. Jelača finds the roots of self-Balkanisation in unresolved collective socio-historical traumas:

> The charge of self-Balkanization is at times deployed in too linear a manner that neglects to consider how war and its aftereffects indeed *are* a traumatic legacy that seems to stubbornly recur or haunt our collective unconscious. Perhaps it is worth considering, for a moment, why it might be that war recurs and violence becomes instigated in such veracious manner rather than pushing against the fact of its existence altogether. Post-Yugoslav cinema is, without a doubt, frequently haunted by this question. Its consideration does not automatically infer that violence is somehow inherent to local "mentality" (a problematic term in its own right), but might open doors for new insight, such as that violence perhaps recurs as a result of the suppressed, unresolved traumas of the past—traumas that have not been meaningfully worked through, but rather emplotted into ethnocentric discourses, passed on, and mistaken for ancient hatreds. (Jelača 2016: 40–1)

Instead of 'some commercial self-branding that can be sold to the Western audience', Radović (2014) considers self-Balkanisation as a political question. According to her, it functions as a form of criticism of the Western gaze and at the same time, it expresses frustration with the involvement of the West in the Balkan wars. She also notes that self-Balkanisation is acceptable in Serbia for it supports the view that the war is a consequence of local people's mentality rather than extreme political ideologies (Radović 2014: 127). Whether it is a trans-historical construction (Jelača 2016), a suppressed reaction upon the West's military and political interference (Radović 2014) or a mere commercial strategy to sell the cultural products of the region (Žižek 1997), the Balkan screen is brimming with hyper-masculine male characters and it seems that (self)-Balkanisation is a profitable strategy. Financed by Western companies (Iordanova 2001: 10–11), the majority of (war) films, such as *No Man's Land* (*Nicija Zemlja*, Tanovic 2001), *The Living and the Dead* (*Zivi i mrtvi*, Milic 2007), *The Blacks* (*Crnci*, Devic and Jurić 2009) or *Ordinary People* (Perisic 2009), have been praised by foreign audiences. As Murtic aptly summarises:

> With the persistent and *irresistible* visualisation of the hyper-masculine man, with whom both the Balkans and the West have become familiar, one might (cynically) ask: who needs a fascinating female character from the Western Balkans anyway? (Murtic 2015: 87)

Post-Yugoslav Cinema: The Cinema of Anger

Less surprising, the post-Yugoslav nationalist discourse used patriarchal narratives to resuscitate the old hegemonic and patriarchal mechanisms and the post-war cinematic context continued the tradition to portray violence on screen. For most filmmakers, war was a lived and traumatic experience and the news media that broadcasted this spectacle, also influenced the choice of topic (Murtić 2015: 78; Krstić 2000).[4]

This new 'cinema of normalization' (Pavičić 2014) resisted the tendency of the 1990s and addressed the realistic burden of women after the conflicts.[5] In contrast to Yugoslav cinema's representation of women as '*mother* and/or *whore*' (Murtić 2015), and post-socialist cinema's suppressed female characters who became marginalised due to the historio-political conditions (Iordanova 1996), the cinema of normalisation has destabilised the old-school misogynist, violent narratives. In recent years, however, an extreme tendency in Serbian cinema has seemingly been playing out the self-Balkanisation metaphor by focusing on sexually super-active male characters, extra-violent scenes, and female characters in suppressed, humiliated roles. *A Serbian Film*, *Porno Gang*, *Clip* and *Tilva Ros* all are examples of this trend. According to the film critic Dejan Ognjanović, these films reflect the collective angry imagination of Serbia:

> These directors were formed by a daily bombardment of images of genuine conflict and physical abuse in their teenage years, which they translate into a bleak post-Milosevic landscape of eroded moral values and sexually explicit imagery. Sentiments of injustice and abandonment ... 'and motifs of orphans or absent parents, scar ... an entire wave of recent movies from the country'. (Dejan Ognjanović in Kerekes and Slater 2016: 132)

The anger of this new generation, as argued below, uses the self-Balkanisation metaphor to criticise the Western imagining of the Balkan. More specifically, it uses self-exoticism and the stereotype of violent Serbians as the spectacle of/for the Western gaze. On the one hand, it internalises the (Western) representation of the local population during the war, while it also serves to criticise Europe's interference into the country's internal politics. The bombings endorsed by the European Union and NATO made a pro-European, pro-Western position 'almost schizophrenic' while the common standpoint of people also rejected nationalism(s) in the region (Daković 2006: 98). The third way, which Daković describes as 'essential humanism', sees the war as a great national tragedy and divides guilt and blame between all the parties involved (NATO, Serbia, Croatia, Bosnia) (Ibid., 98). Essential humanism offers a more objective moral standpoint which equally criticises Milosevic's nationalist politics and the interference of the West. The post-2000 extreme film tendency is part of this ideological view. Fuelled by the frustration and anger caused by wars, NATO bombing, corruption, sanctions and their Western image of 'the Serbs as evil' (Ognjanović 2015: 82), these films feature anti-heroes who are 'lost between guilt, self-pity and violent attempts at working out their own – as opposed to prefabricated identity' (Ibid., 82).

Intermedial Torture: *The Life and Death of a Porno Gang*

Mladen Djordjević's *The Life and Death of a Porno Gang* (*Život i smrt porno bande*, 2009) tells the story of the freshly graduated film director Marko (Mihajlo Jovanović) who desperately wants to shoot his first feature (art) film. After his meeting with porn director Cane (Srdjan Miletić), his attention soon shifts towards adult cinema. Although Cane warns Marko to 'make something Serbian, something simple', the young director decides to shoot a short art film and set up the 'Balkan's first porno theatre' to 'sexually educate Serbs and expand their horizon'. He manages to gather eight members (who are mainly porn stars) but Cane and his policeman brother sabotage the group's premiere and Marko's gang are soon forced to leave Belgrade and go on a (porno) tour around Serbia. After one of their porn shows, Franz (Srboljub Milin), a German-Serbian journalist makes Marko the offer to shoot snuff films because 'the Balkans are still fruitful grounds for the mix of cruelty and creativity' and because the West is hungry for such spectacle. In desperate need of money, the group eventually agrees to explore the unknown territory of 'porn and death'. Although all their agents voluntarily accept death, the snuff business soon takes its toll on the porn group. Whether through suicide, accident or murder, they all die by the end of the film.

With its explicit, pornographic content, bestiality and violent, bloody images, *The Life and Death of a Porno Gang* stirred strong controversy. Some critics praised it as 'horrifying and disgusting, provoking and ... [a] necessary film' which 'shakes you to the core' (Bambray 2010), while others called it 'exploitation cinema at its most exploitive' (Sammons 2012) which is 'only recommended for the most daring viewers who are looking to gross themselves out' (Chowen 2012, also see Kerekes 2016). Without a doubt, Djordjević's intention was to strike controversy and shake the spectator into political consciousness. His film exploits the self-Balkanisation brand but at the same time references the identity crisis and self-exoticism in a uniquely self-reflexive form which, similar to other examples of the New Serbian Wave, questions the very authenticity of pro-filmic reality.

Intermediality plays a key role in Djordjević's film. *The Life and Death of a Porno Gang* references several other mediums, including theatre and television, as well as film and photography. Marko's graduate film, *When the Pig Cried* and his second film (*Oblivion Grass from Svem*) are both parts of intradiegetic narration. While narrating his life, *The Life and Death of a Porno Gang* visually cross-references both films by making their footage part of the diegesis. The black and white *When the Pig Cried* features Marko who eats from the still living and crying head of a pig. While facing the bleeding head at the dinner table, he suddenly grabs a knife and cuts his chest. *Oblivion Grass from Srem*, a 'socio-political porno-horror' (as the intertitle says), narrates the story of a peasant who, after importing genetically modified soybeans from Bulgaria, faces the very poor harvest of his farmland. Out of fury, the peasant sexually penetrates the soil of the land. The mix of sperm and soil gives birth to a magical plant which, when smoked, causes sexual hallucinations. The dealer soon runs out of plants and his customers' withdrawal symptoms cause physical mutations and uncontrolled aggression. The zombie-like crowd attacks the dealer, but he manages to kill one of them by putting a whiskey bottle into his mouth.

Screened in the first quarter of *The Life and Death of a Porno Gang*, *When the Pig Cried* and *Oblivion Grass from Srem* establish the very sarcastic-exploitative atmosphere of Djordjević's film. Both Marko and Djordjević himself clearly play on the self-Balkanisation metaphor which gets turned upside down throughout the film. *When the Pig Cried* deals with an empty metaphor (thus recalling many examples of extreme cinema) and assembles a film that contains self-mutation, animal torture, violence and blood. The lack of colour, narrative coherence and dialogue and/or monologue in the film, together with its very short length – which Williams (1999: 73) names 'stag film' – all serve to foreground the spectacle and create a simple sensual connection between the spectator and the film's narrative space. Marko ironically identifies this receipt of cinema with his very 'artistic ambition' but with *Oblivion Grass from Srem*, he finally reveals the sarcasm behind his statement. His independent art films resemble what Sconce (1995) termed paracinema: that is, a counter-cinematic 'alternative vision of cinematic art' which ... [attacks] the established canon of 'quality' cinema and [questions] the legitimacy of reigning aesthete discourse on movie art' (374). In contrast to camp, this 'aesthetic of vocal confrontation' goes against the economic and cultural elites 'who are responsible for making the contemporary cinema ... so completely boring' (Ibid., 374). By focusing on a film's 'formal bizarreness and stylistic eccentricity', as Sconce puts it,

> the material identity of the film ceases to be a structure made invisible in service of the diegesis, but becomes instead the primary focus of textual attention. It is in this respect that the paracinematic aesthetic is closely linked to the concept of 'excess'. (Sconce 1995: 386)

Sconce also draws attention to the significance of non-diegetic, extratextual discourses that surround a paracinematic example and overall, the cultural and sociological context that frames paracinematic aesthetic valuations: 'the trash aesthetic serves as a reminder that all forms of poetics and aesthetic criticism are ultimately linked to issues of taste; and taste, in turn, is a social construct with profoundly political implications' (Sconce 1995: 392). Taste in *The Life and Death of a Porno Gang* becomes a key word in this context of aesthetic deviance. The intermedial references in Djordjević's film not only allude to the very medium of the film as an aesthetic device but question the (Western) conception of ('highbrow') art. The close-up penetration of the peasant into the soil in *Oblivion Grass from Srem* – a meat shot (Williams 1993: 73) – together with the exploitation-styled, provocative set of pornographic, violent and often-amateurish images stand as a counter-narrative against (self-)Balkanisation and Western exploitation. In contrast to pornography, the films do not aim for the arousal or excitement of the spectator, rather, both *Oblivion Grass from Srem* and *When the Pig Cried* stand as caricatures of the South Slav prototype of man. This is even more obvious in Marko's theatre play. His porn cabaret takes place in 2010, when 'Serbia has problems with the southern neighbours' and the growing matriarchy – together with women's enlarged breasts and proliferation of homosexuality – embitters the lives of Serbians. All this is caused by aliens from the planet 'Eroticon 6' who came to Serbia to start the reign of women. They announce that 'Serbians beware, patriarchy is out of fashion' but before any concrete actions, the show ends by the interruption of Cane and his policeman brother.

Marko wants to expand his creativity by making provocative films and plays which are brimming with alcohol, sex, violence and self-harm – all elements that, in his understanding, are needed for him to be categorised as an artist. *The Life and Death of a Porno Gang* constitutes the third part of this *mise-en-abyme* formula which incorporates both films as intermedial references to create a final, third one which ultimately criticises the (Western) conception of Balkan art. The Western influence is emphasised via the figure of Franz, a German-born Serbian war correspondent who now lives from selling 'black market movies of war and terror' to the Western audience. He urges Marko to mix pornography 'with violence, story plot and politics' to please the 'clients of [the] West and America'. After some snuff films, Franz organises a live snuff show for Western clients. The theatre is played in English for well-suited, wealthy businessmen but, as in the first case in Belgrade, this show gets cancelled by the authorities. In the end, Franz makes an idea to 'film freaks in Serbia, humans and beasts', because 'some people would jerk off even to that'. This exploitation of the Serbian spectacle by Western powers is a very direct message in Djordjević's film. Franz even shows Marko snuff footage from the war where soldiers behead the mujahideen in Bosnia and play football with one of the heads. The young director clearly gets upset by the sight of the brutality but after he witnesses the cruelty of Serbian villagers, he accepts Franz's offer.

The rape of the band by locals is one of the most disturbing scenes of the film. The violent sequence portrays elderly men who immobilise the group with guns and knives in the middle of the forest (Figure 5.1). With long beards and wearing military clothes, the hypermasculine villagers rape all the men and women of the gang. Yet, Djordjević's camera mainly focuses on the man-to-man rapes. The naked butts of the villagers and their rhythmical movement are intercut with the close-ups of the men whose facial expressions mirror disgust and pain. When Dzoni surprisingly starts laughing, the camera again records all the faces and

Figure 5.1 Family portrait: *The Life and Death of a Porno Gang*, Serbia: Film House Bas Celik, 2009.

leaves the scene with a fixed wide shot of the group and the villagers. This photography-like final composition of the family-like group stands in the narrative as a tableau of the war. Men fight against and rape men, women get sexually humiliated, and violence gives birth to a never-ending circle of aggression. The circle continues with Marko's acceptance of Franz's offer. Repellent in the beginning, the young artist eventually accepts the needs of the market, and he identifies with his role, in this way becoming a cold-headed director who only focuses on capturing the more and more gruesome killings. The evolution of the murders thus clearly demonstrates Djordjević's circle of aggression and the effect the wars had on the (Serbian) population/family.

Marko's first snuff film captures a suicide where, just like *When the Pig Cried*, a man is featured who cuts his chest open with a razor. The second snuff piece is about a family man who suffers from AIDS and liver cancer. He reveals his violent experiences of the war where he witnessed the rape of a young girl and expresses his regrets that he killed children and civilians. Instead of the snuff-element of the scene, Djordjević emphasises the confession of the ex-soldier who faces the camera and admits his war crimes. With this very direct reference to the war, the story of *The Life and Death of a Porno Gang* and the travelling family changes. The group consumes more and more drugs, lose their sexual appetite and become depressed. The turning point is the family's third snuff film. Marko and his team decide to punish a local war hero/rapist by cutting off his head with a chainsaw. This is the first time that the young director is only concerned with the spectacle and focuses on how the scene can become 'fucking great, fucking great'. His loss of humanity starts a series of deaths in the film. One of the actors is shot by the police, his ex-boyfriend hangs himself, another two members die in a car accident and the transvestite actress who has just joined the cohort overdoses on heroin. The cameraman of the group is murdered by Cane's policeman brother who rapes Marko's photographer. In the end, it is the young director who reckons with Cane and with his brother as well as Franz, thus killing the ultimate authorities in the film. The circle of aggression ends with the death of the porno family: Marko and his girlfriend cut their wrists.

The self-reflexive filmmaking form and intermedial references convey a deep political message. Djordjević himself noted that his film portrays the consequences of the wars 'when seeing uncensored shots of war atrocities on TV was a normal thing' (Djordjević, quoted in Kendall 2016: 272):

> For several years, the audience that tuned to Channel 1 of the state television around 8pm was treated to a programme called *The News Addendum*, comprised of footage of the latest atrocities committed against Serbian civilians in Croatia and Bosnia and where the audience could see appalling images of entire families being slaughtered. However, these images were abused and falsified both by domestic and foreign media for their own propaganda purposes so that their documentary nature is highly compromised. The young people could perceive the disparity between their immediate reality and the one mediated and constructed by the media. The situation became more complex when a number of new films attempted to depict Serbia's grim reality, which often led to different types of compromised or questionable 'truths'. (Ognjanović: 2015: 82)

The Balkanisation and the Othering of the post-Yugoslav region is most evident in the media portrayal of the war-torn Balkans in Western media (see Bahador 2007; Goldsworthy 2002) which, as Ognjanović outlines, reduced the history of the region 'to a simple interplay between 'victims' and 'villains' (Ibid., 81). Longinović (2002) blames the US-led Western media coverage for transforming Serbia into the Other of Europe. He argues that the televised narratives about the Yugoslav wars turned Serbia into a collectively genocidal nation which formed a strategic part of the West's takeover of the region. The portrayal of 'the serbs'[6] as a 'symptom of the return of that ancient being that thrives on the suffering of others, 'whose violence, less civilised, abominable practices, rape and ethnic killings, have all justified the political, diplomatic and military interventions of NATO governments' (Longinović 2002: 48). Longinović uses the metaphor of vampirism to describe the global and local forms of (media) strategies and the very gothic imaginary that out forward 'the serbs' as necessary evil:

> Represented as the major predatory race in Europe, "the serbs" have resurrected the vampire's eternal hunger in [their] Balkan home, or so the producers of our daily world of information would have us believe. Most of the present knowledge of the Balkans is tied to this excessive violence, which marks the return of "old centuries". (emphasis original, Longinović 2002: 48)

The global media interpreted the events in the Balkans as genocide motivated by ancient ethnic hatreds that implied a need for military intervention which, as Longinović has it, 'would provide those peoples unable to rule themselves with the guidance and protection of "Western democracies"' (emphasis original, Ibid., 53). The televised narratives thus served to justify the violent military intervention of NATO countries by portraying the victory of the West as a humanitarian intervention. Longinović goes as far as to state that 'without the gaze of the Western media and the good intentions of NATO leaders, the gothic imaginary could have stayed limited to horror films and pulp fiction' (54) and that 'if the ethics of "infinite responsibility" could be enacted globally, the specter of the "vampires like us," "the serbs," needs to be supplemented by the "vampires like U.S.," the spectre of the well-intentioned viewers and interveners in the Balkans' (emphasis original, Longinović 2002: 57):

> Despite the fact that "the serbs" have been defeated and cleansed in Croatia, quarantined in Bosnia-Herzegovina, and punitively bombed by NATO in Serbia, they continue to be targeted by the U.S.-led West because they have been doubly Orientalised. As members of the shrinking world of Orthodox Christianity who also bear the postcolonial legacy of Ottoman servitude, they have been transformed into the Other of Europe within Europe ... While ... contaminating its environment with chemical and radioactive pollutants, the Western military alliance touted the superiority of its technology, claiming the moral high ground through various forms of psychological operations and electronic warfare that news consumers in the West accepted as "reality." (emphasis original, Longinović, 2002: 49–56)

The disappointment in the West can be clearly spotted in Longinović's writing whose subjective tone radiates wrath, anger and a huge distress. He argues that the war crimes were committed by post-communist nomadic clones and instead of blaming 'the serbs' who were 'both the fiercest perpetrators and the most numerous victims of these anti-Yugoslav forces' (56), Western nations should also take responsibility for mirroring a one-sided, false televisual image of the Balkan wars and, instead of sticking to the narrative of 'ancient hatred', look for the reasons of the conflict in the constitutional experiments of the Yugoslav political establishment (Goldsworthy 2002: 31).

The basic metaphor of *The Life and Death of a Porno Gang* plays along a very similar argument and, in a similarly heated way, reflects on the (falsified) knowledge-production and phantasmic projections that, according to Serbian voices, characterised the Balkan conflict. *The Life and Death of a Porno Gang* – and the other examples of this wave of Serbian extreme cinema – create counter-narratives against manipulated, falsified and edited aspects of domestic media and the films of Balkanisation by questioning the truth of the (cinematic) medium. The films-within-the-films narrative; the observational, handheld camera; the subjects' straight looks into the device; the extra-diegetic narration; intertexts (dates); and jump cuts not only strengthen the self-reflexive nature of the film but, through this low-budget (video)documentary-like formula, they all draw attention to the (in) authentic recording of pro-filmic events. The staged deaths which, in contrast to Japanese and American snuff films where physical violence happens against the will of the victim, are here predominantly psychological-spiritual executions which become an affectionate, touching experience (Ognjanović 2015: 90). This poignancy is the result of the viewer's identification with the victim who participates in his own death for economic and/or traumatic reasons, while the executioners do the same to please the Western audience. The vision of deaths, as argued by Kendall (2016: 72) are framed by the crew's 'implicated and empathetic gazes' which undermines the scene's aim of voyeuristic titillation. Indeed, the snuff performances function as an ideological platform to confront the viewer with the after-effects of the wars and the very subjugated position of Serbians in the mediated process of violence.

This metaphor is also pronounced via the portraits of the family. The group's fourth snuff film, which fails due to the police's intervention, centres upon a grandfather whose granddaughter suffers from the effects of war. The young girl's face is severely burned, and the grandfather blames NATO's uranium bombs for the scars. Demonstrating the radiation, he also shows his five-legged cow to the group. Similar to the post-rape tableaux, Djordjević uses an identical aesthetic structure to frame the effects of the war (image). The five members of the family, including the five-legged cow, are portrayed standing in the living room and face Marko's camera (*screenshot*). With this single image, the director summarises all the tragedies of the war: the physical-physiological changes that is reflected in the granddaughter's facial expression and the extra leg of the cow, and the poverty and hopelessness that are radiated by the physiognomy of the characters. In the end of *The Life and Death of a Porno Gang*, Franz demands Marko deliver more stories and images like the grandfather's story for he 'fucking loved the five-legged cow'. The mediated family portrait functions as a symbolic, mediated unit of Serbian society which, when captured from a Western point-of-view, generalises a Balkanised gaze (Figure 5.2).

Figure 5.2 Balkan portrait: *The Life and Death of a Porno Gang*, Serbia: Film House Bas Celik, 2009.

Pornography, the other ingredient of the taboo-breaking spectacle, also serves ideological functions. Following the system change, pornography in Eastern Europe 'became a fetish of the free market, an expression of newly found freedom' (Lobodzińska 1995: 40). Soft erotica, the Western magazines' nude images of women, together with the television's pornographic content, got translated into wider availability in the post-socialist countries (Ibroscheva 2013: 96). In Serbia, unregulated, private television channels and local media outlet industries used pornographic content to compete for audience attention and recognition (Ibroscheva 2013: 96). The post-Yugoslav, blooming and unregulated (hard-core) porn and trafficking industry in Belgrade further flourished during the Balkan conflicts and 'had become the number one growth industry in the former Yugoslavia as a result of the war' (Kesić 1999: 191). Interestingly, the explosion of the sex industry and pornography were also used as political tools by nationalists who, in the hope of increasing birth rates, deregulated media questionable content (Jogan 1995: 233). As a consequence, the wide availability of sexual content 'blurred the boundaries between what is considered obscene and what is considered pornographic' (Ibroscheva 2013: 96).

The explicit pornographic content in recent Serbian extreme cinema reflects upon and criticises the spectacle of nationalism(s) by using sexuality as part of the films' grotesque fiction. The criticism of the amateurish porn industry in Serbia is explicitly depicted in the behind-the-scenes porn-sequence of *The Life and Death of a Porno Gang*. In Cane's porn, the characters of a serviceman, a chimneysweep and a housewife are supposed to have a threesome but the chimneysweep (who is fully dressed in black, with chimney brush in his hands), nervously grabs the back of the actress who bursts out in pain. The furious Cane yells at the crew not to be 'like [an] elephant in a teahouse' and not to 'go for that dick like crazy' which endows the scene with a very grotesque tone. The conversation in the porn scene ('it doesn't leak there, it leaks here', points the female character to her vagina); the badly lit, old-school socialist kitchen set; and the characters' very bad acting in the scene all mock Serbia's amateurish porn industry. As Kerekes has it, 'Porn in Serbia remains creatively and technically stilted. ... [It is] evidently uncomfortable playing matters straight and opts instead for the puerile or broadly comic, with jokes told or staged during sex scenes. Consequently, porn consumers tend to favour more competent and more serious overseas products' (Kerekes 2016: 134).

The reason why recent Serbian extreme cinema prefers to mix up pornographic images and hard-core sequences of violent, bloody deaths can be traced back to the wars and the televisual representation of Serbia. Death became a common nominator for the Balkan spectacle and, together with pornography, the juxtaposition of the two created a controversial, taboo-inflicted imaginary. This is to say that, thanks to the Western images that interconnected sexual identity, rape and violent conflicts in global media, the phantasmatic projections from the West became part of the development of Serbian identity (Bjelić and Cole 2002: 303). Sex and violence thus became common nominators in Serbian popular culture through which the trauma and history of the nation could be expressed (Kimber 2014). In this regard, the very graphic and shocking sexual violence and the snuff-brimmed bloodshed in *A Serbian Film* (2010) summarise Serbia's national traumas. The themes of necrophilia, paedophilia and pornography not only reflect upon the immense political and economic changes after the fall of Yugoslavia and the wars that followed, but they also mirror the very present of the Western, neoliberal capital that dictates Serbia's (pornographic) media market.

S(n)uffocating Eastern Europe: *A Serbian Film*

Co-written by Aleksander Radivojević and independently financed by Contra Film, Spasojević's directorial debut narrates the story of Miloš (Srdjan Todorović), a middle-aged, retired porn star whose financial struggles drive him to participate in a last porn movie directed by the unknown auteur, Vukmir (Sergej Trifunović). Hoping to improve the economic situation of his wife Marija (Jelenda Gavrilović) and their son Petars, he even agrees not to see the script or know any details about the shooting. As expected, Miloš soon finds himself in a pornographic nightmare where snuff, torture, sadism, paedophilia and rape make up the upmarket 'art porn' of Vukmir. Miloš tries to escape but Vukmir's team drugs him with animal aphrodisiacs. The narcotics turn the porn actor into an insatiable sex machine. What follows from here in the story is a series of shocking, horrifying acts which turn the production into a snuff film. *A Serbian Film* features child sex abuse, necrophilia and a rich repertoire of sexual violence. In one of the scenes, Miloš decapitates a woman with a machete and uses it for oral sex. In another, we see him being sodomised by Vukmir's military-dressed men. Scenes also include images of an under-aged girl whose lolly-licking is intercut with a scene of fellatio and Miloš's policeman brother as he gets fellated by a woman while watching a happy family video of Miloš, Marija and Petar. In the film's final horror-scene, Miloš and his brother rape two hooded figures who turn out to be Marija and Petar. After killing Vukmir and his entire crew, the family eventually decides to commit suicide. As the family lays dead, we see a new film crew enter the bedroom. Implying necrophiliac sex with the corpses, the unknown man orders the thugs to 'start with the little one'.

In terms of pornography and the trope of filmmaking, Spasojević's film shares many dominant features with *The Life and Death of a Porno Gang*, but Djordjević's film is far less explicit in its on-camera taboo-breaking content. This might be the reason why *The Life and Death of a Porno Gang* is stingily accepted in most circles, while for most critics and viewers, *A Serbian Film* 'remains an ugly duckling' (Kerekes 2016). It is less surprising that, because of representations and juxtaposition of rape and horror, the film's uncut version was banned in numerous countries. In the United Kingdom, the cuts made Spasojević's film the most heavily censored mainstream non-pornographic film of the last sixteen years. The authorities required cuts to material which, according to them, endorsed sexual violence and eroticised children (Kimber 2014). Eventually, the British board acknowledged the director's artistic intentions and with over four minutes of cuts, passed the film with certificate 18. The controversy around the film's premier in both Serbia and other countries (including the arrest of the Sitges Film Festival's director for child pornography charges), seemed to be a good advertisement for *A Serbian Film*; it became the bestseller movie of the distributor Invincible Pictures. Interestingly, it was only after the foreign scandals that Serbia's attention turned towards the film and began to engage in what Kimber (2014) calls 'transgressive edge play' (121). The circulation and regulation of the film led to polarised reactions from critics and audience. Supporters of *A Serbian Film* praised the film's artistic merit and 'intellectual exercise' to unfold the socio-political allegory of the narrative (Ognajović 2015; Kimber 2014: 119). Because many view the explicit pornographic content of the film as a vehicle for 'the historical exploitation of Serbian people' (Kimber 2014: 120), the on-camera atrocities got classified as a legitimate choice to convey deep socio-political traumas.

Negative comments on the film criticised Spasojević's debut for being a poorly made and boring piece, with bad acting, 'crude pop video aesthetics', predictability and lack of suspense (Kimber 2014: 119). Interestingly, most of the critics and even scholars categorised the film as a classic horror movie (see for instance Featherstone 2013; Kimber 2014; Jurković 2020). Scholars have often drawn parallels between the *Saw*-saga (2004–10) or the *Hostel* series (2005–11) and only a few researchers labelled *A Serbian Film* an example of European extreme cinema (Kerner 2016; Frey 2016; McGillvray 2019) or torture porn (Jurković 2020). This clearly demonstrates the genre confusions around this relatively new phenomenon. What makes *A Serbian Film* an extreme example and how does it differ from horror or exploitation?

Newborn Art?

It has often been argued that, in contrast to pornography, recent arthouse films which display explicit sexual intercourse, use sex as a form of storytelling to highlight the ups and downs of a relationship.[7] The main argument, however, focuses on the mise-en-scéne of sex-art films. Frey (2016) for instance argues that, in contrast to pornography's little editing and extremely long takes, films of the aesthetic embrace use various shot scales, editing and shot length, while also avoiding point-of-view shots (167–9). Thus, the representation of sex happens in a more sophisticated filmic form. This stylish aesthetics, as argued by other scholars, gets supplemented by philosophical and intellectual dialogues (Krzywinska 2006); aggressive and alienated sex (Williams 2008); and pessimistic representations of intimacy which subvert social norms about identity and sexuality (Frey 2016: 170). When watching through the lenses of the claims above, the highly stylised mise-en-scéne of *A Serbian Film* seems to allow us to identify the film as a sex-art film. But is the sophisticated form enough to classify a film 'art'?

Even the critical voices acknowledged that Spasojević's film is of great technical expertise. Shot on a RED One HD Digital camera, *A Serbian Film* employs extended tales, handheld camcorder footage, an extravagant colour pallet, well-staged compositions, flashbacks, shadow lighting and carefully constructed, heightened sound effects, as well as polished editing (see Kimber 2014: 113–15). More striking is, however, the film-in-the-film form which, similar to *The Life and Death of a Porno Gang*, plays with spectatorial positions. The constant switch between the diegetic and non-diegetic layers of the film and the play with the spectatorial positions of witness, torturer and tortured describe the devastating nature of torture (Jones 2018: 99). While the first part of the film follows a linear chronology, the second half operates with flashbacks, montage-episodes and memory-images that all help the viewer (and Miloš) to piece the puzzle of the story together. Waking up covered in blood and bruised in his bed, Milos tries to reconnect to the happenings of the previous days. Having been heavily drugged, he barely remembers anything from the bloody porn acts he had to perform. His confusion is expressed via memory-images which include blurry-flashing cuts of a naked butt, a knife held onto his erected penis, blood on the wall, and then Miloš's subjective point-of-view shot as he is peeing blood. The narrative structure of the film from this point on embraces a postmodern, disjointed, mosaic-like storytelling formula which explains the porn star's bruises and bloody t-shirt when he wakes up from his drugged nightmare. These very explicit, episodic montage-sequences include several snuff-scenes. In one of these, Miloš rapes and then decapitates a woman with a machete and continues the rape of the headless corpse. In another one, a woman whose teeth have been removed with pliers is suffocated by oral sex. The peak of these flashback-hall-of-horrors is the film's final scene that places Miloš in a warehouse where he and his brother violently rape two hooded figures who turn out to be his son and wife (Figure 5.3). In the bloody battle that follows, Miloš lobotomises a man by his erected penis that stabs through his eye socket. At the same time, Marija mashes the head of Miloš's brother and then kills

Figure 5.3 Hall of blood in *A Serbian Film*. Serbia: Contra Film, 2010.

Vukmir and the whole crew. The film then returns to a linear chronology and narrates the suicide of Miloš's family.

Because the mosaic-like narrative plot structure indicates that all the violence and damage have already happened before Miloš woke up, Spasojević removes numerous layers of tension and diminishes the suspense in the dramaturgy (Kimber 2014: 113). Instead of narrative comprehension, he focuses on a series of shock-effects which Kendall (2016) calls 'the aesthetic of expenditure' (2016: 263), a 'showy, over-the-top, hyperbolic aesthetic [which puts] ... the spectacle of death on full display ... characterised by a mood of hysteria and excess, which [the film] uses as a form of affective contagion to implicate the spectator' (263). According to Kendall, the aesthetic of expenditure emphasises the viewer's voyeuristic superiority but at the same time disavows her/his participation in the text. In this way, the cinematic spectacle and sight of death foregrounds ethical reflexivity and affect by inviting the audience to reflect on their own involvement as viewing subjects and subjects to extreme cinema's immense diffusion (Ibid., 274–5). This ethical strategy of extremity mediates terror via disturbing and heinous images but at the same time offers satisfaction and enjoyment as the viewer can distance herself/himself from the diegetic vision.

Spasojević's play with the forms of spectatorial positions places the viewer in the shoes of the torturer, the tortured and the witness, in this way setting up a complex triangle of intermedial, critical perspectives (Figure 5.4). First, Miloš witnesses his monstrous sexual actions on the screen of Vukmir's video camera that he finds in the director's office. This double framing structure puts Miloš both into the perpetrator as well as the witness and victim positions. He witnesses his own rape by one of Vukmir's military men and his escape from the house of the underage

Figure 5.4 Spectatorship and intermediality in *A Serbian Film*.
Serbia: Contra Film, 2010.

girl where Vukmir tries to force him to have sex with the child. He also watches the footage where Vukmir explains the 'extasy of free fuck' to Lejla (Katarina Zutić), an ex-colleague of the man who, in response, answers the director by saying that what he does is not art anymore. Miloš's reaction to this clandestine footage juxtaposes with the viewer's disgust. Miloš bites his hands in self-disgust and vomits when he recognises his wrongdoings. Thanks to the intermedial structure of the film which at the same time places Miloš inside and outside of the diegesis, the sequences strengthen his own as well as the viewer's passive position. To enhance the feeling of shock and confusion in the spectator, Spasojević supports the 'found footage' images with Miloš's own subliminal-subjective sequences. This gets special attention in the scene where the man is approached by the grandmother of the underage girl and tells him to 'govern' their house 'as a man', 'take care' of the young daughter and 'make her a woman'. The grandmother, the girl and even the crew of Vukmir that records the events, are shown through Miloš's subjective point-of-view in a way that, thanks to the jumping perspectives of the man and the narrator, breaks the fourth wall (Figure 5.5). The third-person flashbacks and Miloš's empirical first-hand perspective of the events, together with the constant jumps between the diegetic and non-diegetic inner layers of the filmic text, offer a multi-faceted witnessing position for the viewer. This postmodern structure not only represents the way in which the position of the protagonists and the violence of torture porn 'create moral fissures that defy straightforward resolution' (Jones 2018: 99) but, similar to *The Life and Death of a Porno Gang*, also questions the viewer's ethical stance and responsibility via the metaphoric play of experimental-experiential perspectives. This is to say that *A Serbian Film* references the media representation of war via the ideological, multi-focalised construction of the narrative.

Figure 5.5 Witnessing positions: *A Serbian Film*, Serbia: Contra Film, 2010.

POST-WAR EXTREMISM: SUBVERSIVE SERBIA 121

The infamous scene of 'newborn porn' is the epitome of this critique. When Miloš announces his retirement to Vukmir for, as he puts it, he 'can't do such stuff in the kindergarten', the director performs a prolonged, complex speech in which he calls Serbia 'one big shitty kindergarten'. In this country, he adds, 'you have to do whatever it takes to survive'. Vukmir calls the porn crew a family, 'the only warrant for the nation's survival', the 'backbone of the country's economy' that can prove that the nation is 'useful for anything'. When Miloš asks Vukmir with sudden confusion what these all have to do with pornography, the director ironically adds that it's 'not porn but life itself ... the flash and soul of the victim ... transmitted live to the world [that is] now paying to watch ... from the comfort of an armchair'. Vukmir also accentuates that 'victims are the priciest sell in this world and that the whole of Serbia is a victim. To demonstrate 'the power of a real victim', the director then shows Miloš 'newborn porn' footage where one of Vukmir's henchman is seen raping an infant. Less surprisingly, the most disturbing (and most censored) scene of the film led to polarised responses from critics and the audience. Kerekes for instance notes that 'in a catalogue of inflammatory scenes that pull no punches, [the newborn porn scene] overshadows all. What is an audience supposed to make of it? Run away in a funk like Miloš, gauging from responses online?' (Kerekes 2016: 190). Yet, he seems to defend the sequence:

> We can argue that the newborn porn episode shouldn't have been given cinematic shape; it is a fictional grotesque that oversteps common sensibility. But so it is with transgressive ideas. Allegory is demanded of such shocking images. That's how critics validate them. In the case of *A Serbian Film*, we have allegory in abundance. The movie is a metaphor for the political, moral and psychological downfall of Serbia and the world at large, according to first time director Spasojević. But does it ring true? (Kerekes 2016: 190)

While most scholars agree that the scene has a metaphorical stance, the explanations of what it is supposed to represent, differ greatly. Featherstone (2013) sees *A Serbian Film* as 'a traumatic symptom of the Milosevic and immediate post-Milosevic period'. He contrasts the film to 'its American counterparts *Saw* and *Hostel*' and argues that Spasojević's film is a representation of neoliberal globalisation in that it 'adopts a critical perspective on both Serbian and global systemic violence' (140). Featherstone sees the phallus (and rape) in *A Serbian Film* as weapons of war which, as emphasised by Kimber (2014) and Kendall (2016) as well, reflect national traumas and renegotiated identities. It is no wonder that at the film's premier at the South by Southwest Festival, the audience in Austin were called on the stage to '[snort] lines of salt, [squeeze] lime juice into their

122 THE EXTREME CINEMA OF EASTERN EUROPE

eyes, and [take] shots of tequila' to 'understand what Serbians have been through to create a culture of Serbian film' (Kohn 2010). The sadism of the wars, the Milosevic-era, the political transition, corruption and poor post-war governmental leadership are all highlighted as implicit messages in *A Serbian Film*. The shock thus mediates 'the suffering of Serbian people through extreme violence and taboos (most likely for the purpose of financial gain)' (Jurković 2020: 721).

Conversely, Ognajović (2015) argues that 'foreign critics ... lack sufficient insight into the complexities of Serbia's recent history' which is why the deeper, connotative layers of *A Serbian Film* often get overlooked (84). The Serbian critic emphasises the demand of the Western film festival market and one's adjustment to the tastes of the Western audience. In his view, the newborn porn scene symbolises the Serbian film industry (as wonderful family) which makes profit out of its own Balkanism. Although Spasojević himself added that the viewer does not have to have any previous knowledge of Serbia to understand the film (Reed 2010), he also pinpoints Eastern Europe and Serbia's exploited position within world film industries:

> In Eastern Europe, you cannot get your film financed unless you have a barefoot girl who cries on the streets, or some story about war victims in our region. But of course, you should never go too deep, or show tough scenes, or point out the problems. ... European film funds and festivals, some of them, are looking for those kinds of films from Eastern Europe because it's a problematic region with war and suffering. And that's exploitation. Those films are real exploitation. It's spiritual pornography. ... Also because the Western world has lost feelings, so they're searching for false ones, they want to buy feelings. It's like they'll feel more human if they see victims ...' (Spasojević in Selavy, 2010)

The survival of the nation (the Serbian cinema) thus means to obey the demands of Western audience. Pornography in this sense stands for 'a morally and aesthetically bankrupt idea of pseudo-documentary and pseudo-realist "art-cinema" exploiting the real-life suffering through the process of Balkanism' (Ognajović 2015: 84). A new-born porn scene in *A Serbian Film* thus reflects the director's 'spiritual prostitution' (Ibid., 84), that is, the exploitation of Serbians and the self-victimising cliché on the altar of attracting foreign funds. The rape of the infant by the henchmen and the mother's smiling face all comply with Ognajović's reading as symbols of the 'curse upon generations created by the unscrupulous or unthinking peddlers of worthless festival fare':

> The Cinema of Self-Victimisation, epitomised by the snuff footage of "the newborn porn", seems to be Serbian cinema's potential future in a global market where the local "Art of Atrocity" and "Tradition of Terror", together with "Pain and Perversion

from the Balkans", will be saleable commodities for as long as Serbia is perceived as Europe's excremental Other. (Emphasis in the original, Ognajović 2015: 92)

It is no doubt that artistic allegory forms a large base in the connotative structure of *A Serbian Film*. Still, the intermedial structure of the film suggests a deeply-rooted political metaphor which questions art's authenticity and value when it comes to politico-ideological standpoints. Similar to *The Life and Death of a Porno Gang*, the presence of the camcorder in the diegesis of the film foregrounds the representation of war in global media and the value of realism when it comes to mediated images. The implication of the West in the Eastern European process of degradation has been highlighted by the director himself who stated that his film expresses 'honest personal sentiments about the region [and] the last two decades of war', as well as the contemporary 'moral and political nightmare' which all can constitute the 'horrors of history' that can now be experienced by the audience (Spasojević in Kendall 2016: 275). Similar to Featherstone's (2013) argument who sees *A Serbian Film* as a manifestation of Serbia's troubled past and neoliberal present where 'fucking the other is perfectly normal and indeed the best way to ensure competitive advantage' (128), Spasojević often argues for a very local reading of the film. He states that the newborn porn sequence represents the Serbian reality that is, the molestation of the monolithic Serbian government (Kohn 2010) that uses violent images of death and dismemberment as propaganda in state television (see Kerekes 2016: 192).[8] He also accentuates the role of NATO bombings whose global media representation featured Serbs as sadistic Others. But Featherstone (2013) makes a relevant point, noting:

Coming to the party late, what do the Serbs have to offer Europe? ... But clearly this is not new to the West, which has itself a thriving market in sadism and sexual violence. Sadism sells. ... I think we must recognize the fact that it also represents the Serbs' excremental position within a globalized market where they have nothing to offer but their meat, their ability to be humiliated ... (138)

Here, Featherstone seems to agree with Ognajović's self-Balkanising theory and the apprehension of the West as an Orientalist construction. Given the statement of Spasojević, it is likely that the director had the dual intention of reckoning with the 'Balkan wild man' (Ognajović 2015:85) by turning Miloš's 'superhuman phallic properties' inside out and deconstructing his superstar masculine oeuvre. At the same time, Spasojević follows the intermedial referential structure of the new Serbian cinema to criticise what Radović (2008: 175) called 'the image of a Serbian warrior' whose figure in the local media stood for the glorified, honourable, and courageous national hero whose hideous crimes are justified by the war and suffering citizens. *A Serbian Film's* film-in-a-film structure thus questions the very authenticity of representation that often happens in the pursuit of financial gain. The victim (as so the Serbian nation) has to sell the Balkanised image to fulfil the Western demands of global market. The family, just like in the case of *The Life and Death of a Porno Gang*, is doomed to death, which clearly references the Western infiltration, and also the consequences of the NATO bombings that murdered so many families but brought about profit via the circulating footage of death in global media.

A Serbian Film, similar to *The Life and Death of a Porno Gang*, can be seen as an angry parody that reflects upon Serbia's subjected position within political-representational power games. The question is, as always: does the audience gets this connotative layer or see the film as an example of nasty filmmaking? Or, to quote Chowen (2012), who asks in disbelief: why do we put ourselves through disgusting and brutal scenes of cinema?

Raping the Senses of the Spectator

The difficult comprehension of *A Serbian Film* is further exacerbated by Spasojević's confusing and often contrasting arguments on the allegoric aspect of his film. In some interviews, as seen above, he accentuates that the film is an honest expression of Serbia's past and current states, while in other forums, he states that *A Serbian Film* is a universal production that mirrors the problems of the modern world (Reed 2010). In contrast to many of his statements, he emphasises that the film rests on the foundation of a global phenomenon that is the exploitation of citizens by corrupt authorities by whom 'you're raped from birth, and it doesn't even stop after your death' (Selavy 2010). The blurry statements of Spasojević on what the film *is really* about seem to indicate that the director himself has a vague idea what his object of criticism really is. His confusing answers at the film's Q&A sessions[9] only support the claim that Spasojević's primarily aim with the film was more to shock the audience than serve any kind of political allegory.

Out of the 597 reviews on IMDb[10], only 18 mention having looked up the (socio-political and/or historical) connotations of *A Serbian Film*. These comments also reflect on Spasojević's aim to capture the consequences of Yugoslav wars and/or the capitalist present of Serbia. Out of the 18 reviews, only one dissects the way *A Serbian Film* reflects upon how the character of Miloš resembles a 'puppet of government' who listens to instructions through an earpiece. The other 17 reviewers, albeit aware of

POST–WAR EXTREMISM: SUBVERSIVE SERBIA 125

the political allegory, consider the film an example of exploitation that only 'exists to shock the viewers in the name of art' (CinemaClown). The very common standpoint of the reviews is that the spectacle and shock defeat the allegorical layer of the film:

> Apparently, the movie is meant to show, or well, be an allegory as to how Serbian people are forced into doing things, am I getting this right or what? How their Government (sic) is meant to be controlling & how violent Serbia is? But all I seen (sic) was rape after rape in this so called movie that is trying to make this important "political statement", but we know underneath that's just a guise for its cheap exploitative purpose. (TodayIsTheDayOurSinsWillBeOver)

Most of the reviewers who dig up some background information on the film agree that

> if this is an allegory of the Serbian government and how it exploits people ... there are millions of better ways to go about it ... Unless the Serbian government sends people to your house to force you to rape your own children, while they're raping you, then the filmmakers failed at their goal to create a governmental allegory. (mrhs612-1)

Others add that the film 'delivers something without substance' (hkmsimmons) and 'if this very dark film is only an allegory ... put the Iron Curtain back up' (melvelvit-1). It is no doubt that, as Klapka (2014) has argued, common audience members require an explanation of the film to effectively understand it. But as we see, even if they are aware of Spasojević's artistic intentions, most of the reviewers consider *A Serbian Film* cheap shock cinema. It seems that the director's goal to unmask the Serbian (and/or global) realities of the contemporary Zeitgeist turned the film into a great example of the self-Balkanisation strategy. With his attempt to subvert the Western understanding of Serbia 'by virtue of exaggeration', Spasojević achieves the opposite (Klapka 2014) and the film's 'potential for dramatic impact and satirical relevance ... ultimately [gets] lost amongst rambling scenes of anal sex and "newborn porn"' (Green 2010).[11] After all, what is the goal of art if its deeper message is not understood by the audience?

Spasojević has very often expressed that he did not plan to shock, stake controversy, or break any records with *A Serbian Film*. Rather, his very intention was to 'make the most honest and direct film' (Reed 2010) and emphasise the pornographic aspect of life. Also, his intention was to face the topic of violence against women and children in Serbia (Seavy 2010). He states that if someone does not get the message of the film, that is because 'that part of the audience doesn't know how to watch the film ... because the movie language that we use ... is actually closer to ... Western films than our own' (Selavy 2010). Spasojević seems to angrily defend his film that not only upset critics, viewers, censors and authorities but the Serbian government[12] as well.

It seems that, irrespectively of its aesthetic quality, the snuff-device and the very explicit imagery of sexual taboos were just too much for the common audience, yet the film achieved its attempt to engineer public debate around its subject matter.[13] Although both *A Serbian Film* and *The Life and Death of a Porno Gang* aim to set up an allegorical frame based on the intermedial play with camcorders and double-framing, the films are strongly divided by their reception. In contrast to the 'campy excess' and 'hallucinatory hyperrealism' of *A Serbian Film*, *The Life and Death of a Porno Gang* remains more naturalistic and less edited for the shock value (Shapiro 2011) which might be a reason why, opposed to *A Serbian Film*, it has a DVD edition in many countries. Both films are hyperbolic and frame an 'artistic' spectacle for Western buyers through plots of a porn director who sinks into the world of the snuff industry. With their self-reflexive style, they invoke the explicitness of the Yugoslav Black Wave and the films of Makavejev as well as the productions of the 'New Serbian Wave'. In that, they follow a very local-national Serbian filmmaking tradition that forms an anti-establishment message via upsetting imagery. Conversely, Spasojević himself disagrees with the presence of any new waves in Serbian cinema and calls the phenomenon of similarly violent and sexually explicit films which play along an intermedial structure in the country 'an accident' (Reed 2010). He argues that the similarity might be because of European film funds and festivals that 'are looking for the same ... stories' in Serbia and Eastern Europe. Also, in contrast to Makavejev's Freudian-Marxist tone that combined reflexive montage sequences and sexually explicit, but aestheticised images to set up an allegorical construction that originates from a totalitarian ideology – be that capitalism or communism, Spasojević's fusion of sexploitation, horror, hard-core porn and melodrama and the thematic and audio-visual excesses that accompany this mix – give the film a parodical atmosphere (Batori 2017). With its more grounded style and lesser desire to shock, the extremity of *The Life and Death of a Porno Gang* is composed in an aesthetically-thematically less intrusive way and has a more coherent narrative flow. That is, it exemplifies the old truism that less is more. What is striking still, is that both films address non-Serbian audiences by recycling 'Western clichés of Eastern European primitivism' (Kendall 2016: 272) and use porn/snuff as markers of victimised national identities to sell 'Serbia's blood and sperm' to the West.

CHAPTER 6

Towards Contemporary Extreme Forms of Double Colonialism

The marriage of power, sex and violence aimed at portraying politically incorrect manifestations of the ruling-ruled dichotomy on the Eastern European screen, has resulted in an even greater and more explicit pornographic fantasy in the post-2004 neoliberal epoch in the region. Following the hardship of the capitalist transition and the high hopes that accompanied it, the post-2007 neoliberal crisis has even further deepened the old West-East dichotomy. Supererogation, self-colonisation and emasculation, and the graphic violence against females became normalised parts of Eastern European filmmaking practices.

The present chapter investigates the patterns of neoliberal crisis in contemporary Eastern European cinema. By introducing the post-2010 Eastern European narrative structure known as the 'double form of neoliberal subjugation', this section of the book examines heavily gendered visual formations through selected case studies. While dissecting four films from four different Eastern European countries – the Slovenian Damjan Kozole's *Slovenian Girl* (*Slovenka*, 2009), the Romanian Ruxana Zenide's *Ryna* (2005), the Czech directors' Matěj Chlupáček and Michal Samir's *Touchless* (*Bez doteku*, 2013), and the Hungarian Szabolcs Hajdu's *Bibliothèque Pascal* (2010) – the study sets up a visual-narrative method to neoliberal (self-)colonisation. It argues that, along with the nostomanic resurrection of the socialist male figure, there is a tendency in the region's cinema that features Western male figures as powerful, authoritative and often violent characters who exploit Eastern European women by sexual trafficking and/or other forms of corporeal violence that render these females obedient to them. The coloniser power, however, uses the socialist father figure as mediator to succeeding this act, which creates a double-formed oppressive structure: that of the father and his female relatives.

Crisis of Neoliberalism in Eastern Europe

The 2007 global financial crisis put Eastern Europe into the centre of economic recession (Kattel 2010). In view of this, it is not surprising that, being disappointed in the post-1989 neoliberal reforms – with relatively less chance to reach the Western development level (Kornai 2006; Kattel 2010), the region entered the age of what Boyer (2012:19) defines as *nostomania* – a desire to recapture the old socialist way of life.

The economic doctrine of neorealism that originally aimed to develop market economies and proposed practices to promote human well-being 'within an institutional framework characterised by private property rights, individual liberty, unencumbered market and free trade' (Harvey 2007: 22), has had to face many crises since the 1970s and has been heavily criticised by Western as well as East European economists (Davies 2016; Kornai 2006). For instance, Stuart Hall calls the present socio-economic situation an 'unresolved rupture of that conjuncture' which he defines as the 'long march of the Neoliberal Revolution' (2011: 705). According to him, the neoliberal model is based on a tyrannical state structure that oppresses individuals by prevailing over private and corporate interest.

As Harvey (2007) has it, 'the profoundly antidemocratic nature of neoliberalism' (2007: 42) has entailed 'much destruction, not only of prior institutional frameworks and powers ... but also of division of labor, social relations, welfare positions, technological mixes, ways of life, attachment to the land, habits of the heart, ways of thought, and the like' (23). The privatisation of public institutions, utilities, social welfare provision and the wholesale commodification of nature, cultural forms, and history – together with the accumulated foreign debt, the monetisation of exchange and taxation and austerity measures (Harvey 2007) – gave birth to a crisis-laden 21st century Eastern Europe.

This is not to say, of course, that the neoliberal free-market ideology and foreign support only caused damages. Without the support of the European Union and Western capital, the region would be still at the 1989 economic level (Berend and Bugaric 2015). Foreign companies established retail networks, high-tech industrial sectors and domestic and occidental workplaces, while the post-socialist countries' landscape is slowly shifting towards a modernised, capitalist territory. On the other hand, however, the neoliberal transformation and crisis caused severe economic decline, massive unemployment, migration and dependence on foreign capital (Lane 2010). As Berend and Bugaric troublesome summarise, Eastern European countries that 'joined the EU in 2004 and 2007 have declined, rather than improved since accession' (2015: 777). The current crisis led to 'a rediscovery of the economic role of nation states' (Dale and Hardy 2011) and authoritarian populism that goes hand in hand with Euroscepticism, neoconservative and chauvinistic movements and militarism (Polyakova and Shekhovtsov 2016).

Populism and Self-Colonising Structures in Eastern Europe

The penetration of multinational companies into the Eastern European economic structure and the immense outmigration from the region into wealthier European countries set up a new centre-periphery socio-geographic structure, with the West being the object of desire and East the marginal brother that will never catch up to its sibling. The discursive practices that blame Eastern Europe for the region's economic difficulties (Dale and Hardy 2011), and identify post-socialist countries as 'backward, inefficient, underproducing, politically juvenile, oppositional to [Western] identities and generally untrustworthy' (Dauphinée 2003: 194), only emphasise the region's suppressed socio-economic position and Orientalist reading. In this way, the post-1989 transition and European neoliberal crisis resurrected the old West-East dichotomy. With the concentrated Western geopolitical power on one side, and its 'socially stigmatized brother' (Buchowski 2006: 474) on the other, the hierarchy between the centre and periphery became more and more sharp, thus giving way to a new orientalist mind-set (Buchowski 2006) and self-colonising social imagination.

In the midst of a severe economic state, populism became a defining political strategy in Eastern Europe. While there is no doubt that the phenomenon grew out of the crisis and failure of neoliberal reforms, the role of the socialist past must not be forgotten in this regard. I argue that people in Eastern Europe have been on a quest for a personal leader who would stand for national values, and citizens' security and protection. As Weyland (1999) emphasises, in a populist structure, the leader reaches the mass in a direct way, while building a new or old populist party with a low level of institutionalisation. In this manner, populism in Eastern Europe acts as a form of *nostomania*, a return to the old totalitarian socialist system whose main paternalistic figure promises wealth and safety to his citizens, while abusing them. The periphery-centre dichotomy and self-colonisation imaginary thus not only signal the very economic recession but a certain nostalgia for the past to re-set the gender-differentiated parental socio-political structure.

130   THE EXTREME CINEMA OF EASTERN EUROPE

While the representation of women in the films of the socialist period pinpoints the very Other-coloniser and subjected-ruler dichotomies through sexual assault or bodily violence against them, it also communicates a metaphoric message: the punishment and death of the nation by socialist powers. In the films of transition, however, these roles undergo a dramatic change whose main attribute is the very lack of the father figure and so the caring, paternalist state. Instead of the righteous, strong male character that would dominate over cinematic narratives, the post-1989 film corpus has given way to weakening worker heroes, anomic individuals (Andreescu 2013) and continued female supererogation. Lucian Pintilie's *The Oak* (*Balanta*, 1992) for instance, starts with the death of the communist ex-politician father of the main protagonist, Nela (Maja Morgenstein). She decides to donate the dead body for research and education, but the hospital rejects her offer and the wish of the deceased. The middle-aged daughter then decides to escape Bucharest and travel through Romania where she almost gets raped by unknown factory workers in the countryside. In Pintilie's film, the body of the dead father – the corpse of the state – becomes an unwanted object, while the daughter gets into dangerous situations in which she is incapable of protecting herself. The process of emasculation – the death of the father figure and growing tendency of violent males on screen – thus starts at the very beginning of the new capitalist transformation.

The process of emasculation as the region's reaction to the failure to meet the European ideals (Imre 2002) kept women and other national minorities in the internally colonised position. In this discourse, the insecure colonised masculinities inflict sexual violation on them. The post-2000 Eastern European film corpus that features an increasing tendency toward violence against women, signals a dramatic change in gender relations in cinema that is illustrated by the resurrection of the lost socialist father figure as the Western capitalist male (Andreescu 2013). In this way, the inflicted neoliberal policy and crisis in the region go hand in hand with the repatriarchalisation of its cinematic discourse. That is, after the death of the socialist father, a new narrative was born that embraces women with a new identity on screen. Instead of heroic mothers, films often portray women in highly sexualised and subordinated contexts, with sexual trafficking and prostitution as main concepts, be that rape – like in Titus Muntean's *Kino Caravan* (2009), Peter Calin Netzer's *Maria* (2003) from Romania; Jan Cvitkovič's *Gravehopping/Odgrobadogroba* (2005) Matej Chlupacek's *Touchless/Bez doteku* (2005) from the Czech Republic; or Kornél Mundruczó's *Delta* (2008) from Hungary – or trafficking and prostitution – like in the Romanian Cătălin Mitulescu's *Loverboy* (2011),

Myroslav Slaboshpytskyi's *The Tribe/Plemya* (2014) from Ukraine or the Serbian Vinko Bresan's *Will Not End Here/Nije Kraj* (2008) – or other forms of mental and physical abuse against women, as Srdjan Spasojević's *A Serbian Film/Srpski Film* (2012) and Maja Miloš's *Clip/Klip* (2012) illustrate. All in all, women get into oppressed, subjected positions in Eastern European narratives.[1]

Besides the revival of the patriarchal system by violent Western male characters, the post-2004 film corpus illustrates the (self)-colonised structure and crisis-laden position of the region by the resurrection of the socialist father figure in the form of an impotent male character who is obliged to cooperate with the Western, colonising power by betraying his family. I call this narrative a 'double form of neoliberal subjugation' whereby the internally colonised, emasculated male figure uses his powers to oppress his wife, daughter and other female characters on screen. These women then undergo a series of physical and sexual assaults that – portrayed in explicitly violent and pornographic sequences on screen – eventually transforms their bodies and very identity into a self-colonised imaginary. As I argue, in the post-2004 Eastern European discourse, corporeal violence against women and its extreme visual representation on screen symbolise a double form of neoliberal subjugation – a growing tendency of nostomania, populism and neoliberal dissatisfaction.

Extreme Corporal Violence in Contemporary Eastern European Cinemas

Ruxana Zenide's *Ryna* (2005) focuses on the titular teenager heroine who runs her father's gas station in a small village in the Romanian Danube Delta. Because of her father's desire to have a son, Ryna (Dorotheea Petre) has been brought up a boy: she must dress as a man, not wear make-up and have short hair. While she assists her alcoholic father's suspicious, illegal businesses in town (that involves initiating mechanical failures in cars at night so that they will have more clients the next day), Ryna's desire to dress as a woman and go to local parties constantly grows. At the same time, she becomes the centre of male attention in the village. Besides the mayor of the town and the young postman who have a crush on her, she gets into the centre of the attention of the newly-arrived French anthropologist looking for the roots of Latinity in Romania. The man asks Ryna to participate in his research by letting him measure her body and she eventually agrees to do so. They slowly grow a close relationship but after a failed kiss-attempt, the young girl chooses to go home and returns to her father. The old man, however, decides to sacrifice Ryna's virginity on the

132 THE EXTREME CINEMA OF EASTERN EUROPE

altar of prolonging his gas station contact with the village and let her be raped by the mayor.

The film illustrates a closed world where women's identity is prescribed as inferior (Doru 2014). Ryna stands under the control of her emasculated father whose violent behaviour chases away the girl's mother. The teenager thus gets stuck in a very patriarchal society, with male figures dominating over her life. First, it is her repressive father, then the French anthropologist and finally the mayor who take advantage over her body. While Ryna finds rescue in photography, her passion also signifies a highly gendered structure.

In the opening sequence of the film, the girl is portrayed capturing a bull that eventually attacks her so that she has to run away. This highly symbolic scene puts Ryna in contrast to the testosterone-fuelled social context that rules the narrative of the film. Wherever she goes, she gets objectified by male powers. First, it is her father that oppresses the teenager by demanding a male behaviour and look from her. Ryna obediently agrees to work as a car mechanic and hide any trace that would signal her femininity. She keeps her jewellery in a box far from home and wears oily, dark mechanics overalls and dark clothes throughout the film. Her male iconography only changes when she goes to the party: her pink dress and bright kerchief emphasise her female features that lead to tragedies in her life. While the French anthropologist uses a genuine way to get close to Ryna, the local mayor brutally rapes her in the presence of the girl's father. Being a haemophiliac, the teenager soon gets sent to hospital to survive the blood loss where the men of town accuse the French doctor of rape. Dressed as a man, Ryna suddenly appears just to state that the sexual violence was committed by an unknown person and leaves the hospital. After the rape, she thus re-positions herself in the male-role, which gives her a safe position in town.

The peripheral Romanian village in *Ryna* demonstrates a halt in the socialist era: it is not only the very setting of the film – with depilated, grey buildings, dusty roads and old cars – but the very grid of gender hierarchy that reawakens the epoch. The town is led by a corrupt totalitarian figure who, in exchange for Ryna's virginity, promises to keep the gas station and save the father's business from the penetration of a multinational chain. As the main capitalist power in the film, the mayor threatens the mechanic with the establishment of foreign companies in town. Eventually, Ryna, the untainted young girl and the only woman in the film, pays the price of the capitalist transformation. Her body – like the nation's – gets scarred by the emasculated father figure whose response to the globalist change is selling out his daughter. Ryna thus stands in a doubly subjected position. Not knowing how to react upon the neoliberal transformation, the socialist father figure betrays his own child, while he himself also stands under the supervision of the mayor.

The appearance of the French doctor – and so the foreign power – starts a series of tragedies in Ryna's life. Dressed in his white uniform, the anthropologist's iconography stands in strong contrast with the portrayal of other men in the town. His colonising character – the intelligent, civilised Western doctor – takes palm-prints and photos of the locals – the uncivilised tribe – which sharpens the periphery-central dichotomy. In this self-colonising process, the inhabitants of the town succumb to his cultural power, and so does Ryna by starting learning French to get closer to his authority. While the girl first rejects his wish to be measured, she eventually lets the doctor to touch her body, which only exacerbates her subjected position in the film. From this moment, she sinks deeper in her colonised, oppressed role. Still, while the Western power's penetration into her intimate sphere is soft violence, her rape by the mayor is a brutal deed. Her self-colonising process thus ends with the violent extermination of her female body, which outlines the oppressive power-structure of the current Romanian socio-political establishment.

Similar to Ryna, the Czech *Touchless* represents the double neoliberal subjugation via the tropes of the emasculated father figure, the lack of the mother and a dominating capitalist power. The teenager Jolana (Teresa Vítu) lives with her mother and stepfather in Prague. During the day, she lives the life of an average school girl but at nights, she gets raped by her stepfather. First, her mother looks away and tries not to notice the change in her daughter's behaviour. Later, when realising the situation, she succumbs to the wish of the man and sacrifices Jolana on the altar of her marriage. Later, the stepfather decides to sell the girl to the manager of a brothel where she gets constantly beaten up and raped. It seems however, that Jolana becomes identified with her subjected role to the extent where she cannot think of herself as a free individual. When she is offered freedom, she hesitates whether to accept it and stay in the brothel, or start a new life. While the film has an open ending, *Touchless* suggests the former: in the grid of male domination, she has taken on the role of the objectified, sex worker-role that she cannot leave behind.

Like *Ryna*, *Touchless* represents a deeply patriarchal society with the absence of maternal roles. Jolana stands under the absolute control of her policeman stepfather who does suspicious business with the Czech underworld. After getting pregnant, the teenager loses the very right to her body: she is obliged to have an abortion and then work in a brothel. The last maternal bond to her mother and her own unborn child thus gets finally broken: deprived of her reproductive rights and access to her own womb, she succumbs to the will of her stepfather to be a sex worker. In the brothel, however, she acquires another father-figure. Kleiner (Ondrej Malý), the German-Czech manager of the place has an ambivalent relationship with Jolana: as the head of the business, the older man pretends to take care of the girl, but he also brutally rapes her over and over again. Stuck in this male-dominated world, Jolana gets humiliated by all the protagonists in the film. Sold by her stepfather, she has to work in a deeply profit-oriented world brimming with Western clients where she faces daily physical and mental abuse. The colleague of her stepfather who tries to save her only aggravates this crisis. First, he pretends to be a client in order to get Jolana out of the brothel. Later, however, he decides to live in the sex club to sleep with the girl. Disappointed in her 'prince', Jolana leaves the bedroom and continues working, while the man gets thrown out of the place.

Touchless illustrates the mental and corporeal transformation of Jolana from an innocent school girl to a sex worker. In the first half of the film, she is dressed as an average teenager with a natural look and loose clothes. In the brothel, her figure gets heavily fetishised. It is not only her heavy make-up and provocative outfit that signal the change but her very behaviour too, as she endures the daily abuse without resistance. Her dependence on older, male father-like figures throughout the film signals her absolute subjected role: sold by her emasculated stepdad, she steps into the world of capital acquired through female rape. Jolana's transformation thus signals the very neoliberal changes in the region: from the crisis-laden socialist home, she moves into a profit-oriented space based on bodily exploitation. Interestingly, while the mise-en-scène of the film changes – with fluorescent lights and vivid colours dominating the screen – the gender roles depicted in *Touchless* do not alter. Whether in the socialist home, or the brothel, Jolana gets stuck in her doubly subjected role by succumbing to her stepfather and then to Kleiner, the neoliberal power in the film.

"This EU, It Costs Us a Lot of Money": *Slovenian Girl* and *Bibliothèque Pascal*

While *Ryna* and *Touchless* follow the roads of two teenagers, the film *Slovenian Girl* features a university student who decides to step on the road of prostitution in order to acquire a flat and have a stable financial background. The twenty-three-year-old Aleksandra (Nina Ivanišin) advertises herself as the 'Slovenian Girl' (*Slovenka*) in the newspapers and has a prosperous business with foreign clients. She soon buys a luxury flat in the heart of Ljubljana, but gets threatened by the local underworld and is blackmailed to join their circles. Aleksandra escapes the city and decides to temporarily reside in her father's home in the countryside to get time to find a solution to her problems. She eventually changes her nickname to 'Naïve' and re-starts her business in the city, but her income does not cover the monthly bank loan she took to pay for her flat. Losing her friends, clients and home, she finally moves in with her father.

Besides her struggles with the Slovenian underworld and mortgage, Aleksandra is wanted by the police for questioning regarding the death of a German politician. This narrative line runs through the whole film as it causes a national scandal in the country. Aleksandra is constantly followed by journalists – be that from television or other media platforms – that want to disclose the identity of the 'Slovenian Girl'.

The German politician and member of the European Parliament dies of cardiac arrest after he takes Viagra before meeting Aleksandra. In the film's opening shot, the girl enters the hotel room of the gasping man and, noticing his critical state, calls the reception for help. Before escaping the room, she takes all the money of the dying politician and only learns of his death from the news. In the next scene, Aleksandra is portrayed sitting in a cab whose driver complains about the European Union that, according to him, only causes headaches and financial trouble for Slovenians. The film's establishing shot thus makes a clear statement of an abusive Western power which is further illustrated by the visual depiction of the German politician. While Aleksandra's natural look – her black hair, white skin and slim figure – radiate elegance, the representation of the overweight, grasping old man mediates greed and wealth. The German politician is incapable of answering the girl's questions and, although she tries to help by bringing a glass of water, Aleksandra's facial expressions remain numb. She lacks any emotional feedback when it comes to business and in this regard, she does not differ much from her clients.

As representative of the nation, the Slovenian Girl takes on a contradictory position in the narrative. On the one hand, she is sexually exploited by visiting Westerners, while on the other, she deliberately chooses to serve them. Aleksandra's only goal is to have enough money for her flat and expensive lifestyle and, as an English literature university student, she steps on the road of self-colonisation. Realising that her only way to achieve capital is the commodification of her body, she starts playing according to neoliberal rules. She uses her English to do business with Western customers and her body to achieve what she wants from society. Knowledge and corporeality thus merge in the capitalist space of the city that brings her prosperity and satisfaction.

However, as the *Slovenian Girl*, Aleksandra eventually gets punished for her colonised, semi-subjected identity – the local sex worker who serves

136   THE EXTREME CINEMA OF EASTERN EUROPE

Western clients – and the local gangsters soon blackmail her for money. Unlike Aleksandra's clients who are older, less attractive males from Italy, Germany and other EU-countries, the pimps are young, well-built young Slovenians who demand the Slovenian Girl's part-income. Aleksandra's already threatened and vulnerable state caused by the police warrant and media attention thus gets even more complicated: while the Slovenian forces chase her, she still has to serve Western clients to pay her debt.

In this multi-layered colonising structure, Alexandra, the national female figure, succumbs to Western powers but, when threatened by her countrymen, she becomes a helpless, panicky woman. In this way, as *Slovenian Girl* suggests, the nation gets exploited by foreign influence and, while slowly going bankrupt, the Slovenian state makes no profit from the monetary exchange.

Besides the Western-periphery and colonised-coloniser dichotomies, *Slovenian Girl* sets up a further opposition by contrasting Ljubljana with rural Slovenia. In her father's remote village, people are altruistic, genuine citizens who closely watch after each other. In this space, Aleksandra changes to a naïve young girl who is supported by her divorced father: the man does the housework, cleans, cooks and washes and irons his daughter's clothes. While he takes on a maternal identity, the man is deprived of his role as the head of the family: in the capitalist framework, he is incapable of supporting his daughter's studies and living, and escapes into music and drinking. As the resurrected socialist father figure, he enters an emasculated role and, even though he learns about Aleksandra's prostitution, he remains silent. For the young girl however, the rural setting brings peace and security which changes when, after going back to Ljubljana, she faces her father's best friend in the hotel room. After the first shock, the obese man demands Alexandra have sex with him, but he does not pay for the service. Thus, whenever the call girl meets Slovenian men, she gets deprived of money and enters a dangerous system of bribes and greed. Similar to her ex-boyfriend who threatens Aleksandra by telling her father about the girl's business, the best friend blackmails the woman to reveal the truth to her only family if she does not sleep with him. This is the end of her self-colonising process: Aleksandra decides to give up prostitution and move back to her father's village. By leaving behind the capital and its centralised Western powers, she eventually relocates to the periphery and chooses the old Slovenian traditional space as her future setting.

In contrast to *Ryna*, *Touchless* and *Slovenian Girl*, Szabolcs Hajdu's *Bibliothèque Pascal* uses a cross-border narrative and physical travel to demonstrate neoliberal subjugation. The film narrates the story of Mona (Orsolya Török-Illyés), a single Transylvanian mother who gets trafficked to England to work in a luxury brothel. Dressed as Joan of Arc and later as Desdemona, she must fulfil the fantasies of Western customers. Slowly, her body goes through a drastic transformation: from an Eastern European mother she turns into the fantasy of foreign clients, with heavy make-up, extravagant costumes and witty sexual games (Figure 6.1). During her oppression, Mona also learns English by studying her erotic roles and talking to Pascal (Shamgar Amram), the head of the brothel. Thus, while she is forced to work as a sex worker, she slowly succumbs to the Western powers by self-colonising herself. Her daily rape and forced heroin consumption, together with the physical-psychological assault by Englishmen transforms Mona into an object. She loses the very right to her own body that gets exploited at every level.

The colonising power structures are further illustrated by the portrayal of Mona's home country, Romania and her cell in England. The Eastern European country is depicted as a godforsaken space, with muddy roads and criminals that create an Orientalist image of the area. It is this socialist Balkan space where the woman's colonising journey begins. Mona is sold by her estranged father who asks her to accompany him to Germany where he would undergo an operation. Instead of any surgery, he exchanges his daughter for money and gets eventually murdered by traffickers. Germany thus functions as a changing point in the story that seals Mona's very fate in the West. Interestingly, in the daughter's dream at the end of the film, it is the father who saves her from the brothel. In this phantasmagorical scene, he arrives to England with an orchestra and opens the doors to

Figure 6.1 Western gaze: *Bibliothèque Pascal*, Hungary: Katapult Film, 2010.

all the prisoners in the sex club. In this way, the socialist father figure gets literally resurrected in a phantasy where he overcomes the colonising Western powers to save his daughter – and so the nation from further Western exploitation.

In the selected examples, the prolonged takes of brutal bodily violence strengthen the vulnerability of female embodiment. The way content and themes are broached in these films – the inflated sequences of bio-logically realistic violence, blood and suffering which are all exhibited in prolonged, often, handheld-take form and lingering close-ups – frame femininity as being formed in a process of ritualised supererogation. Even if images are aestheticised, form never overcomes the pro-filmic violence of the sequences. Everything in these examples is corporeal, grounded in the intersection of Eastern subjugation and Western supremacy. Although the excessive spectacle offers a sensual challenge to the viewer, *Slovenian Girl*, *Ryna*, *Bibliothèque Pascal* and *Touchless* are all pregnant with meaning. Although raw and uncomfortable, the rape sequences are encoded in emphatic alignment with the suffering of female characters. On the one hand, this is due to the films' smoothly unfolding narratives and the syuzhet's clear cause-and-effect chain which helps our identifica-tion with the suppressed characters. On the other hand, I see some growth in the representation of female suffering. That is, the one-sided, masculine perspective that rendered the emphatic alignment with the female charac-ters almost impossible in the socialist examples as well as the epoch of the transition, slowly gives way to more self-reflexive filmic form that casts doubt over hypermasculine point of views. Instead of eliminating all pos-sibilities of sympathy for the victim, there is a shift (although minimal) in representation that, instead of normalising rape as 'men's nature', finally emphasises the physical and psychological effects that such action has on the (female) victim.

Conclusion

In *Public Rape: Representing Violation in Fiction and Film*, Horeck (2004) provides a detailed analysis on an infamous US rape trial that was broadcasted on CNN and received immense publicity in the media. The question she poses – similar to one of the most crucial focus points of studies on extreme cinema – centres on people's interest in consuming images of rape and violence. She argues that, as the 'phantom public' watches the 'Big Dan's' rape trial (named after the bar in which the rape took place), the act of viewing becomes a form of participation in that crime. Although this highly problematic statement dismisses the role of taboos in societies – that is, one's curiosity of the unknown or unexperienced – Horeck's argument on spectatorship, trauma and the civic bond alludes to a new form of collective voyeurism. This 'socio-sexual contract', as she calls this phenomenon, is 'violently reproduced over an image of the raped woman's body', in which the 'spectacularization of reality' and communal spectatorship intend to serve the ends of civic justice (85). It is through *re-presentation* of the rape at the trial and television that the communal failure to protect the victim gets revealed and leads to a collective thirst for justice. In Eastern European extreme cinema, this socio-sexual contract plays along the supererogation/emasculation/loss-of-femininity axis, but in contrast to the salvation value of *re-presentation*, it only deepens the gender and equality gap in the cinema of the region. Rape, a recurring metaphor of political, social, ideological, and economic repression, becomes a central motif and a narrative driving force of Eastern Europe cinemas.

Because the book sees the filmic positioning of women as symbols of the nation and men as representatives of the state, the metaphoric role of rape and the constant corporeal and verbal humiliation of female protagonists have been attributed to different types of colonialisms in the region.

In terms of marketing, sexuality has always been a well-received topic in cinema. However, by reaching the limits of spectatorship whose somatic-emotional experience makes the films unforgettable, filmmakers

140   THE EXTREME CINEMA OF EASTERN EUROPE

during socialism manipulated viewers to step into a critical stance in which they could witness how ideology eradicates sexual gratification and sub-jectivity. Unfortunately, as with Makavejev, the radical potential of desire was reduced to a dictatorial treatment of spectatorial subjectivity, which hindered the understanding of the film.

Also, as most of the presented filmmakers are male, the selected produc-tions have a one-sided, masculine view on sexuality and rape. While the critical eye might comprehend the connotative level of these productions and decode women's position as martyrs of the socialist state structure, I doubt that this message was (or had the potential to be) understood in every case. It is especially because of the very explicit portrayal of sexuality and nudity on screen which, as taboos, have stimulated spectatorship – and made us remember that all cinema aims for commercial gain. By paying attention to the shock on screen, however, subversivism often eradicated the ideological message of these films.

As argued within this book, post-1989 violence on screen functions as a reflection on the new forms of colonialism that, inaugurated by Western capitalism, caused severe financial damages to citizens. The re-colonialisation process of the nation is emphasised on the visual level of extreme images that feature rape, torture and other transgressive deeds on screen. The 'cinema of castration' (*Conjugal Bed*, *Pleasant Days*, *She-Shaman*) foregrounds violent and extreme sexual acts against women which demonstrates a patriarchal society on the road of emasculation. The role of violence and female supererogation reach such a level that, as Chapters 3 and 4 have illustrated, they slowly establish their own filmic canons of animal cruelty. In the post-2000 extreme cinema of Eastern Europe, this trend gets split. On the one hand, filmmakers connect con-troversial acts and images to femininity and convey the message of the death of the nation (*Somnambulance*, *Andel Exit*, *Alone*). On the other, the genre evolves into exploitation cinema that, with its sustained focus on shock, dwells on sensationalist topics and non-narrative storytelling methods (*Baklava*, *Marble Ass*). *The Life and Death of a Porno Gang* and *A Serbian Film*, as chapter 5 has illustrated, fuse exploitation and art cinema. With their counter-narrative (paracinematic) form, the two films mock the apparatus of the South Slav family by centring their plots on the very kern of domestic sphere. The violence committed by and on the porn-family of *The Life and Death of a Porno Gang* and *A Serbian Film* both suggest the infinite development of violence which embraces more generations. The sexual abuse, humiliation and torture of women in the very graphic sequences de-mythologises females as mothers of homeland and nation. The torment and rape of these characters happens for the sake

CONCLUSION 141

of Western buyers which clearly mirrors Serbia's post-NATO bombing disappointment and wrath. In a paradoxical way, however, these films reflect on the falsified knowledge-production and phantasmic projections of global media war-broadcast by featuring violent (hyper)masculine characters who, as aggressive, untamed and wild people, cause the death of female characters and themselves die after. This self-Balkanised gesture presents and accentuates the stereotype of violent Serbs as spectacle for the Western gaze while at the same time, it also criticises that very gaze via the self-reflexive film forms, snuff-performances and the death of Serbian male heroes. It seems that the real identity crisis of Serbian extreme cinema rests on the very confusion of mixing standpoints: that is, whether to serve the Western gaze and produce violent, self-Balkanised (angry) art and receive attention, and/or 'secretly' demonise the Other through the self-eroticised forms of sex and violence.

The explicit pornographic content of the sexual and physical abuse in the neoliberal cinema (*Slovenian Girl*, *Bibliothèque Pascal*, *Touchless*, *Ryna*) only underline the East-West colonised-coloniser dichotomy by causing discomfort in the viewer to achieve political spectatorship. Thus, similar to socialist rape-films and the cinema of castration, this contemporary extreme tendency in Eastern European cinema communicates a metaphoric message that points toward the exploitative nature of the current neoliberal framework. As a symbol of populism and *nostomania*, the elder socialist father figure in the selected examples only stands as mediator between the exploiting West and his home country. The increasing number and amount of female rapes, domestic violence and physical abuse on the contemporary Eastern European screen suggest a new re-patriarchised social structure that resurrects the socialist father figure as an emasculated, impotent male who, while being colonised by Western powers himself, oppresses his female relatives by their sexual exploitation. In this patriarchal context, women stand under the double burden of internal colonisation against the older male parent while they also take on a self-colonised imaginary and succumb to Western powers. In this double form of neoliberal subjugation, *nostomania*, the base of the Eastern European populist structure, plays a crucial role. The female characters in *Ryna*, *Slovenian Girl*, *Touchless* or *Bibliothèque Pascal* all have a loving-hate relationship with their fathers who eventually deceive them. Hoping in the wealth and security provided by these elder figures, the female protagonists have absolute trust in their male parents. Instead of supporting their daughters, however, these figures all step into business relations with Western and/or local capitalist forces that demand female sacrifice or, as in the case of *The Call Girl*, the silent supervision of their child's deterioration.

142   THE EXTREME CINEMA OF EASTERN EUROPE

The fusion of pornography and violence as common ground to express the trauma of the region can be seen as an inherited aesthetic tradition that, as in the Yugoslav Black Wave, criticised the political establishment via shocking and awakening images. The lack of censorship and the wide availability of pornographic content in Yugoslavia and then Serbia and its fusion with war images, can also be indicators for such extreme cinematic language. Indeed, as Kerekes (2016) argues, allegories might need subversive images and very often, shock-effects to mediate the message of narratives. But what's the point if, as argued within the book, the audience do not understand the connotative message behind brutal sequences? Besides looking at the more or less sophisticated aesthetics of extreme films, scholarship should also reassess whether such violent images deliver on their aims.

The Future Dangers of Extreme Cinemas

In light of the increasing number of festival films that deploy violent sexual encounters, we can argue that sex has indeed became to art cinema what 3D or IMAX is to blockbusters (Frey 2016: 205). The market-oriented approach to (European) cinemas is in danger of legitimising and validating s(exploitation) tactics in auteurist visions and assert a higher cultural value to explicit, violent and pornographic sexual imagery. While there is no doubt that taboo-breaking representation can function as legitimate metaphor, this book called for a narrative demarcation between pure commercial tactics (exploitation traditions) and modern art narratives (auteur cinema). The two are, of course, not mutually exclusive. However, as demonstrated within these chapters, narrative incoherence might easily overset the balance between 'wannabe art' and the connotative, deeper layers of cinema. In other words, the balance of cinematic codes (explicit sexual content) and extra-cinematic codes (ideology, cultural contextualisation) must be taken into account before we group all films with pornographic-violent content *art*. One can of course argue that in the case of film directors only using cinematic codes, as is the case of avantgarde productions, they can still communicate diverse codes about film form, apparatus, national psyche and/ or spectatorship. Still, as the book illustrated, when cinematic codes solely focus on pornographic content (without narrative justification), 'wannabe art' reduces itself to pure sexual spectacle. This is not to judge the content of these films or differentiate between high and low cultural values. Rather, this book questioned our critical stance and criticism's often superficial cult of the (European) auteur cinema and its thirst for realism.

Overall, the categorisation of extreme cinema as an example of modern realist tendency has many dangers. Especially because, as Hayworth (2000)

CONCLUSION   143

accentuates, realism on film 'not only suppress[es] certain truths but produce[s] others' (311). The festival hits and academic acclaim of extreme films have the dangerous potential of normalising the representation of transgression and creating a new kind of 'social truth'. If so, art cinema is moving towards pornography and (s)exploitation. Scholars, critics and cultural commentators have a special responsibility to define boundaries, contexts and discourses that can be deemed fruitful for future discussion on extreme cinemas. As emphasised within this book, the unwritten rule in scholarship and film criticism that pronounces all films of renowned European art directors as valuable art or cinema comes with a danger of oversimplification, hypocritical behaviour, and the chance that such critical canons reinforce and normalise extreme representations. Moreover, the praise of all extreme forms, be that 'wannabe art' or extreme cinema, advertises a possible career pathway for future filmmakers, especially from smaller national industries and the Eastern European region that exploit transgression to rise to worldwide fame (as *A Serbian Film* illustrated).

The third danger concerns Eastern European extreme cinema. As Jelača (2016) has it, the destabilised gender roles which identify men as aggressors and womanhood as identical to victims risks the re-stabilisation of binary and traditional gender roles and reiterate the dichotomy of gendered violence. The generalisation and understanding of men as aggressors and women as victims of (sexual) abuse only strengthen the static notion of Eastern Europe as a backward, chauvinist, dangerous and uncivilised territory. While the market of self-exoticism and victimisation seems to work, this self-Orientalist approach (together with the festival demand to advertise such imagery) hinders the birth of any new mimetic canon in/of the region. Not only do such representations leave Eastern Europe in the never-ending secondary, suppressed and backward position but they also reinforce female supererogation and hypermasculine tendencies as forms of regional self-identification and self-presentation.

Sensationalist bodily representations – as, *inter alia*, the recent festival success of Julia Ducournau's *Titane* (2021), Ninja Thyberg's *Pleasure* (2021) or the Netflix-success of the Polish *365 Days*-saga (2022) demonstrate – have become number one focus points of festivals, distributors and filmmakers. The end of extreme cinemas is nowhere near. On the contrary, as an institutionalised artform, it will define the upcoming decade(s) and go as explicit, pornographic and violent as critical commenters, journalists, film critics and scholars let it – or to put it in another way, unconditionally praise such forms.

Bibliography

Abel, M. (2007), *Violent Affect. Literature, Cinema, and Critique after Representation*, Lincoln and London: University of Nebraska Press.

Alexander, E. (2016), 'The Titular Nation in (Post-)Yugoslav Cinema', in A. Virginás (ed.), *Cultural Studies Approaches in the Study of Eastern European Cinema. Spaces, Bodies, Memories*, Newcastle upon Tyne: Cambridge Scholars Publishing, 85–112.

Allen, B. (1996), *Rape Warfare: The Hidden Genocide in Bosnia-Herzegovina and Croatia*, Minneapolis: University of Minneapolis Press.

Anachkova, B. (1995), 'Women in Bulgaria', in B. Łobodzińska, (ed.), *Family, Women and Employment in Central-Eastern Europe*, Westport, Connecticut, London: Greenwood Press, 56–69.

Andreescu, F. (2013), *From Communism to Capitalism. Nation and State in Romanian Cultural Production*, New York: Palgrave Macmillan.

Andrew, G. (2015), 'Anatomy of Hell', *Time Out*, 9 January 2015, <https://www.timeout.com/movies/anatomy-of-hell> (last accessed 2 October 2022).

Andrews, D. (2013), *Theorizing Art Cinemas. Foreign, Cult, Avant-garde, and Beyond*, Austin: University of Texas Press.

Antoniou, A. K. and D. Akrivos (2017), *The Rise of Extreme Porn. Legal and Criminological Perspectives on Extreme Pornography in England and Wales*, Cham: Palgrave Macmillan.

Arason, C. (2015), 'Abject Anatomy: Catherine Breillat's *Anatomy of Hell*', Off Screen, 19:9, <https://offscreen.com/view/abject-anatomy-catherine-breillat> (last accessed 2 October 2022).

Archer, N. (2011), 'Beyond Anti-Americanism, Beyond Euro-Centrism: Locating Bruni Dumont's *Twentynine Palms* in the Context of European Cinematic Extremism', in T. Horeck and T. Kendall (eds), *The New Extremism in Cinema. From France to Europe*, Edinburgh: Edinburgh University Press, 55–69.

Aretov, N. (2010), 'Bulgarian Émigrés and Their Literature: A Gaze from Home', in E. Agoston-Nikolova (ed.), *Shoreless Bridges. South East European Writing in Diaspora*, Amsterdam and New York: Rodopi, 65–83.

Arthur, P. (2011), 'Escape From Freedom: The Films of Dusan Makavejev', *Cinéaste*, 27:1, 11–15.

Ashley, T. (2004), 'Too Scary for Stalin', *The Guardian*, 26 March, <https://www.theguardian.com/music/2004/mar/26/classicalmusicandopera.russia> (last accessed 2 October 2022).

BIBLIOGRAPHY

Attwood, F. (2009), 'Introduction: The Sexualization of Culture', F. Attwood (ed.), *Mainstreaming Sex. The Sexualization of Western Culture*, London and New York: I. B. Tauris, xi–xiii.

Baban, A. (1999), 'Romania', in by H. P. David (ed.), *From abortion to contraception. A resource to public policies and reproductive behaviour in Central and Eastern Europe from 1917 to the present*, London: Greenwood Press, 191–222.

Bacon, H. (2015), *The Fascination of Film Violence*, New York: Palgrave Macmillan.

Badley, L. (1995), *Film, Horror and the Body Fantastic*, Westport, Connecticut, London: Greenwood Press.

Bahador, B. (2007), *The CNN Effect in Action: How the News Media Pushed the West toward War in Kosovo*, New York and London: Palgrave Macmillan.

Bakács, T. S. (2003), 'Szép napok. Félrehagyott gyermekek' (Pleasant Days. Neglected children), *Filmvilág*, 3, 10–11.

Baker, M. (2011), 'Watching Rape, Enjoying Watching Rape...: How Does a Study of Audience Cha(lle)nge Mainstream Film Studies Approaches?', in. T. Horeck and T. Kendall (eds), *The New Extremism in Cinema. From France to Europe*, Edinburgh: Edinburgh University Press, 105–17.

Baker, M. (2013), 'Embracing Rape: Understanding the Attractions of Exploitation Movies', in F. Attwood, V. Campbell, I. Q. Hunter and S. Lockyer (eds), *Controversial Images. Media Representations on the Edge*, New York: Palgrave Macmillan, 217–39.

Bakic-Hayden, M. (1995), 'Nesting Orientalisms: The Case of Former Yugoslavia', *Slavic Review*, 54:4, 917–31.

Bakic-Hayden, M. and R. M. Hayden (1992), 'Orientalist variations on the theme "Balkans": Symbolic geography in Yugoslav cultural politics since 1987', *Slavic Review*, 51:1, 1–15.

Balázs, P., A. Bozóki, Ş. Catrina, A. Gotseva, J. Horvath, D. Limani, B. Radu, Á. Simon, Á. Szele, Z. Tófalvi, and K. Perlaky-Tóth (eds, 2014), *25 Years After the Fall of the Iron Curtain. The state of integration of East and West in the European Union*, European Commission: Directorate-General for Research and Innovation Inclusive, Innovative and Reflective Societies.

Banski, J. and M. Mazur (2021), *Transformation of Agricultural Sector in the Central and Eastern Europe after 1989*, Cham: Springer.

Banski, J. (2018), 'Phases to the transformation of agriculture in Central Europe – Selected processes and their results', *Agric. Econ. – Czech*, 64:12, 546–53.

Bansky, J. (2008), 'Agriculture of Central Europe in the Period of Economic Transformation', available at <https://www.researchgate.net/publication/237810436_AGRICULTURE_OF_CENTRAL_EUROPE_IN_THE_PERIOD_OF_ECONOMIC_TRANSFORMATION> (last accessed 10 August 2022).

Barber, S. (2010), 'The Films of the Vienna Action Group', in R. G. Weiner and J. Cline (eds), *Cinema Inferno. Celluloid Explosions from the Cultural Margins*, Lanham, Toronto, Plymouth: The Scarecrow Press, 217–25.

Barefoot, G. (2017), *Trash Cinema. The Lure of the Low*, New York: Columbia University Press.

Barker, J. M. (2009), *The Tactile Eye. Touch and the Cinematic Experience*, Berkeley: California University Press.

Batori, A. (2017), 'Newborn-Porn and the Wannabe-Art Film of the Future. Srdan Spasojevic's *A Serbian Film* (Srpski Film, 2010)', *East European Film Bulletin*, Vol. 78, <https://eefb.org/perspectives/srdan-spasojevics-a-ser bian-film-srpski-film-2010/> (last accessed 2 October 2022).

Batori, A. (2018), *Space in Romanian and Hungarian Cinema*, New York: Palgrave Macmillan.

Batori, A. (2020), 'The Double Form of Neoliberal Subjugation', in T. Austin and A. Koutsourakis (eds), *Cinema of Crisis. Film and Contemporary Europe*, Edinburgh: Edinburgh University Press, 164–80.

Beller, J. (1998), 'Capital/Cinema', in E. Kaufman and K. J. Heller (eds), *Deleuze and Guattari: New Mappings in Politics, Philosophy, and Culture*, Minneapolis: University of Minnesota Press.

Benson-Allot, C. (2013), *Killer Tapes and Shattered Screens. Video Spectatorship from VHS to File Sharing*, Berkeley, Los Angeles, London: University of California Press.

Berend, I. T. and Bugaric, B. (2015), 'Unfinished Europe: Transition from Communism to Democracy in Central and Eastern Europe', *Journal of Contemporary History*, 50:4, 768–85.

Bergan, R. (2019), 'Dušan Makavejev obituary', *The Guardian*, 6 February, <https://www.theguardian.com/film/2019/feb/06/dusan-makavejev-obit uary> (last accessed 20 May 2021).

Bernard, M. (2016), 'The Only Monsters Here Are the Filmmakers': Animal Cruelty and Death in Italian Cannibal Films', in Stefano Baschiera and Russ Hunter (eds), *Italian Horror Cinema*, Edinburgh: Edinburgh University Press, 191–207.

Betz, M. (2003), 'Art, Exploitation, Underground,' in M. Jancovich, A. L. Reboli, J. Stringer and A. Willis (eds), *Defining Cult Movies: The Cultural Politics of Oppositional Taste*, Manchester: Manchester University Press, 204–5.

Betz, M. (2009), *Beyond the Subtitle: Remapping European Art Cinema*, Minneapolis and London: University of Minnesota Press.

Beugnet, M. (2007), *Cinema and Sensation: French Film and the Art of Transgression*, Carbondale: Southern Illinois University Press.

Beugnet, M. (2011), 'The Wounded Screen', in. T. Horeck and T. Kendall (eds), *The New Extremism in Cinema. From France to Europe*, Edinburgh: Edinburgh University Press, 29–43.

Beugnet, M. and L. Mulvey (2015), 'Film, Corporeality, Transgressive Cinema: A Feminist Perspective', in L. Mulvey and A. B. Rogers (eds), *Feminisms. Diversity, Difference and Multiplicity in Contemporary Film Cultures*, Amsterdam: Amsterdam University Press, 187–202.

Betz, M. (2013), 'High and Low and In Between', *Screen* 54: 4, 495–513.

BIBLIOGRAPHY

147

BHM (2016), 'Baklava', *Boyhood Movies*, 23 April 2016 <https://boyhoodmov ies.org/baklava-2007/> (last accessed 13 July 2022).

Birn (2008), 'Controversial Bulgarian Documentary Triggers Prosecution', *Balkan Insight*, 24 January 2008, <https://balkaninsight.com/2008/01/24/ controversial-bulgarian-documentary-triggers-prosecution/> (last accessed 13 July 2022).

Bjelic, D. (2003), 'Introduction: Blowing Up the "Bridge"', in D. Bjelic and O. Savic (eds), *Balkan as Metaphor: Between Globalization and Fragmentation*, Cambridge, MA: MIT Press, 1–22.

Bjelic, D. I. and L. Cole (2002), 'Sexualizing the Serb', in D. I. Bjelic and O. Savic (eds), *Balkan as Metaphor. Between Globalization and Fragmentation*, Cambridge, Massachusetts and London: England, 279–311.

Bloom, C. (1988), 'Grinding with the Bachelors: Pornography in a Machine Age', in G. Day and C. Bloom (eds), *Perspectives on Pornography. Sexuality in Film and Literature*, New York: St. Martin's Press, 9–26.

Boose, L. (2002), 'Crossing the River Drina: Bosnian Rape Camps, Turkish Impalement, and Serbian Cultural Memory', *Signs* 28, 71–96.

Booth, K. (ed. 2005), *The Kosovo Tragedy: The Human Rights Dimensions*, London and Portland: Frank Cass.

Bordun, T. (2017), 'The End of Extreme Cinema Studies', *Canadian Review of Comparative Literature* 1:44, 122–36.

Bordun, T. (2017b), *Genre Trouble and Extreme Cinema. Film Theory at the Fringes of Contemporary Art Cinema*, New York: Palgrave Macmillan.

Bordun, T. (2018), *Genre Trouble and Extreme Cinema. Film Theory at the Fringes of Contemporary Art Cinema*. Cham, Switzerland: Palgrave Macmillan.

Bordwell, D. (1985), *Narration in the Fictional Film*, London: Routledge.

Bordwell, D. (2008), *Poetics of Cinema*, New York and Oxon: Taylor and Francis.

Bordwell, D. (2012), 'The Art Cinema as a Mode of Film Practice, in. C. Flower (ed.), *The European Cinema Reader*, London and New York: Routledge, 94–103.

Boyer, D. (2012), 'From Algos to Autonomos: Nostalgic Eastern Europe as Postimperial Mania', in M. Todovora and Zs. Gille (eds), *Post-Communist Nostalgia*, New York, Oxford: Berghahn Books, 17–29.

Boyle, K. (ed., 2010), *Everyday Pornography*, London: Routledge.

Bozelka, K. J. (2010), 'Exploitation Films and Success. The Half-Told Melodramas of Andy Milligan', in R. G. Weiner and J. Cline (eds), *Cinema Inferno. Celluloid Explosions from the Cultural Margins*, Lanham, Toronto, Plymouth: The Scarecrow Press, 171–90.

Bradshow, P. (2005), '9 Songs', *The Guardian*, 11 March 2005, <https://www. theguardian.com/film/News_Story/Critic_Review/Guardian_Film_of_the_ week/0,4267,1434764,00.html> (last accessed 12 December 2021).

Brick, E. (2012), '*Baise-Moi* and The French Rape-Revenge Film', in P. Allmer, E. Brick and D. Huxley (eds), *European Nightmares. Horror Cinema in Europe Since 1945*, London and New York: Wallflower Press, 93–103.

Bridges, A. J. (2010), 'Methodological considerations in mapping pornography content', in K. Boyle (ed.), *Everyday Pornography*, London: Routledge, 34–50.

Brottman, M. (1997), *Offensive Films. Toward an Anthropology of Cinéma Vomitif*, Westport, London: Greenwood Press.

Brown, W. (2010), 'Negotiating the Invisible', in W. Brown, D. Iordanova and L. Torchin (eds), *Moving People, Moving Images: Cinema and Trafficking in the New Europe*, St Andrews Film Studies (with College Gate Press), 16–48.

Brown, W. (2015), *Supercinema. Film-Philosophy for the Digital Age*, London: Berghahn Books.

Brzozowska, Z. (2015), 'Female Education and Fertility under State Socialism in Central and Eastern Europe', *Population*, 70 (4), 689–725.

Buchowski, M. (2006), 'The Specter of Orientalism in Europe: From Exotic Other to Stigmatized Brother', *Anthropological Quarterly*, 79:3, 463–82.

Buckland, W. (2021), *Narrative and Narration: Analyzing Cinematic Storytelling*, New York: Columbia University Press.

Buckley, M. (1989), '*Woman and Ideology in the Soviet Union*', Michigan: The University of Michigan Press.

Buden, B. (2008), 'Behind the Velvet Curtain. Remembering Dušan Makavejev's W.R.: Mysteries of the Organism', *Afterall: A Journal of Art, Context and Enquiry*, 18, 118–26.

Bukatman, S. (2006), 'Spectacle, Attractions and Visual Pleasure', in Wanda Strauven (ed.), *The Cinema of Attractions Reloaded*, Amsterdam: Amsterdam University Press.

Bumbray, C. (2010), 'Review: The Life and Death of a Porno Gang (Fantasia)', JoBlo, 21 July 2010, <https://www.joblo.com/fantasia-review-the-life-death-of-a-porno-gang/> (last accessed 23 May 2022).

Burts, J. (2002), *Animals in Film*, London: Reaction Books.

Butler, A. (2012), 'Sacrificing the Real Early 20th Century Theatrics and the New Extremism in Cinema', *Cinephile*, 8:2.

Butler, E. (2012b), 'Catherine Breillat: Anatomy of a Hard-Core Agitator', in X. Mendik (ed.), *Peep Shows. Cult Film and the Cine-Erotic*. London and New York: Wallflower Press, Chapter 10.

Bystydzienski, J. M. (1995), 'Woman and Families in Poland: Pressing Problems and Possible Solutions', in B. Łobodzińska' (ed.), *Family, Women and Employment in Central-Eastern Europe*, Westport, Connecticut, London: Greenwood Press, 193–205.

Cámara, C. (1997), 'The Labor Market in Central and Eastern Europe: Transformations and Perspectives', *Eastern European Economics*, 35:1, 76–93.

Campbell, H. (2014), '"Anatomy of Hell" Was the Film That Made Me Fear My Own Vagina', *Vice*, 22 December, <https://www.vice.com/en/article/8gd33x/anatomy-of-hell-was-the-film-that-made-me-fear-my-own-junk-820> (last accessed 2 October 2022).

BIBLIOGRAPHY

149

Canby, V. (1975), 'Politics with Syrup', *The New York Times*, 10 October, <https://www.nytimes.com/1975/10/10/archives/in-sweet-movie-politics-with-syrup.html> (last accessed 20 May 2021).

Carol, J. C. (1992), *Men, Women and Chainsaws: Gender in the Modern Horror Film*, Princeton: Princeton University Press.

Carrol, B. (2016), *Feeling Film. A Spatial Approach*, New York: Palgrave Macmillan.

Carter, D. R. (2010), 'It's Only a Movie? Reality as Transgression in Exploitation Cinema, in. J. Cline and R. G. Weiner (eds), *From the Arthouse to the Grindhouse. Highbrow and Lowbrow Transgression in Cinema's First Century*, Plymouth: The Scarecrow Press, 297–317.

Carter, O. (2018), *Making European Cult Cinema. Fan Enterprise in an Alternative Economy*, Amsterdam: Amsterdam University Press.

Cavell, S. (1979), 'On Makavejev, on Bergman', *Critical Inquiry*, 6(2), 305–30.

Chocano, C. (2004), 'Anatomy of a film both graphic, abstract', *Los Angeles Times*, 27 September 2004 <https://www.latimes.com/archives/la-xpm-2004-sep-27-et-breillat27-story.html> (last accessed 14 September 2022).

Chowen, B. (2012), 'Blue-ray Review: The Life and Death of a Porno Gang', *Inside Pulse*, 9 September 2012 <https://insidepulse.com/2012/09/09/blu-ray-review-the-life-and-death-of-a-porno-gang/> (last accessed 24 May 2022).

Chowen, B. (2015), 'Movie Review-Branden Chowen on The Life and Death of a Porno Gang (2009)', *Cinefessions*, 10 February 2015, <https://www.cinefessions.com/2015/02/movie-review-branden-chowen-on-the-life-and-death-of-a-porno-gang-2009/> (last accessed 2 October 2022).

Christos, M. (2003), *Orthodox Fundamentals: The Quest for an Eternal Identity*, Budapest: Central European University Press.

Church, D. (2015), *Grindhouse Nostalgia Memory, Home Video and Exploitation Film Fandom*, Edinburgh: Edinburgh University Press.

Cook, P. (1976), 'Exploitation Films and Feminism', *Screen*, 17(2), 122–27.

Corrington, R. S. (2003), *Wilhelm Reich: Psychoanalyst and Radical Naturalist*, New York: Farrar, Straus and Giroux.

Coulthard, L. (2011), 'Interrogating the Obscene: Extremism and Michael Haneke', in T. Horeck and T. Kendall (eds), *The New Extremism in Cinema. From France to Europe*, Edinburgh: Edinburgh University Press, 180–92.

Coulthard, L. and Birks, C. (2015), 'Desublimating Monstrous Desire: The Horror of Gender in New Extremist Cinema', *Journal of Gender Studies*, 25(4), 461–76.

Cramer, Michael (2016), 'Battle with history: Carlos Reygadas and the cinema of being', in S. Jeong and J. Szaniawski (eds), *The Global Auteur. The Politics of Authorship in 21st Century Cinema*, New York and London: Bloomsbury Academic, 235–53.

Cranny-Francis, A. (2009), 'Touching Film: The Embodied Practice and Politics of Film Viewing and Filmmaking', *The Senses and Society*, 4:2, 163–78.

Crémieux, A. (2015), 'Exploitation Cinema and the Lesbian Imagination', *Transatlantica*, 2, 14 July 2016 <http://journals.openedition.org/transatlantica/7869> (last accessed 29 April 2021).

Csaki, Csaba and Laura Tuck (2000), 'Rural Development Strategy. Eastern Europe and Central Asia', *World Bank Technical Paper: Europe and Central Asia Environmentally and Socially Sustainable Rural Development Series*. Washington: The World Bank Washington, no. 484.

Dakovic, N. (2006), 'Europe lost and found: Serbian cinema and EU integration', *New Cinemas: Journal of Contemporary Film*, 4:2, 93–103.

Dale, G. and Fabry, A. (2018), 'Neoliberalism in Eastern Europe and the Former Soviet Union', in D. Cahill, M. Cooper, M. Konings and D. Primrose (eds), *The SAGE Handbook of Neoliberalism*, London: Sage Publications, 234–48.

Dale, G. and Hardy, J. (2011), 'Conclusion: The "Crash" in Central and Eastern Europe', in G. Dale (ed.), *First the Transition, then the Crash: Eastern Europe in the 2000s*, London: Pluto Press, 251–64.

Dalore, A. (2019), 'Transition in Serbian Film Industry in the Example of Female Producers and Directors', in N. Marinchevska (ed.), *Post-totalitarian Cinema in Eastern European Countries: Models and Identities*, Sofia: Institute of Art Studies, Bulgarian Academy of Sciences, 127–35.

Daniel. M. (2015), *Extreme Asia. The Rise of Cult Cinema from the Far East*, Edinburgh: Edinburgh University Press.

Dapena, G. (2010), 'Reveries of Blood and Sand. The Cinema of Jean Rollin', in R. G. Weiner and J. Cline (eds), *Cinema Inferno. Celluloid Explosions from the Cultural Margins*, Lanham, Toronto, Plymouth: The Scarecrow Press, 226–43.

Dauphinée, E. (2003), 'Faith, Hope, Neoliberalism: Mapping Economies of Violence on the Margins of Europe', *Dialectical Anthropology*, 27:3–4, 189–203.

David, A. (2010), 'Toward an Inclusive, Exclusive Approach to Art Cinema', in. R. Galt and K. Schoonover (eds) *Global Art Cinema. New Theories and Histories*, Oxford: Oxford University Press, 62–75.

Davies, W. (2016), *The Limits of Neoliberalism. Authority, Sovereignty, and the Logic of Competition*, London: Sage Publications.

De Luca, T. (2014), *Realism of the Senses in World Cinema: The Experience of Physical Reality*, London and New York: I. B. Tauris.

De Luca, T. (2016), 'Natural Views: Animals, Contingency and Death in Carlos Reygadas's *Japón* and Lisandro Alonso's *Los Muertos*', in T. De Luca and N. B. Jorge (eds), *Slow Cinema*, Edinburgh: Edinburgh University Press, 219–30.

De Ville, D. (2010), Menopausal Monsters and Sexual Transgression in Argento's Art Horror', in R. G. Weiner and J. Cline (eds), *Cinema Inferno. Celluloid Explosions from the Cultural Margins*, Lanham, Toronto, Plymouth: The Scarecrow Press, 53–76.

DeCuir, G. Jr. (2010), 'Black Wave polemics: rhetoric as aesthetics', *Studies in Eastern European Cinema*, 1(1), 85–96.

BIBLIOGRAPHY

Deighan, S. (2016), 'An Andrzej Żuławski Retrospective: Szamanka', *Diabolique Magazine*, 25 June 2016 <https://diaboliquemagazine.com/andrzej-zulawski-retrospective-szamanka/> (last accessed 8 September 2022).

Devine, P. (2010), 'BBFC Release More Information on Why a Serbian Film was Classified' <https://thepeoplesmovies.com/2010/12/a-serbian-film-uk-trailer/> (last accessed 23 May 2022).

Donev, A. (2019), 'On the typology of self-financed Bulgarian feature films after 1990', in N. Marinchevska (ed.), *Post-Totalitarian Cinema in Eastern European Countries: Models and Identities*, Sofia, Bulgaria: Institute of Art Studies, 59–71.

Dumancic, M. (2013), 'Hiding in Plain Sight? Making Homosexuality (In)Visible in Post-Yugoslav Film, in N. Fejes and A. P. Balogh (eds), *Queer Visibility in Post-socialist Cultures*, Chicago: University of Chicago Press, 57–81.

Duncan, P. (2016), *The Emotional Life in Postmodern Film: Affect Theory's Other*, Oxon: Routledge.

Durnell, D. (2006), 'Woman's Body as an Anatomy of Hell: Nihilism, Recursion and Tragedy in Breillat's *Anatomy of Hell*. Sex as Body Politics', *Off Screen*, 10:7, <https://offscreen.com/view/anatomy_of_hell> (last accessed 2 October 2022).

Eaton, A. W. (2012), 'What's Wrong with the (Female) Nude?', in H. Maes and J. Levinson (eds), *Art and Pornography. Philosophical Essays*, Oxford: Oxford University Press, 277–308.

Ebert, R. (1975), '*Sweet Movie*', <https://www.rogerebert.com/reviews/sweet-movie-1975> (last accessed 21 May 2021).

Ebert, R. (2017), *Your Movie Sucks*, Kansas City: Andrews McMeel Publishing, LLC.

Elduque, A. (2017), 'Hungry Gazes, Digesting Closeups: Pasolini, *Porcile* and the Politics of Consumption', *Screen* 58(2), 119–40.

Eliade, M. (1970), *Zalmoxis: The Vanishing God*, Chicago: Chicago University Press.

Elliott-Smith, D. (2016), *Queer Horror Film and Television. Sexuality and Masculinity at the Margins*, London and New York: I. B. Tauris.

Elsaesser, T. (2005), *European Cinema Book: Face to Face with Hollywood*, Amsterdam: Amsterdam University Press.

Feaster, F. (1994), 'The Woman on the Table: Moral and Medical Discourse in the Exploitation Cinema', *Film History*, 6:3, 340–54.

Feaster, F. and B. Wood (1999), *Forbidden Fruit. The Golden Age of the Exploitation Film*, Baltimore: Midnight Marquee Press.

Featherstone, M. (2010), 'Body, Image and Affect in Consumer Culture', *Body & Society*, 16:1, 193–221.

Featherstone, M. (2013), '*Coito ergo sum*: Serbian sadism and global capitalism in *A Serbian Film*', *Horror Studies*, 4:3, 127–41.

Featherstone, M. and B. Johnson (2012), 'Ovo Je Srbija: The horror of the national thing in *A Serbian Film*', *Journal of Cultural Research*, 16:1, 63–79.

Ferroni Brigade, The (2012), 'Beginnings Are Useless: A Conversation with Andrzej Żuławski', Notebook Interview, *MUBI*, 12 March 2012 <https://mubi.com/notebook/posts/beginnings-are-useless-a-conversation-with-andrzej-zulawski> (last accessed 14 September 2022).

Filippo, M. S. (2010), 'Unthinking Heterocentrism: Bisexual Representability in Art Cinema', in R. Galt and K. Schoonover (eds) *Global Art Cinema. New Theories and Histories*, Oxford: Oxford University Press, 75–92.

Fojtova, S. and Sokolova, V. (2013), 'Strategies of Inclusion and Shifting Attitudes towards Visibility in the Gay, Lesbian, and Queer Discourse in the Czech Republic after 1989', in N. Fejes and A. P. Balogh (eds), *Queer Visibility in Post-socialist Cultures*, Chicago: University of Chicago Press, 105–31.

Formanek, C. (2008), 'Mundruczó Kornél: Delta. Klasszikusabban gondolkodom, mint feltételezik rólam' (Kornél Mundruczó: Delta. I Think in a More Classic Way than People Would Assume)', *Film.hu* <https://magyar.film.hu/filmhu/magazin/mundruczo-kornel-delta-interju-werk> (last access 01 February 2022).

Foster, G. A. (2016), '*Anatomy of Hell*: A Feminist Fairy Tale', Senses of Cinema, 2006:80 <https://www.sensesofcinema.com/2016/cteq/anatomy-hell/> (last accessed 2 October 2022).

Fréire, P. (2005), *The Pedagogy of the Oppressed*, trans. Myra Bergman Ramos, New York and London: Continuum.

Frey, M. (2016), *Extreme Cinema. The Transgressive Rhetoric of Today's Art Film Culture*, New Brunswick, New Jersey and London: Rutgers University Press.

Fuery, P. (2004), *Madness and Cinema. Psychoanalysis, Spectatorship and Culture*, New York: Palgrave Macmillan.

Gal, S. (1994), Gender in the Post-Socialist Transition: The Abortion Debate in Hungary, *East European Politics and Societies*, 8:2, 256–86.

Galt, R. and K. Schoonover (2010), 'Introduction: The Impurity of Art Cinema', in R. Galt and K. Schoonover (eds), *Global Art Cinema. New Theories and Histories*, Oxford: Oxford University Press, 3–29.

Gaut, B. (2010), *The Philosophy of Cinematic Art*. Cambridge: Cambridge University Press.

Georgi (2011), 'Baklava', *The SkyKid* <https://theskykid.com/baklava-2007/> (last accessed 13 July 2022).

Gervai, A. (1995), '*Mozi az alagútban. A kilencvenes évek* [The Hungarian Cinema of the 1990s]', Budapest: Pelikán.

Ghodsee, K. (2021), 'The Enemy of My Enemy in My Friend: The Curious Tale of Feminism and Capitalism in Easter Europe', in K. Bluhm, G. Pickhan, J. Stypinska, A Wierzcholska (eds), *Gender and Power in Eastern Europe. Changing Concepts of Femininity and Masculinity in Power Relations*, Cham: Springer, 15–25.

Glucklich, A. (2010), *Sacred Pain. Hurting the Body for the Sake of the Soul*, Oxford: Oxford University Press.

BIBLIOGRAPHY

Goddard, M. (2011), 'Eastern Extreme: The Presentation of Eastern Europe as a Site of Monstrosity in *La Vie nouvelle* and *Import/Export*', in. T. Horeck and T. Kendall (eds), *The New Extremism in Cinema. From France to Europe*, Edinburgh: Edinburgh University Press, 82–93.

Goddard, M. (2012), 'The Impossible Polish New Wave and its Accursed Émigré Auteurs: Borowczyk, Polanski, Skilomowski, and Zulawski', in Imre, A. (ed.), *A Companion to Eastern European Cinemas*, West Sussex: Wiley-Blackwell, 291–311.

Goddard, M. (2014), 'Beyond Polish Moral Realism. The Subversive Cinema of Andrzej Żuławski', in. E. Mazierska and M. Goddard (eds), *Polish Cinema in a Transnational Context*, Rochester: University of Rochester Press.

Goldman, M. F. (1997), *Revolution and Change in Central and Eastern Europe: Political, Economic and Social Challenges*, Armonk, New York, London: M. E. Sharpe.

Goldsworthy, V. (2003), 'Invention and In(ter)vention: The Rhetoric of Balkanization', in D. Bjelic and O. Savic (eds), *Balkan as Metaphor: Between Globalization and Fragmentation*, Cambridge, MA: MIT Press, 25–38.

Goodall, M. (2010), 'The Real Faces of Death. Art Shock in *Des Morts*, in J. Cline and R. G. Weiner (eds), *From the Arthouse to the Grindhouse. Highbrow and Lowbrow Transgression in Cinema's First Century*, Plymouth: The Scarecrow Press, 244–64.

Gormley, P. (2005), *The New-Brutality Film. Race and Affect in Contemporary Hollywood Cinema*, Bristol: Intellect Books.

Goulding, D. (1990), 'The Films of Dusan Makavejev. Between East and West', in G. Petrie and R. Dwyer (eds), *Before the Wall Came Down. Soviet and East European Filmmakers Working in the West*, Lanham, New York and London: University of Press America, 143–57.

Goulding, D. J. (1994), 'Makavejev' in D. J. Goulding (ed.), *Five Filmmakers. Tarkovsky, Forman, Polanski, Szabó, Makavejev*, Indiana University Press, 209–64.

Gragovic-Soso, J. (2002), *Saviours of the Nation: Serbia's Intellectual Opposition and the Revival of Nationalism*, London: Hurst and Co.

Green, D. (2010), Film Review: A Serbian Film, *Cinevue*, December, <https://cine-vue.com/2010/12/film-review-a-serbian-film.html> (last accessed 2 October 2022).

Grodal, T. (2016), 'Film, Metaphor and Qualia Salience', in K. Fahlenbrach (ed.), *Embodied Metaphors in Film, Television, and Video Games. Cognitive Approaches*, New York: Routledge, 101–15.

Grønstad, A. (2011), 'On the Unwatchable', in. T. Horeck and T. Kendall (eds), *The New Extremism in Cinema. From France to Europe*, Edinburgh: Edinburgh University Press, 192–209.

Gülçür, L. and İlkkaracan, P. (2002), 'The "Natasha" experience: Migrant sex workers from the former Soviet Union and Eastern Europe in Turkey', *Women's Studies International Forum*, 25 (4), 411–21.

Hagman, H. (2007), 'Every Cannes needs its scandal': Between art and exploitation in contemporary French film', *Film International*, 29, 32–40.

Hall, D. (2015), Antagonism in the Making: Religion and Homosexuality in Post-Communist Poland, in S. Sremac and R. R. Ganzevoort (eds), *Religious and Sexual Nationalisms in Central and Eastern Europe: Gods, Gays and Governments*, Leiden and Boston: Brill, 74–93.

Hall, S. (2011), 'The Neo-liberal Revolution', *Cultural Studies*, 25:6, 705–28.

Hallama, P (2021). 'Questioning Gender Stereotypes Under Socialism: Fatherly Emotions and the Case of Single Fathers', in K. Bluhm, G. Pickhan, J. Stypinska, A. Wierzcholska (eds), *Gender and Power in Eastern Europe. Changing Concepts of Femininity and Masculinity in Power Relations*, Cham: Springer, 209–27.

Haltof, M. (2000), 'The Representation of Stalinism in Polish Cinema', *Canadian Slavonic Papers / Revue Canadienne des Slavistes*: 42: 1–2, 47–61.

Hamblin, S. (2014), 'Cinema of Revolt: Black Wave Revolution and Dušan Makavejev's Politics of Disgust', *Cinema Journal* 53:4, 28–52.

Hames, P. and C. Portuges (2006), 'Introduction', in C. Portuges and P. Hames (eds), *Cinemas in Transition in Central and Eastern Europe after 1989*, Philadelphia: Temple University Press, 1–10.

Hames, P. (2009), *Czech and Slovak Cinema. Theme and Tradition*, Edinburgh: Edinburgh University Press.

Hardy, S. (2009), 'The New Pornographies: Representation or Reality?', F. Attwood (ed.), *Mainstreaming Sex. The Sexualization of Western Culture*, London and New York: I. B. Tauris, 3–19.

Harlan, J. (2022), '"A Serbian Film": We Understand, Grumpire!', 24 February, <https://www.grumpire.com/a-serbian-film-we-understand/> (last accessed 2 October 2022).

Harper, S. (2017) *Screening Bosnia. Geopolitics, Gender and Nationalism in Film and Television of the 1992-1995 War*, London, New York: Bloomsbury.

Harsanyi, D. (1992), 'Women in Romania', in F. Mueller (ed.), *Gender Politics and Post-Communism: Reflections from Eastern Europe and the Former Soviet Union*, London: Routledge, 39–52.

Harvey, D. (2007), 'Neoliberalism as Creative Destruction', *The Annals of the American Academy of Political and Social Science*, 610, 22–44.

Hashamova, Y. (2012), 'War Rape: (Re)Defining Motherhood, Fatherhood and Nationhood', in H. Goscilo and Y. Hashamova (eds), *Embracing Arms – Cultural Representation of Slavic and Balkan Women in War*, 233–53.

Hawkins, J. (2000), *Cutting Edge. Art-Horror and the Horrific Avant-garde*, Minnesota: Minnesota University Press.

Hayworth, S. (2000), *Cinema Studies. The Key Concepts*, London and New York: Routledge.

Heitlinger, A. (1995), 'Women's Equality, Work and Family in the Czech Republic', in B. Łobodzińska (ed.), *Family, Women and Employment in Central-Eastern Europe*, Westport, Connecticut, London: Greenwood Press, 87–101.

BIBLIOGRAPHY

Heitlinger, A. (1995), 'Women's Equality, Work and Family in the Czech Republic', in B. Lobodzinska (ed.), *Family, Women and Employment in Central-Eastern Europe*, London, Westport, Connecticut: Greenwood Press, 87–100.

Heller-Nicholas, A. (2014), *Found Footage Horror Films: Fear and the Appearance of Reality*, Jefferson, North Carolina: McFarland.

Henry, C. (2014), *Revisionist Rape-Revenge: Redefining a Film Genre*, New York, London: Palgrave Macmillan.

Hester, H. (2017), 'Perverting the Explicit: Catherine Breillat's Visual Vocabulary of Desire', in D. Kerr and D. Peberdy (eds), *Tainted Love. Screening Sexual Perversion*, London and New York: I. B. Tauris, 47–63.

Heyns, B. (2005), 'Emerging Inequalities in Central and Eastern Europe', *Annual Review of Sociology*, 31, 163–97.

Higashi, S. (1990), '*Night of the Living Dead: A Horror Film about the Horrors of the Vietnam Era*', in L. Dittmar and G. Michaud (eds), *From Hanoi to Hollywood. The Vietnam War in American Film*, New Brunswick and London: Rutgers University Press, 175–89.

Higgins, L. A. (1991), 'Screen/Memory: Rape and Its Alibis in Last Year at Marienbad', in L. A. Higgins and B. R. Silver (eds), *Rape and Representation*, New York: Columbia University Press, 303–23.

Hilary, A. and M. A. Orenstein (2016), 'Why did Neoliberalism Triumph and Endure in the Post-Communist World?', *Comparative Politics*, 48:3, 313–31.

Hobbs, S. (2015), 'Reconceptualising extreme art film as transnational cinema', *Transnational Cinemas*, 6:1, 33–48.

Hobbs, S. (2016), 'Animal Snuff', in. N. Jackson, S. Kimber, J. Walker and T. J. Watson (eds), *Snuff. Real Death and Screen Media*, London: Bloomsbury, 63–81.

Hobbs, S. (2018), *Cultivating Extreme Art Cinema. Text, Paratext and Home Video Culture*, Edinburgh: Edinburgh University Press.

Holden, S. (2005), 'The Story of a Love Affair, in the Language of the Body', *The New York Times*, 22 July 2005 <https://www.nytimes.com/2005/07/22/movies/the-story-of-a-love-affair-in-the-language-of-the-body.html> (last accessed 12 December 2021).

Horeck, T. (2004), *Public Rape: Representing Violation in Fiction and Film*, London: Routledge.

Horeck, T. (2011), '"A Passion for the Real": Sex, Affect and Performance in the Films of Andrea Arnold', in. T. Horeck and T. Kendall (eds), *The New Extremism in Cinema. From France to Europe*, Edinburgh: Edinburgh University Press, 169–80.

Horeck, T. and Kendall, T. (2011), 'Introduction', in. T. Horeck and T. Kendall (eds), *The New Extremism in Cinema. From France to Europe*, Edinburgh: Edinburgh University Press, 1–18.

Horeck, T. and Kendall, T. (2012), 'The New *Extremisms*: Rethinking Extreme Cinema', *Cinephile*, 8:2, 6–10.

Horeczky, K. (2002), '"Bármi megtörténhet. Beszélgetés Mundruczó Kornéllal" (Anything can happen. A conversation with Kornél Mundruczó', *Filmkultúra* <http://www.filmkultura.hu/regi/2002/articles/profiles/mundruczok. hu.html> (last accessed 12 January 2022).

Horton, A. J. (2001), 'Hard Stuff: Vladmír Michálek's *Anděl Exit*', *Central European Review*, 3:4, 29 January 2001, <https://www.pecina.cz/files/www. ce-review.org/01/4/kinoeye4_horton.html> (last accessed 13 July 2022).

Houston, B. and Marsha Kinder (1978), 'Sweet movie', *Quarterly Review of Film & Video*, 3:4, 545–67.

Hubner, L. (2011), 'A Taste for Flesh and Blood? Shifting Classifications of Contemporary European Cinema', in L. Hubner (ed.), *Valuing Films. Shifting Perceptions of Worth*, New York: Palgrave Macmillan, 198–214.

Hutchings, P. (2004), *The Horror Film*, London: Routledge.

Hyland, R. (2009), 'A Politics of Excess: Violence and Violation in Miike Takashi's *Audition*', in J. Choi and M. Wada-Marciano (eds), *Horror to the Extreme. Changing Boundaries in Asian Cinema*, Hong Kong: Hong Kong University Press, 199–218.

Ibroscheva, Elza (2013), *Advertising, Sex and Post-Socialism. Women, Media and Femininity in the Balkans*, Lanham, Boulder, New York, Toronto, Plymouth: Lexington Books.

Imre, A. (2001), 'Gender, Literature, and Film in Contemporary East Central European Culture', CLCWeb: *Comparative Literature and Culture* 3:1 <http:// docs.lib.purdue.edu/clcweb/vol3/iss1/6> (last accessed 12 January 2022).

Imre, A. (2002), 'Introduction. Eastern European Cinema from No End to the End (As We Know It)', in Imre, A. (ed.), *A Companion to Eastern European Cinemas*, The Atrium, Southern Gate, Chichester, West Sussex: Wiley-Blackwell, 1–21.

Imre, A. (2009), *Identity Games: Globalization and the Transformation of Media Cultures in the New Europe*, Cambridge, MA: MIT Press.

Iordanova, D. (1996), 'Women in New Balkan Cinema: Surviving on the Margins', *Film Criticism*, 21:2, 24–39.

Iordanova, D. (1999), 'Kusturica's *Underground* (1995): Historical Allegory or Propaganda?' *Historical Journal of Film, Radio and Television*, 19(1), 69–86.

Iordanova, D. (2000), 'Cinema of the Dispersed Yugoslavs: Diaspora in the Making', *CineAction* 52, 68–72.

Iordanova, D. (2001), *Cinema of Flames: Balkan Film, Culture, and the Media*, London: British Film Institute.

Iordanova, D. (2003), *Cinema of the Other Europe. The Industry and Artistry of East Central Europe*, London: Wallflower Press.

Iordanova, D. (2006), 'Bulgarian Cinema: Optimism in Moderation', in. C. Portuges and P. Hames (eds), *Cinemas in Transition in Central and Eastern Europe after 1989*, Philadelphia: Temple University Press, 10–40.

Iordanova, D. (2007), 'Whose is this Memory?: Hushed Narratives and Discerning Remembrance in Balkan Cinema'. *Cineaste*, Summer 2007: 22–7.

BIBLIOGRAPHY 157

Iordanova, D. (2013), 'Bulgarian Cinema: Optimism in Moderation', in A. Imre (ed.), *Cinemas in Transition in Central and Eastern Europe after 1989*, Philadelphia: Temple University Press, 10–39.

Jackson, N. (2016), 'Introduction: Shot, Cut, and Slaughtered: The Cultural Mythology of Snuff', in N. Jackson, S. Kimber, J. Walker and T. J. Watson (eds), *Snuff. Real Death and Screen Media*, London and New York: Bloomsbury Publishing, 1–23.

Jackson, N. (2016b), 'Wild Eyes, Dead Ladies: The Snuff Filmmaker in Realist Horror', in N. Jackson, S. Kimber, J. Walker and T. J. Watson (eds), *Snuff. Real Death and Screen Media*, London and New York: Bloomsbury Publishing, 189–211.

Jagodzinski, J. (2007), 'The Inverted Drive in Andrzej Żuławski's Szamanka: A Lacanian Reading of the Post Femme-Fatale', *Canadian Review of Comparative Literature*, 34:3, 316–28.

Jameson F. (2004), 'Thoughts on Balkan cinema', in A. Egoyan and I. Balfour (eds), *Subtitles: On the Foreignness of Film*, London and Cambridge: MIT Press.

Janisse, K. (2012), *House of Psychotic Women. An Autobiographical Topography of Female Neurosis in Horror and Exploitation Films*, Gadalming, Surrey: FAB Press.

Jelaca, D. (2012), 'Cinematic Images of Women at a Time of National(ist) Crisis: The Case of Three Yugoslav Films', in L. Khatib (ed.), *Storytelling in World Cinema: Contexts*, London: Wallflower Press, 133–43.

Jelaca, D. (2016), *Dislocated Screen Memory. Narrating Trauma in Post-Yugoslav Cinema*, New York, London: Palgrave Macmillan.

Jensen, R. (2010), 'Pornography is what the end of the world looks like', in K. Boyle (ed.), *Everyday Pornography*, London: Routledge, 105–14.

Jeung, S. H. and D. Andrew (2008), 'Grizzly Ghost: Herzog, Bazin, and the Cinematic Animal', *Screen* 49:1, 1–12.

Jogan, M. (1995), 'Redomestication of Women and Democratization of Postsocialist Slovenia', in. B. Łobodzińska (ed.), *Family, Women and Employment in Central-Eastern Europe*, Westport, Connecticut, London: Greenwood Press, 229–37.

Jones, S. (2013), *Torture Porn. Popular Horror after Saw*, Hampshire: Palgrave Macmillan.

Jones, S. (2013b), 'The Lexicon of Offence: The Meaning of Torture, Porn and "Torture Porn"', in F. Attwood, V. Campbell, I. Q. Hunter and S. Lockyer (eds), *Controversial Images. Media Representations on the Edge*, New York: Palgrave Macmillan, 186–201.

Jones, S. (2018), 'Sex and Horror', in C. Smith, F. Attwood and B. McNair (eds), *The Routledge Companion to Media, Sex and Sexuality*, New York: Routledge, 290–99.

Jouzeliuniene, I. and Kanopiene, V. (1995) 'Women and Family in Lithuania', in B. Łobodzińska (ed.), *Family, Women and Employment in Central-Eastern Europe*, Westport, Connecticut, London: Greenwood Press, 155–65.

Juricic, T. (2022), 'And the Marble Ass saw the second coming of Tito: Želimir Žilnik's cinematic representations of a transitional society through the revolutionary carnivalesque', *Studies in Eastern European Cinema*, DOI: 10.1080/2040350X.2022.2041368.

Jurkovic, T. (2020), 'The Horror Genre in Balkan Cinema', in C. Bloom (ed.), *The Palgrave Handbook of Contemporary Gothic*, New York and London: Palgrave Macmillan, 711–25.

Kalmar, G. (2017), *Formations of Masculinity in Post-Communist Hungarian Cinema. Labyrinthian Men*, New York: Palgrave Macmillan.

Kaplan, A. E. (2010), 'European Art Cinema. Affect, and Postcolonialism: Herzog, Denis, and the Dardenne Brothers', in. R. Galt and K. Schoonover (eds) *Global Art Cinema. New Theories and Histories*, Oxford: Oxford University Press, 285–303.

Kasdovasili, S. A. (2019), '*Sweet Movie*', https://transnational-queer-under ground.net/sweet-movie/ (last accessed 23 May 2021).

Kattel, R. (2010), 'Financial and economic crisis in Eastern Europe', *Journal of Post Keynesian Economics*, 33:1, 41–59.

Kavka, M. (2016), 'The Affective Reality of Snuff', in N. Jackson, S. Kimber, J. Walker and T. J. Watson (eds), *Snuff. Real Death and Screen Media*, London and New York: Bloomsbury Publishing, 47–63.

Keesey, D. (2010), 'Split Identification: Representations of Rape in Gaspar Noé's *Irréversible* and Catherine Breillat's *À ma sœur/Fat Girl*', *Studies in European Cinema*, 7:2, 95–107.

Keesey, D. (2017), *Twenty First Century Horror Films*, Harpenden, Herts: Kamera Books.

Kendall, T. (2016), 'Affect and the Ethics of Snuff in Extreme Art Cinema', in N. Jackson, S. Kimber, J. Walker and T. J. Watson (eds), *Snuff. Real Death and Screen Media*, London and New York: Bloomsbury Publishing, 257–77.

Kennedy-Pipe, C. and P. Stanley (2005), 'Rape in War: Lessons of the Balkan Conflicts in the 1990s', in K. Booth, (ed.), *The Kosovo Tragedy: The Human Rights Dimensions*, London and Portland: Frank Cass, 67–87.

Kerekes, D. and D. Slater (2016), *Killing for culture: From Edison to ISIS: A New History of Death on Film*, London: Headpress.

Kern, L. (2011), 'Short Takes: *A Serbian Film*', *Film Comment*, May-June, <https://www.filmcomment.com/article/a-serbian-film-review/> (last accessed 2 October 2022).

Kerner, A. M. and J. I. Knapp (2016), *Extreme Cinema: Affective Strategies in Transnational Media*, Edinburgh: Edinburgh University Press.

King, G. (2019), *Positioning Art Cinema: Film and Cultural Value*, London and New York: I. B. Tauris.

King, R. (1992), 'To Have or Not to Have Sex in Critical Theory: Sexuality in the Early Writings of Wilhelm Reich and Erich Fromm', *Mid-American Review of Sociology*, 16(2), No. 2, 81–91.

BIBLIOGRAPHY 159

Kiossev, A. (2011), 'The Self-Colonizing Metaphor', *Atlas of Transformation*, <http://monumenttotransformation.org/atlas-of-transformation/html/s/self-colonization/the-self-colonizing-metaphor-alexander-kiossev.html> (last accessed 21 January 2021).

Kipp, J. (2011), 'No Room for Love: Andrzej Zulawski's Szamanka', *Slant Magazine*, 21 October 2011, <https://www.slantmagazine.com/film/no-room-for-love-andrzej-zulawskis-szamanka/> (last accessed 12 December 2021).

Kiss, A. (2018), 'Censorship Revisited', in Florian Kührer-Wielach and Michaela Nowotnick (eds), Aus den *Giftschränken* des *Kommunismus*: *Methodische Fragen* zum *Umgang* mit *Überwachungsakten* in *Zentral-* und *Südosteuropa*, Regensburg: Verlag Friedrich Pustet, 233–70.

Klapka, A. (2014), 'Understanding A Serbian Film: The Effect of Censorship and File-sharing on Critical Reception and Perceptions of Serbian National Identity in the UK', *Frames Cinema Journal*, 6, <https://framescinemajournal.com/article/understanding-a-serbian-film-the-effects-of-censorship-and-file-sharing-on-critical-reception-and-perceptions-of-serbian-national-identity-in-the-uk/> (last accessed 2 October 2022).

Kligman, G. (1998), *The Politics of Duplicity: Controlling Reproduction in Ceauşescu's Romania*, Berkeley, Los Angeles and London: University of California Press.

Kohn, E. (2010), '"A Serbian Film" Shocks Midnight Audiences At SXSW', *The Wall Street Journal*, 15 March 2010, <https://www.wsj.com/articles/BL-SEB-27420> (last accessed 8 October 2022).

Koncz, K. (1995), 'The Position of Hungarian Women in the Process of Regime Change', in B. Łobodzińska (ed.), *Family, Women and Employment in Central-Eastern Europe*, Westport, Connecticut, London: Greenwood Press.

Kornai, J. (2006), 'The Great Transformation of Central Eastern Europe', *Economics of Transition*, 14:2, 207–44.

Kourtova, P. (2013), 'Imitations and Controversy: Performing (Trans)Sexuality in Post-Communist Bulgaria', in F. Attwood, V. Campbell, I. Q. Hunter and S. Lockyer (eds), *Controversial Images. Media Representations on the Edge*. New York: Palgrave Macmillan, 52–67.

Kovács, A. B. (2007), *Screening Modernism. European Art Cinema, 1950-1980*, Chicago and London: University of Chicago Press.

Kozma, K (2012), 'Champaign, Boredom. Dušan Makavejev's *Sweet Movie* (1974)', *East European Bulletin* (18) <https://eefb.org/retrospectives/dusan-makavejevs-sweet-movie-1974/> (last accessed 10 November 2021).

Kragić, B. (2011), 'Lukas Nola: Celestial Body (Nebo, sateliti, 2000); Alone (Sami, 2001)', 11 April 2011, *Kinokultura* <http://www.kinokultura.com/specials/11/R-celestialbody-alone.shtml> (last accessed 12 December 2021).

Krakus (2018), *No End in Sight. Polish Cinema in the Late Socialist Period*, Pittsburgh, PA: Pittsburgh University Press.

Krizsán, A. and Roggeband, C. (2018), 'Introduction: Mapping the Gendered Implications of Democratic Backsliding in the Countries of the CEE Region',

160 THE EXTREME CINEMA OF EASTERN EUROPE

in A. Krizsán and C. Roggeband (eds), *Gendering Democratic Backsliding in Central and Eastern Europe*. A Comparative Agenda, Budapest: Central European University Press, 4–31.

Kronja, I. (2008), 'Women's rights in Serbian cinema after 2000', *New Review of Film and Television Studies*, 6:1, 67–82.

Kronja, K. (2006), 'The Aesthetics of Violence in Recent Serbian Cinema: Masculinity in Crisis', *Film Criticism*, 30:3, 17–37.

Krstic, I. (2000a). 'Serbia's Wound Culture: Teenage Killers in Miloševic's Serbia: Srdan Dragojevic's *Rane*', in A. J. Horton (ed.), *Celluloid Tinderbox: Yugoslav Screen Reflections of a Turbulent Decade*, Shropshire: New Europe Review, 89–102.

Kunicki, M., N Davokic, and D. Leppla (2018), 'Cultural Position and Filmmaking in Communist East Central Europe: Lessons from Poland and the Former Yugoslavia', in B. Apor, P. Apor, H. Sándor (eds), *The Handbook of COURAGE: Cultural Opposition and its Heritage in Eastern Europe*, Budapest: Hungarian Academy of Sciences, 267–89.

Laine, T. (2011), *Feeling Cinema. Emotional Dynamics in Film Studies*. New York, London: Continuum.

Lane, D. (2010), 'Post-Socialist States and the World Economy: The Impact of Global Economic Crisis', *Historical Social Research / Historische Sozialforschung*, 35:2, 218–41.

Lanis, B. (2010), 'The Neorealist Transgressions of Pier Paolo Pasolini', in R. G. Weiner and J. Cline (eds), *Cinema Inferno. Celluloid Explosions from the Cultural Margins*, Lanham, Toronto, Plymouth: The Scarecrow Press, 3–10.

Lanthier, J. L. (2011), Review: A Serbian Film, Slant, 12 May, <https://www.slantmagazine.com/film/a-serbian-film> (last accessed 2 October 2022).

Lawrence, M. (2010): 'Haneke's Stable. The Death of an Animal and the Figuration of the Human', in B. Price and J. D. Rhodes (eds), *Michael Haneke*, Wayne State University Press, Detroit, 63–87.

Legge, J. S. and Alford, J. R. (1986), 'Can Government Regulate Fertility? An Assessment of Pronatalist Policy in Eastern Europe', *The Western Political Quarterly*, 39:4, 709–28.

Levi, P. (2009), *Disintegration in Frames. Aesthetics and Ideology in the Yugoslav and Post-Yugoslav Cinema*. Stanford: Stanford University Press.

Levi, P. and Iordanova, D. (1999), 'Eastern European Cinema', *Journal of Film and Video*, 51:1, 56–76.

Haltof, M. (2000), 'The Representation of Stalinism in Polish Cinema', *Canadian Slavonic Papers / Revue Canadienne des Slavistes*, 42:1/2, 47–61.

Levine, P. B. and D. Staiger (2004), 'Abortion Policy and Fertility Outcomes: The Eastern European Experience', *Journal of Law and Economics*, 47 (4), 223–43.

Levy, E. (2010), 'B is for Bile, Blood, and Bones. On Corporeal Bodies in the films of Peter Greenaway', in R. G. Weiner and J. Cline (eds), *Cinema Inferno. Celluloid Explosions from the Cultural Margins*, Lanham, Toronto, Plymouth: The Scarecrow Press, 193–216.

BIBLIOGRAPHY

Lindner, K. (2017), *Film Bodies: Queer Feminist Encounters with Gender and Sexuality in Cinema*, London and New York: I. B. Tauris.

Lippit, A. M. (2002), 'The Death of an Animal', *Film Quarterly*, 56:1, 9–22.

Lišková, K. and Holubec, S. (2020), 'Women between the private and public spaces', in Borodziej, S. Holubec, J. Puttkamer (eds), *The Routledge History Handbook of Central and Eastern Europe in the Twentieth Century, Volume 1: Challenges of Modernity*, London and New York: Routledge, 183–235.

Lobodzinska, B. (1995), 'The Family and Working Women during and after Socialist Industrialization and Ideology' in. B. Łobodzińska (ed.), *Family, Women and Employment in Central-Eastern Europe*, Westport, Connecticut, London: Greenwood Press, 1–47.

Lobodzinska, B. (1995), 'The Family and Working Women during and after Socialist Industrialization and Ideology', in B. Łobodzińska (ed.), *Family, Women and Employment in Central-Eastern Europe*, Westport, Connecticut, London: Greenwood Press, 1–47.

Longinovic, T. (2011), *Vampire Nation: Violence as Cultural Imaginary*, Durham, NC: Duke University Press.

Longinovic, T. Z. (2002), 'Vampires Like Us: Gothic Imaginary and "the serbs"', in D. I. Bjelic and O. Savic (eds), *Balkan as Metaphor. Between Globalization and Fragmentation*, Cambridge, Massachusetts and London: England, 39–61.

Longinović, T. Z. (2005), 'Playing the Western Eye: Balkan Masculinity and Post-Yugoslav War Cinema', in A. Imre (ed.), *East European Cinemas*, New York: Routledge, 35–48.

Lóránd, Zs. (2018), *The Feminist Challenge to the Socialist State in Yugoslavia*, New York and London: Palgrave Macmillan.

Lowenstein, A. (2005). *Shocking Representation: Historical Trauma, National Cinema, and the Modern Horror Film*. New York: Columbia University Press.

Lübecker, N. (2011), 'Lars von Trier's *Dogville*: A Feel-Bad Film', in. T. Horeck and T. Kendall (eds), *The New Extremism in Cinema. From France to Europe*, Edinburgh: Edinburgh University Press, 157–69.

Lübecker, N. (2015), *The Feel-Bad Film*, Edinburgh: Edinburgh University Press.

Lykidis, A. (2020), *Art Cinema and Neoliberalism*, New York and London: Palgrave Macmillan.

Lynch, A. (2012), *Porn Chic: Exploring the Contours of Raunch Eroticism*, London: Bloomsbury Publishing.

Maas, S. C. (2019), 'The Gaze of Shame: A Conversation with Catherine Breillat', *MUBI: Notebook Interview*, 21 October 2019, <https://mubi.com/notebook/posts/the-gaze-of-shame-a-conversation-with-catherine-breillat> (last accessed 2 October 2022).

MacBean J. R. (1972), 'Sex and Politics: Wilhelm Reich, World Revolution, and Makavejev's WR', *Film Quarterly*, 25:3, 2–13.

MacDougall, D. (2006), *The Corporeal Image. Film, Ethnography, and the Senses*, Princeton and Oxford: Princeton University Press.

MacKenzie, S. (2002), '*Baise-moi*, Feminist Cinemas and the Censorship Controversy', *Screen*, 43(3), 315–24.

Maes, H. (2012), 'Who Says Pornography Can't Be Art?', in H. Maes and J. Levinson (eds), *Art and Pornography. Philosophical Essays*, Oxford: Oxford University Press, 16–47.

Mahmoud, T. M. and Trebesch, C. (2010), 'The Economics of Human Trafficking and Labour Migration: Micro-Evidence from Eastern Europe', *Journal of Comparative Economics*, 38 (2), 173–88.

Manning, E. (2006), *Politics of Touch. Sense, Movement, Sovereignty*, Minnesota: Minnesota Press.

Marcus, T. (1998), 'Short story', *Journal of Storytelling*, 5:2, 23–7.

Mardorossian, C. M. (2014), *Framing the Rape Victim. Gender and Agency Reconsidered*, New Brunswick, New Jersey and London: Rutgers University Press.

Marks, L. (2000), *The Skin of the Film. Intercultural Cinema, Embodiment and the Senses*, Durham and London: Duke University Press.

Marks, L. (2002), *Sensuous Theory and Multisensory Media*, Minnesota: University of Minnesota Press.

Martin, A. (2018), *Mysteries of Cinema. Reflections on Film Theory, History and Culture 1982-2016*, Amsterdam: Amsterdam University Press.

Mazierska, E. (2010), *Masculinities in Polish, Czech and Slovak Cinema. Black Peters and Men of Marble*, New York, Oxford: Berghahn Books.

Mazierska, E. (2014), 'Makavejev's uses of history in *Innocence Unprotected*, *Sweet Movie* and *Gorilla Bathes at Noon*', *Studies in Eastern European Cinema*, 5:1, 16–30.

Mazierska, E. (2015), 'The East Meets the West in Contemporary Eastern European Films', in I. Bondebjerg, E. N. Redvall and A. Higson (eds), *European Cinema and Television. Cultural Policy and Everyday Life*, Hampshire: Palgrave Macmillan, 151–68.

Mazierska, E., L. Kristensen and E. Naripea (2014), 'Postcolonial Theory and the Postcommunist World', in Mazierska, E., L. Kristensen and E. Naripea (eds), *Postcolonial Approaches to Eastern European Cinema. Portraying Neighbours On-Screen*, London and New York: I. B. Tauris, 1–41.

McGillwray, M. (2019), 'It's so easy to create a victim. Subverting gender-stereotypes in the New French Extremity', in S. Holland, R. Shail and S. Gerrard (eds), *Gender and Contemporary Horror Film*, Bingley: Emerald Publishing, 7–22.

McIntyre, Robert J. (1992), 'The Phantom of the Transition: Privatization of Agriculture in the Former Soviet Union and Eastern Europe', *Comparative Economic Studies*, 34, 81–95.

McLennan, J. (2003), 'Andel Exit', *Film Blitz*, 31 December 2003, <https://filmblitz.org/andel-exit-2000/> (last accessed 12 December 2021).

McMahon, L. (2019), *Animal Worlds: Film, Philosophy and Time*, Edinburgh: Edinburgh University Press.

BIBLIOGRAPHY

McNair, B. (2009), 'From Porn Chic to Porn Fear: The Return of the Repressed?', in F. Attwood, (ed.), *Mainstreaming Sex. The Sexualization of Western Culture*, London and New York: I. B. Tauris, 55–77.

McNair, B. (2013), *Porno? Chic! How pornography changed the world and made it a better place*, London and New York: Routledge.

Menik, X. (2012), 'Introduction. Pervasive Peeping: New Ways to Survey the Cine-Erotic', in X. Mendik (ed.), *Peep Shows. Cult Film and the Cine-Erotic*, London and New York: Wallflower Press.

Mihailović, K. (2014), 'From a priest into a clown: Makavejev's critical transformation of Bergman', *Studies in Eastern European Cinema*, 5:1, 31–44.

Mikuš, M. (2015), '"Faggots Won't Walk through the City": Religious Nationalism and LGBT Pride Parades in Serbia', in S. Sremac and R. R. Ganzevoort (eds), *Religious and Sexual Nationalisms in Central and Eastern Europe: Gods, Gays and Governments*, Leiden and Boston: Brill, 15–33.

Milivojevic, M. (2015), 'Introducing Wounds: Challenging the 'Crap Theory of Pain' in Nikola Lezaic's *Tilva Ros*', in D. Sharma and F. Tygstrup (eds), *Structures of Feeling. Affectivity and the Study of Culture*, Berlin, Munich, Boston: De Gruyter.

Millett-Gallant, A. (2010), *The Disabled Body in Contemporary Art*, New York: Palgrave Macmillan.

Milojević, I. (2012), 'Transforming Violent Masculinities in Serbia and Beyond', in O. Simic, Z. Volcic, C. R. Philpot (eds), *Peace Psychology in the Balkans. Dealing with a Violent Past while Building Peace*, New York: Springer, 57–75.

Minagawa, Y. (2013), 'Inequalities in Healthy Life Expectancy in Eastern Europe', *Population and Development Review*, 39:4, 649–71.

Minagawa, Y. (2013), 'The Social Consequences of Postcommunist Structural Change: An Analysis of Suicide. Trends in Eastern Europe', *Social Forces*, 91:3, 1035–56.

Miroiu, M. (1996), 'Ana's Land. The Right to be Sacrificed', in T. Renne (ed.), *Ana's Land. Sisterhood in Eastern Europe*, Boulder: Westview Press, 136–41.

Moore, L. J. and J. Weissbein (2010), 'Cocktail Parties: Fetishizing Semen in Pornography Beyond Bukkake', in K. Boyle (ed.), *Everyday Pornography*, London: Routledge, 77–90.

Morag, R. (2020), *Perpetrator Cinema. Confronting Genocide in Cambodian Documentary*, New York: Columbia University Press, Wallflower Press.

Moravcsik, A. (2012), 'Europe After the Crisis: How to Sustain a Common Currency', *Foreign Affairs*, 9:3, 54–68.

Morawska, E. (2007), Trafficking into and from Eastern Europe', in. Maggy Lee (ed.), *Human Trafficking*, London: Willan, 92–115.

Morrison, B. (2021), *Complicating Articulation in Art Cinema*, Oxford: Oxford University Press.

Morrison, S. (2018), 'Sex and the Soviets: Depiction of Rape in Soviet Cinema and Literature', *The Thetean: A Student Journal for Scholarly Historical Writing*, 47:1, 123–33.

Mortimer, L. (2002), 'Our Carnal Nature and Cosmic Flow', *The Massachusetts Review*, 43:1, 107–34.

Mortimer, L. (2008), 'The World Tasted: Dušan Makavejev's Sweet Movie', *Senses of Cinema*, 47, <http://sensesofcinema.com/2008/feature-articles/sweet-movie-mortimer/> (last accessed 20 May 2020).

Mortimer, L. (2009), *Terror and Joy. The Films of Dusan Makavejev*, London, Minneapolis: University of Minnesota Press.

Moss, K. (1995), 'The Underground Closet: Political and Sexual Dissidence in East European Culture', in E. Berry (ed.), *Post-communism and the Body Politic*, New York: New York University Press, 229–51.

Mostov, J. (2000), 'Sexing the nation/desexing the body: politics of national identity in the former Yugoslavia', in. T. Mayer (ed.), *Gender Ironies of Nationalism Sexing the Nation*. London, New York: Routledge, 89–113.

Murphy, K. (2005), 'Hell's Angels: An Interview with Catherine Breillat on *Anatomy of Hell*', *Senses of Cinema*, February 2005, <https://www.sensesof cinema.com/2005/on-recent-films-34/breillat_interview/> (last accessed 3 October 2022).

Murtic, D. (2015), *Post-Yugoslav Cinema. Towards a Cosmopolitan Imagining*, London and New York: Palgrave Macmillan.

Nagib, L. (2011), *World Cinema and the Ethics of Realism*, London: Continuum.

Neale, S. (1981), 'Art Cinema as Institution,' *Screen* 22:1, 11–39.

Nergin, L. (2008), *Appearance and Identity. Fashioning the Body in Postmodernity*, New York: Palgrave Macmillan.

Newall, M. (2012), 'The Aesthetics of Transgressive Pornography', in H. Maes and J. Levinson (eds), *Art and Pornography. Philosophical Essays*, Oxford: Oxford University Press, 206–26.

Nicodemo, T. (2012), 'Cinematography and Sensorial Assault in Gaspar Noé's *Irreversible*', *Cinephile*, 8:2, 32–48.

Nieubuurt, B. J. (2021), 'Želmir Žilnik's "Marble Ass": Pioneer of Post-Yugoslav LGBTQ+ Cinema', June 30, 2021, *M Library Blogs*, https://apps.lib.umich.edu/blogs/lost-stacks/%C5%BEelmir-%C5%BEilnik%E2%80%99s-mar ble-ass-pioneer-post-yugoslav-lgbtq-cinema (last accessed 13 October 2022).

Null, C. (2001), '*Sweet Movie Review*', <https://www.contactmusic.com/film/review/sweetmovie> (last accessed 12 February 2020).

O'Brien, D. P. (2019), 'Hap-Tech Narration and the Postphenomenological Film', *Philosophies*, 4, 2–28.

Ognjanovic, D. (2015), '"Welcome to the Reality Studio": Serbian Hand-Held Horrors', in L. Blake and X. A. Reyes (eds), *Digital Horror. Haunted Technologies, Network Panic and the Found Footage Phenomenon*, London: I. B. Tauris, 80–95.

Okólski, M. (1998), 'Regional Dimension of International Migration in Central and Eastern Europe', *Genus*, 54:1–2, 11–36.

Olney, I. (2013), *Euro Horror. Classic European Horror Cinema in Contemporary American Culture*, Bloomington: Indiana University Press.

BIBLIOGRAPHY 165

Olney, I. (2017), *Zombie Cinema*, New Brunswick: Rutgers University Press.

Ostrowska, D. (2006), 'Filmic Representations of the Myth of the Polish Mother', in E. Mazierska and E. Ostrowska (eds), *Women in Polish Cinema*. Oxford, New York: Berghahn Books, 37–54.

Ostrowska, D. (2006a), 'Polish "Superwoman": a Liberation or Victimisation?', in E. Mazierska and E. Ostrowska (eds), *Women in Polish Cinema*. Oxford, New York: Berghahn Books, 55–74.

Ostrowska, E. (2017), 'Women Who Eat Too Much: Consuming Female Bodies in Polish Cinema', in Y. Hashamova, B. Holmgren and M. Lipotevsky (eds), *Transgressive Women in Modern Russian and East European Cultures. Film the Bad to the Blasphemous*, New York and London: Routledge, 128–43.

Outhwaite, W. and L. Ray (2005), *Social Theory and Postcommunism*, Oxford, UK: Blackwell.

Owen, J. (2014), 'From Buñuel to the Barbarogenius: Surrealist and avant-garde traditions in the films of Dušan Makavejev', *Studies in Eastern European Cinema*, 5:1, 3–15.

Paasonen, S. (2013), 'Grains of Resonance: Affect, Pornography and Visual Sensation'. *Somatechnics*, 3:2, 351–68.

Palmer, T. (2006), 'Style and Sensation in the Contemporary French Cinema of the Body', *Journal of Film and Video*, 58:3, 22–32.

Palmer, T. (2012), 'Rites of Passing. Conceptual Nihilism in Jean-Paul Civeyrac's *Des filles en noir*', *Cinephile*, 8:2, 10–18.

Palmer, T. (2015), *Irreversible*, New York: Palgrave Macmillan.

Parvulescu, A. (2011), *The Traffic in Women's Work: East European Migration and the Making of Europe*, Chicago: Chicago University Press.

Pavičić, J. (2010) 'Cinema of Normalization': Changes of Stylistic Model in Post-Yugoslav Cinema After the 1990s', *Studies in Eastern European Cinema*, 1:1, 43–56.

Pavicic, J. (2012), 'From a Cinema of Hatred to a Cinema of Consciousness: Croatian Film After Yugoslavia', in A. Vidan and G. Crnkovic (eds), *In Contrast: Croatian Film Today*, Zagreb: HFS, 49–58.

Pavicic, J. (2014), 'Cinema of normalisation: changes of stylistic model in post-Yugoslav cinema after the 1990s', *Studies in Eastern European Cinema*, 1:1, 43–56.

Pethő, Á. (2011), *Cinema and Intermediality: The Passion for the In-Between*, Newcastle upon Tyne: Cambridge Scholars Publishing.

Petley, J. (2000), 'Snuffed Out: Nightmares in a Trading Standards Officer's Brain', in X. Mandik and G. Harper (eds), *Unruly Pleasures: The Cult Film and its Critics*, Guildford: FAB Press, 205–19.

Petley, J. (2013), 'The Following Content is Not Acceptable', in F. Attwood, V. Campbell, I. Q. Hunter and S. Lockyer (eds), *Controversial Images. Media Representations on the Edge*, New York: Palgrave Macmillan, 131–53.

Petrović, J. (2018), *Women's Authorship in Interwar Yugoslavia: The Politics of Love and Struggle*, New York and London: Palgrave Macmillan.

Polyakova, A. and Shekhovtsov, A. (2016), 'On the Rise: Europe's Fringe Right', *World Affairs*, 179:1, 70–80.

Popan, E. R. (2013), 'The Good, the Bad, and the Gypsy: Constant positive representation and use of reversed negative stereotypes as "sympathy triggers"', Master Thesis, University of Texas at Austin, December 2013.

Portuges, C. (1992), 'Border Crossings: Recent Trends in East and Central European Cinema', *Slavic Review*, 51:3, 531–35.

Portuges, C. (2010), 'Conversation with Yvette Bíró: Interviews Conducted in Paris, 5 July 2008, and New York City, 1 November 2008', *Studies in Eastern European Cinema*, 1:1, 97–107.

Power, N. (2010), 'Blood and Sugar: The Films of Dušan Makavejev', *Film Quarterly*, Vol. 63:3, 42–51.

Projansky, S. (2001), *Watching Rape. Film and Television in Postfeminist Culture*, New York: New York University Press.

Quandt, J. (2004), 'Flesh and Blood: Sex and Violence in Recent French Cinema', *Artforum*, 42:6, 126–32.

Racioppi, L. and O'Sullivan, K. (2009), 'Gender Politics in Post-Communist Eurasia', in L. Racioppi, Linda and K. O'Sullivan (eds), *Gender Politics in Post-Communist Eurasia*, Michigan: Michigan State University Press, 1–47.

Radovic, M. (2008), 'Resisting the Ideology of Violence in 1990s Serbian Film', *Studies in World Christianity*, 14:2, 168–79.

Ranciére, J. (2011), *The Emancipated Spectator*, London: Verso.

Rankovic, R. (2019), 'Migrations of Young People in Serbian Cinema: Go, Stay or Come Back?' in N. Marinchevska (ed.), *Post-totalitarian Cinema in Eastern European Countries: Models and Identities*, Sofia: Institute of Art Studies, Bulgarian Academy of Sciences, 103–12.

Rappas, I. A. C. (2016), 'Corporeal Violence in Art-House Cinemas: Cannes 2009', *Continuum: Journal of Media and Cultural Studies*, 30:6, 670–78.

Reed, B. (2010), 'Interview: A Serbian Film', *DIY*, 8 December, <https://diymag.com/archive/interview-a-serbian-film> (last accessed 2 October 2022).

Rehlin, G. (2004), 'A Hole in My Heart', *Variety*, 8 September 2004, <https://variety.com/2004/film/markets-festivals/a-hole-in-my-heart-1200531223/> (last accessed 12 December 2021).

Reyes, X. A. (2016), 'The Mediation of Death in Fictional Snuff: Reflexivity, Viewer Interpellation, and Ethical Implication', in N. Jackson, S. Kimber, J. Walker and T. J. Watson (eds), *Snuff. Real Death and Screen Media*, London and New York: Bloomsbury Publishing, 211–25.

Reyes, X. A. (2020), 'Abjection and Body Horror', in C. Bloom (ed.), *The Palgrave Handbook of Contemporary Gothic*, New York and London: Palgrave Macmillan, 393–411.

Richter, N. (2015), 'Filming the Impossible: An Interview with Catherine Breillat', *Reverse Shot*, 19 May 2015, <http://reverseshot.org/interviews/entry/2053/breillat_interview> (last accessed 10 September 2022).

BIBLIOGRAPHY

Rivi, L. (2007), *European Cinema after 1989. Cultural Identity and Transnational Production*, New York, London: Palgrave Macmillan.

Roche, R. (2015), 'Exploiting Exploitation Cinema: An Introduction', *Transatlantica*, (2), 14 July 2016, <http://journals.openedition.org/transatlantica/7846> (last accessed 29.04.2021).

Russell, J. (2004), '*Anatomy of Hell (Anatomie De L'Enfer*, 2004)', *BBC Movies*, <https://www.bbc.co.uk/films/2004/11/22/anatomy_of_hell_2004_review.shtml> (last accessed 2 October 2022).

Russell, P. (2013), *Shock Movies: A Guide to Controversial and Disturbing Films*, Bad News Press.

Sammons, B. M. (2012), 'The Life and Death of a Porno Gang – Blu-ray Review', *Hellnotes*, 30 August 2012 <https://hellnotes.com/the-life-and-death-of-a-porno-gang-blu-ray-review/> (last accessed 2 October 2022).

Sarkosh, K. and W. Menninghaus (2016), 'Enjoying Trash Films: Underlying Features, Viewing Stances, and Experiential Response Dimensions', *Poetics* (57), 40–54.

Schober, A. (2009), 'Cinema as Political Movement in Democratic and Totalitarian Societies since the 1960s', In. A. Harutyunyan, K. Hörschelmann, and M. Miles (eds), *Public Spheres after Socialism*, Bristol, Chicago: Intellect, 39–63.

Sconce, J. (1995), 'Trashing the Academy: Taste, Excess, and an Emerging Politics of Cinematic Style,' *Screen* 36:4, 371–93.

Sconce, J. (2007), 'Introduction', in J. Sconce (ed.), *Sleaze Artists. Cinema at the Margins of Taste, Style, and Politics*, Durham and London: Duke University Press, 1–16.

Sconce, J. (2007b), 'Movies. A Century of Failure', in J. Sconce (ed.), *Sleaze Artists. Cinema at the Margins of Taste, Style, and Politics*, Durham and London: Duke University Press, 273–309.

Seibold, W. (2022), 'Why A Serbian Film is Misunderstood, And More Relevant Than Ever', 19 August, *SlashFilm*, <https://www.slashfilm.com/973214/why-a-serbian-film-is-misunderstood-and-more-relevant-than-ever/> (last accessed 2 October 2022).

Sélavy, V. (2010), 'A Serbian Film: Interview with Srdjan Spasojevic', *Electric Sheep*, <http://www.electricsheepmagazine.co.uk/2010/12/05/a-serbian-film-interview-with-srdjan-spasojevic/> (last accessed 2 October 2022).

Šelih, A. (2012), 'Crime and Crime Control in Transition Countries', in A. Šelih and A. Završnik (eds), *Crime and Transition in Central and Eastern Europe*, New York: Springer, 3–37.

Sharrett, C. (2009), 'The Problem of Saw: "Torture Porn" and the Conservatism of Contemporary Horror Films', *Cinéaste*, 35:1, 32–7.

Shaun, K. (2014), 'Transgressive edge play and *Srpski Film/A Serbian Film*', *Horror Studies*, 5:1, 107–25.

Shaviro, S. (1992), *The Cinematic Body*, Minnesota: Minnesota Press.

Shaviro, S. (2011), 'After Hope: The Life and Death of a Porno Gang', *Academic Journal of Film and Media*, <http://www.acidemic.com/id137.html> (last accessed 1 October 2022).

Shinjo, I. (2019), 'Male Sexuality in the Colony. On Toyokawa Zenichi's Searchlight', in M. Inoue and S. Choe (eds), *Beyond Imperial Aesthetics: Theories of Art and Politics in East Asia*. Hong Kong: Hong Kong University Press, 97–116.

Singh, G. (2014), *Feeling Film: Affect and Authenticity in Popular Cinema*, London and New York: Routledge.

Singnorelli, N. (2005), *Violence in the Media*, California: ABC-CLIO.

Siomopoulos, A. (2010), 'Cult-ural Learnings from Borat. A Model of the New Standardized Cult Film', in. J. Cline and R. G. Weiner (eds), *From the Arthouse to the Grindhouse. Highbrow and Lowbrow Transgression in Cinema's First Century*, Plymouth: The Scarecrow Press, 208–23.

Sloat, A. (2009), The Influence of European Union Legislation on Gender Equality in Central and Eastern Europe, in L. Raicoppi and K. O'Sullivan (eds), *Gender Politics in Post-Communist Eurasia*, Michigan: Michigan State University Press.

Smalley, G. (2013), 'Sweet Movie (1974)', *366 Weird Movies*, 10 July, <https://366weirdmovies.com/148-sweet-movie-1974/> (last accessed 20 May 2020).

Smith, H. E. (2022), 'A Serbian Film: Is the Internationally Banned Movie Art of Trash?', *Movieweb*, 16 April, <https://movieweb.com/a-serbian-film-art-or-trash/> (last accessed 2 October 2022).

Smith, I. R. (2020), 'What Is Cult When It's At Home? Reframing Cult Cinema in Relation to Domestic Space', in. S. Baschiera and M. De Rosa (eds), *Film and Domestic Space. Architectures, Representations, Dispositif*, Edinburgh: Edinburgh University Press, 210–25.

Sobchack, V. C. (1984), 'Inscribing ethical space: Ten propositions on death, representation, and documentary', *Quarterly Review of Film Studies*, 9:4, 283–300.

Sobchack, V. C. (2004), *Carnal Thoughts. Embodiment and Moving Image Culture*, Berkeley, CA: California University Press.

Sobchack, V. C. (1977), 'No Lies: Direct Cinema as Rape', *Journal of the University Film Association*, 29:4, 13–18.

Sobchack, V. C. (1992), *The Address of the Eye*, New Jersey: Princeton University Press.

Sobotka, T. (2011), 'Fertility in Central and Eastern Europe after 1989: Collapse and Gradual Recovery', *Historical Social Research*, 36(2), 246–96.

Sobotka, T., V. Skirbekk, V. and D. Philipov (2011), 'Economic recession and fertility in the developed world', *Population and Development Review*, 37:2, 267–306.

Sorfa, D. (2019), 'Seeing Oneself Speak: Speech and Thought in First-Person Cinema'. *JOMEC Journal – Journalism, Media and Cultural Studies*, 13, 104–21.

BIBLIOGRAPHY

Sterritt, D. (2007), 'Sweet Movie: Wake Up!', *The Criterion Collection*, 18 June, <https://www.criterion.com/current/posts/487-sweet-movie-wake-up> (last accessed 12 February 2020).

Sterritt, D. (2010), 'A Shadow Poet: Michael Haneke', in R. G. Weiner and J. Cline (eds), *Cinema Inferno. Celluloid Explosions from the Cultural Margins*, Lanham, Toronto, Plymouth: The Scarecrow Press, 244–69.

Stevenson, J. (2010), 'Grindhouse and Beyond', in. J. Cline and R. G. Weiner (eds), *From the Arthouse to the Grindhouse. Highbrow and Lowbrow Transgression in Cinema's First Century*, Plymouth: The Scarecrow Press, 129–53.

Stevenson, J. (ed. 2002), *Fleshpot. Cinema's Sexual Myth Makers and Taboo Breakers*, Manchester: Critical Vision.

Stőhr, L. (2016), 'Conflicting Forces: Post-Communist and Mythical Bodies in Kornél Mundruczó's films', *Studies in Eastern European Cinema*, 7:2, 139–52.

Stojanova, C. (2006), 'Post-communist Cinema. The Politics of Gender and Genre', in. L. Badley, R. B. Palmer and S. J. Schneider (eds), *Traditions in World Cinema*, Edinburgh: Edinburgh University Press.

Stojanova, C. (2006b), 'Post-Communist Cinema', in L. Badley, R. B. Palmer and S. J. Schneider (eds), *Traditions in World Cinema*, New Brunswick, New Jersey: Rutgers University Press, 95–117.

Stojanova, C. (2006c), 'Memory and Reinvention in Post-Socialist Hungarian Cinema', in. C. Portuges and P. Hames (eds), *Cinemas in Transition in Central and Eastern Europe after 1989*, Philadelphia: Temple University Press, 104–35.

Stojanova, C. (2012), 'A Gaze from Hell: Eastern European Horror Cinema Revisited', in P. Allmer, E. Brick and D. Huxley (eds), *European Nightmares. Horror Cinema in Europe Since 1945*, London and New York: Wallflower Press, 225–39.

Stojanović, N. (2014), 'Makavejev of Our Youth', *Studies in Eastern European Cinema*, 5:1, 75–9.

Stratton, D. (2002), 'Pleasant Days', *Variety*, https://variety.com/2002/film/awards/pleasant-days-1200551489/ (last access 01 February 2022).

Strausz, L. (2017), *Hesitant Histories on the Romanian Screen*, New York: Palgrave Macmillan.

Surtees, R. (2008), 'Traffickers and Trafficking in Southern and Eastern Europe. Considering the Other Side of Human Trafficking', *European Journal of Criminology*, 5:1, 39–68.

Švankmajer, J. (2014), *Touching and Imagining. An Introduction to Tactile Art*, transl. Stanley Dalby, London and New York: I. B. Tauris.

Synder, S. (1994), '*The Transparent I. Self/Subject in European Cinema*', New York, Berlin: Peter Lang, 165–79.

Szulc, L. (2018), *Transnational Homosexuals in Communist Poland: Cross-Border Flows in Gay and Lesbian Magazines*, New York, London: Palgrave Macmillan.

Taylor, A. (2017), *Troubled Everyday: The Aesthetics of Violence and the Everyday in European Art Cinema*, Edinburgh: Edinburgh University Press.

Taylor, R. (2004), 'Sweet Movie', 11 July, <http://www.notcoming.com/reviews/sweetmovie/> (last accessed 12 February 2020).

Taylor, T. R. (2020), 'Torture Porn', in C. Bloom (ed.), *The Palgrave Handbook of Contemporary Gothic*, New York and London: Palgrave Macmillan, 411–31.

Tereškinas, A. (2011) 'Masculinity and male body in the contemporary Lithuanian cinema' *Filosofija. Sociologija*. 22:1, 57–64.

Testa, B. (1990), 'Reflections on Makavejev. The Art Film and Transgression, Between East and West'. *Before the Wall Came Down. Soviet and East European Filmmakers Working in the West*, Lanham, New York and London: University of Press America, 229–47.

Thomas, C. E. (2012), '(Un)sexing Lady Macbeth: Gender, Power, and Visual Rhetoric in her Graphic Afterlives', *The Upstart Crow*, 31, 81–102.

Thomsen, C. B. (1974), '"Let's Put the Life Back in Political Life": An Interview with Dusan Makavejev', *Cinéaste*, 6:2, 14–18.

Todd, L. (2019), 'Music television aesthetics, experimentation, and the evocation of chaos in Serbian film', *Studies in Eastern European Cinema*, 10:2, 129–45, DOI: 10.1080/2040350X.2018.1518616.

Todorova, M. (1997), *Imagining the Balkans*, Oxford: Oxford University Press.

Todorova, M. (2006), *Balkan Family Structure and the European Pattern: Demographic Developments in Ottoman Bulgaria*, Budapest: Central European University Press.

Todorović, N. (2021): 'Želimir Žilnik and the problem called: Reality', 30 June 2021, *LGBTI.ba*, https://lgbti.ba/zelimir-zilnik-and-the-problem-called-reality/ (last accessed 13 October 2022).

Tot, F. (2020), 'Marble Ass, Yugoslavia's first openly queer film, turns 25. Here's why you need to watch it', *The Calvert Journal*, 19 February 2020, <https://www.calvertjournal.com/articles/show/11641/lgbtq-yugoslavia-black-wave-film-serbia-marble-ass> (last accessed 12 December 2021).

Towlson, J. (2014), *Subversive Horror Cinema. Countercultural Messages of Films from Frankenstein to the Present*. Jefferson, North Carolina: McFarland & Company, Inc., Publishers.

Trifonova, T. (2011), 'Between the National and the Transnational: Bulgarian Post-Communist Cinema', *Studies in Eastern European Cinema*, 2:2, 211–25.

Tuck, G. (2009), 'The Mainstreaming of Masturbation: Autoeroticism and Consumer Capitalism', in F. Attwood, (ed.), *Mainstreaming Sex. The Sexualization of Western Culture*, London and New York: I. B. Tauris, 77–93.

Uidhir, M. C. and Pratt, H. J. (2012), 'Pornography at the Edge. Depiction, Fiction, and Sexual Predilection', in. H. Maes and J. Levinson (eds), *Art and Pornography. Philosophical Essays*, Oxford: Oxford University Press, 137–57.

Van Boeschoten, R. (2003), 'The Trauma of War Rapes: A Comparative View on the Bosnian War Conflict and the Greek Civil War', *History and Anthropology*, 14:1, 41–54.

Verdery, K. (1996), *What Was Socialism and What Comes Next?*, Princeton: Princeton University Press.

BIBLIOGRAPHY

Vesi V. (2018), 'Violated sex: rape, nation and representation of female characters in Yugoslav new film and black wave cinema', *Studies in Eastern European Cinema*, 9:2, 132–47.

Vijn, A. (2010), 'Imagine 2010: Life and Death of a Porno Gang Review, *Screen Anarchy*, 21 April 2010, <https://screenanarchy.com/2010/04/imagine-2010-life-and-death-of-a-porno-gang-review.html> (last accessed 2 October 2022).

Vlastimir, S. (2014), 'From switchboard operators to Coca-Cola kids: Transformations of the political left in the films of Dušan Makavejev', *Studies in Eastern European Cinema*, 5:1, 45–58.

Vucetic, R. (2018), *Coca-Cola Socialism: Americanization of Yugoslav Culture in the Sixties*, Budapest-New York: Central European University Press.

Vuković, V. (2019), 'Cinematic Suicide: Representations of Working Women in Yugoslav New Film', *Apparatus. Film, Media and Digital Cultures in Central and Eastern Europe*, 9.

Waddell, C. (2018), *The Style of Sleaze: The American Exploitation Film, 1959–1977*, Edinburgh: Edinburgh University Press.

Wassil R. (2015), 'Films with a Criminal Record: An Investigation of Exploitation Films', *Film Matters*, Winter 2015, 83–6.

Watson, P. (1993), 'The rise of masculinism in Eastern Europe', *New Left Review*, I/198, 71–82.

Watson, P. (1993b), 'Eastern Europe's Silent Revolution: Gender', *Sociology*, 27:3, 471–87.

Watson, T. J. (2020), 'Part of My Soul Did Die When Making This Film': Gothic Corporeality, Extreme Cinema and Hardcore Horror in the Twenty-First Century', in R. J. Hand and J. McRoy (eds), *Gothic Film. An Edinburgh Companion*, Edinburgh: Edinburgh University Press, 218–32.

Waugh, T. (1988), 'Lesbian and Gay Documentary: Minority Self-Imaging, Oppositional Film Practice, and the Question of Image Ethics', in L. Gross, J. S. Katz and J. Ruby (eds), *Image Ethics. The Moral Rights of Subjects in Photographs, Film and Television*, Oxford: Oxford University Press, 248–73.

Weiner, R. G. (2010), 'The Prince of Exploitation', in. J. Cline and R. G. Weiner (eds), *From the Arthouse to the Grindhouse. Highbrow and Lowbrow Transgression in Cinema's First Century*, Plymouth: The Scarecrow Press, 41–57.

Weir K. And S. Dunne (2014), 'The connoisseurship of the condemned: *A Serbian Film*, the *Human Centipede 2* and the appreciation of the abhorrent', *Participations: Journal of Audience and Reception Studies*, 11:2, 78–99.

Weschler, L. (1984), 'Poland's Banned Films', *Cinéaste*, 13:3, 11–12.

Wesley, M. C. (1999), 'Reverence, Rape, Resistance: Joyce Carol Oates and Feminist Film Theory', *Mosaic: An Interdisciplinary Critical Journal*, 32:3.

West, A. (2016), *Film of the New French Extremity. Visceral Horror and National Identity*, Jefferson, North Carolina: McFarland and Company.

Weyland, K. (1999), 'Neoliberal Populism in Latin America and Eastern Europe', *Comparative Politics*, 31:4, 379–401.

Wheatley, C. (2011), 'Naked Women, Slaughtered Animals: Ulrich Seidl and the Limits of the Real', in T. Horeck and T. Kendall (eds), *The New Extremism in Cinema. From France to Europe*, Edinburgh: Edinburgh University Press, 93–105.

Wheatley, C. (2012), '"Le Cineaste d'Horreur Ordinaire": Michael Haneke and the Horrors of Everyday Existence', in P. Allmer, E. Brick and D. Huxley (eds), *European Nightmares. Horror Cinema in Europe Since 1945*, London and New York: Wallflower Press, 207–21.

Whisnant, R. (2010), 'From Jekyll to Hyde: The Grooming of Male Pornography Consumers', in K. Boyle (ed.), *Everyday Pornography*, London: Routledge, 114–34.

Wiegand, E. (2017), 'Who Can Be Eaten? Consuming Animals and Humans in the Cannibal-Savage Horror Film', in. E. E. Wiegand in C. J. Miller and A. B. Van Riper (eds), *What's Eating You? Food and Horror on Screen*, New York, London: Bloomsbury, 253–69.

Wilkins, B. (2012), 'Review: Mladen Djordjevic The Life and Death of a Porno Gang on Synapse Blu-ray', *Slant*, 11 September 2012, <https://www.slant magazine.com/dvd/the-life-and-death-of-a-porno-gang/> (last accessed 25 May 2022).

William, B. (2013), 'Violence in Extreme Cinema and the Ethics of Spectatorship', *Projections*, 7:1, 25–42.

Williams, L. (1999), *Hard Core: Power, Pleasure, and the "Frenzy of the Visible"*, Berkeley, CA: University of California Press.

Williams, L. (2008), *Screening Sex*, Durham and London: Duke University Press.

Williams, L. (2019), 'Motion and e-motion: lust and the 'frenzy of the visible', *Journal of Visual Culture*, 18 (1), 97–129.

Wolchik, S. L. (2000), 'Reproductive Policies in the Czech and Slovak Republics', in S. Gal and G. Kligman (eds), *Reproducing Gender: Politics, publics, and everyday life under socialism*, Princeton: Princeton University Press, 58–92.

Wolff, L. (1994), *Inventing Eastern Europe: The map of civilization on the mind of the enlightenment*, Stanford, CA: Stanford University Press.

Wood, R. (2008), 'Fresh Meat: Diary of the Dead: Diary of the Dead may be the summation of George A. Romero's zombie cycle (at least until the next instalment)', *Film Comment*, January-February 2008, <https://www.filmcomment. com/article/fresh-meat-diary-of-the-dead/> (last accessed 13 July 2022).

Wynnyczuk, V. and Uzel, R. (1999), 'Czech Republic and Slovak Republic', in H. P. David (ed.), *From Abortion to Contraception*, Westport: Greenwood Press, 91–117.

Yu, C-M. (2019), 'Corpo-reality in the Hong Kong New Wave', in M. Inoue and S. Choe (eds), *Beyond Imperial Aesthetics: Theories of Art and Politics in East Asia*. Hong Kong: Hong Kong University Press, 125–47.

Zacijek, A. M. and Calasanti, M. T., (1995), 'The impact of Socioeconomic Restructuring on Polish Women', in B. Łobodzińska (ed.), *Family, Women*

BIBLIOGRAPHY

and Employment in Central-Eastern Europe, Westport, Connecticut, London: Greenwood Publishing, 179–93.

Zahlten, A. (2012), 'Neo-Liberal Avant-Garde Sexploitation in Japan: The Interplay of Collaboration and Revolution in the Pink Film', in X. Mendik (ed.), *Peep Shows. Cult Film and the Cine-Erotic*. London and New York: Wallflower Press, 194–205.

Zahlten, A. (2019), 'The Prerogative of Confusion: Pink Film and the Eroticization of Pain, Flux and Disorientation', *Screen* 60:1, 25–45.

Zajec, S. (2009), 'Boosting the image of a nation: the use of history in contemporary Serbian film', *Northern Lights*, 7, 173–89.

Zielinksa, E. (2000), 'Between Ideology, Politics, and Common Sense: The Discourse of Reproductive Rights in Poland', in S. Gal and G. Kligman (eds), *Reproducing Gender: Politics, publics, and everyday life under socialism*, Princeton: Princeton University Press, 23–58.

Žižek, S. (1997), 'Underground, or Ethnic Cleansing as a Continuation of Poetry by Other Means', *InterCommunication*, 18, <www.ntticc.or.jp/pub/ic_mag/ic018/intercity/zizek_E.html> (last accessed 2 October 2022).

Žižek, S. (1997b). 'Multiculturalism, or the Cultural Logic of Multinational Capitalism', *New Left Review*, September/October: 28–52.

Zvijer N. (2018), 'Film (de)construction of national identity. The case of Serbian films from the 1990s', *Images*, 23:3, 15–23.

Filmography

9 Songs, Michael Winterbottom, UK: Revolution Films, 2004.
Slovenian Girl [*Slovenka*], Damjan Kozole, Serbia: Film House Bas Celik, 2009.
A Hole in My Heart [*Ett hål i mitt hjärta*], Sweden: Memfis Film, 2004.
A Serbian Film [*Srpski Film*], Srdjan Spasojević, Serbia: Contra Film, 2010.
Alone [*Sami*] Lucas Nola, Croatia: Alka-Film Zagreb, 2001.
An Andalusian Dog [*Un Chien Andalou*], Luis Buñuel, France: Les Grands Films Classiques, 1929.
Anatomy of Hell [*Anatomie de l'enfer*], Catherie Breillat, France: Arte France Cinéma 2004.
Angel Exit [*Andel Exit*], Vladimír Michálek, Czech Republic: Buc-Film, 2000.
Apocalypse Now, Francis Ford Coppola, USA: Omni Zoetrope, 1979.
Baklava, Alexo Petkov, Bulgaria: Lost Vulgaros Productions, 2007.
Battleship Potemkin [*Bronenosets Potyomkin*], Sergei Eisenstein, USSR: Mosfilm, 1925.
Benny's Video, Michael Haneke, Austria and Switzerland: Lang Film and Wega Film, 1992.
Bibliothèque Pascal, Szabolcs Hajdu, Hungary: Katapult Film, 2010.
Breakfast with the Devil [*Doručak sa davolom*], Yugoslavia: Neoplanta Film, Miroslav Mika Antić, 1971.
Carne, Gaspar Noé, France: Les Cinémas de la Zone, 1991.
Clip [*Klip*] Maja Miloš, Serbia: Film House Bas Celik, 2012.
Crazy World of Ours [*Bube u glavi*], Miloš Radivojević, Yugoslavia: Ineks Film, 1970.
Custody [*Nadzor*], Poland: Film Group X, Ryszard Bugajski, 1985.
Delta, Kornél Mundruczó, Hungary: Proton Cinema, 2008.
Dogtooth [*Kynodontas*], Yorgos Lanthimos, Greece: Boo Productions, 2009.
Elegy [*Elégia*] Zoltán Huszárik, Hungary: Balázs Béla Stúdió, 1965.
Entr'acte, René Clair, France: Les Ballets Suedois, 1924.
Fat Girl [*À ma sœur!*], Catherie Breillat, France: Arte France Cinéma, 2001.
Fuck Me [*Baise-moi*], Virginie Despentes and Coralie Trinh Thi, France, 2000.
Gravehopping [*Odgrobadogroba*], Jan Cvitkovič, Slovenia: Staragara, 2005.
Handcuffs [*Lisice*], Krsto Papić, Yugoslavia: Jadran Film, 1969.
Hemel, Sacha Polak, Netherlands: Circle Films, 2012.
Hidden [Caché], Michael Haneke, France: France 3 Cinéma, 2005.
Horoscope [*Horoskop*], Yugoslavia: Bosna Film, Boro Drašković, 1969.

FILMOGRAPHY 175

Hostel I-III, Eli Roth, USA: New Entertainment, 2005, 2007, 2011.

I Stand Alone [*Seul contre tous*], Gaspar Noé, France: Canal+, 1998.

In a Year of 13 Moons, [*In einem Jahr mit 13 Monden*], Rainer Werner Fassbinder, Germany: Filmverlag der Autoren, 1978.

In the Realm of the Senses [*Ai no korīda*], France and Japan: Argos Films and Oshima Productions, Ósima Nagisza, 1976.

Interrogation [*Przesłuchanie*], Poland: Film Group X, Ryszard Bugajski 1982.

Irreversible [*Irréversible*], Gaspar Noé, France: StudioCanal, 2002.

Isle [*Seom*], Kim Ki Duk, South Korea: Myung Films, 2000.

Japón, Carlos Reygadas, Mexico: NoDream Cinema, 2002.

Kino Caravan, Titus Muntean, Romania: Libra Film, 2009.

L'Age d'Or, Luis Buñuel, France: Vicomte de Noailles, 1930.

Last Seen Wearing a Blue Skirt [*Gyilkos kedv*], Erdőss Pál, Hungary: Mafilm, 1997.

Last Tango in Paris, Bernardo Bertolucci, Italy and France: Produzioni Europee Assocati, 1972.

Loverboy, Cătălin Mitulescu, Romania: Strada Film, 2011.

Marble Ass [*Dupe od mramora*], Želimir Žilnik, Serbia: Radio B92, 1995.

Maria, Calin Peter Netzer, Romania: Artis Film, 2003.

New Life [*La Vie nouvelle*], Philippe Grandrieux, France: Canal+, 2002.

Night of the Living Dead, George A. Romerto, USA: Image Ten, 1968.

No Man's Land [*Ničija zemlja*], Danis Tanović, Bosnia: Studio Maj, 2001.

Nymphomaniac I-II, Lars von Trier, Denmark: Zentropa Entertainments, 2013.

Ordinary People [*Obični ljudi*], Vladimir Perišić, France and Servia: TS Productions, 2009.

Persona, Ingmar Bergman, Sweden: AB Svensk Filmindustri, 1966.

Piggies [*Swinki*], Robert Glinski, Poland: 42film, 2009.

Plastic Jesus [*Plastični Isus*], Lazar Stojanović, Yugoslavia: Centar Film, 1971.

Pleasant Days [*Szép napok*] Mundruczó, Hungary: Mafilm, 2002.

Pleasure, Ninja Thyberg, Sweden: Plattform Produktion, 2021.

Red Wheat [*Rdeče klasje*], Živojin Pavlović, Yugoslavia: Viba Film, 1970.

Romance [*Romance X*], Catherie Breillat, France: Arte France Cinéma, 1999.

Ryna, Ruxana Zenide, Romania: Elefant Films, 2005.

She-Shaman [*Szamanka*], Andrzej Żuławski, Poland: Canal+Polska, 1996.

Siberian Lady Macbeth [*Siberska Ledi Magbet*] Andrzej Wajda, Poland: Avala Films, 1962.

Skinning [*Šišanje*], Stevan Filipovic, Serbia: Hypnopolis, 2010.

Sombre, Philippe Grandrieux, France: Canal+, 1998.

Somewhere in the East [Undeva in est], Nicolae Margineanu, Romania: Studioul de Creatie Solaris Film, 1991.

Somnambulance [*Somnambuul*], Sulev Keedus, Estonia: F-Seitse, 2003.

State of Things [Stare de fapt], Stere Gulea, Romania: Romania: Studioul de Creatie Solaris Film, 1995.

Strike [*Stachka*], Sergei Eisenstein, USSR: Mosfilm, 1925.

Sweet Movie, Dušan Makavejev, France: V. M. Productions, 1974.

T.T. Syndrome [*T.T. Sindrom*], Dejan Zečević, Serbia: Tangram Entertainment, 2002.

Taxidermia, György Pálfi, Hungary and France: Eurofilm, 2006.

Titane, Julia Ducournau, France: Kazak Productions, 2021.

Touch Me Not [*Nu mă atinge*], Adina Pintilie, Romania, 2018.

The Blacks [*Crnci*], Goran Devic and Zvonimir Jurić, Croatia: Kinorama, 2009.

A Clockwork Orange, Stanley Kubrick, UK: Hawk Films, 1971.

The Conjugal Bed [Patul Conjugal] Mircea Daneliuc, Romania: Alpha Films International, 1993.

The Cove, Louie Psihoyos, USA: Skyfish Films, 2009.

The Last House on the Left, Wes Craven, USA: Lobster Enterprises, 1972.

The Life and Death of a Porno Gang [*Život i smrt porno bande*], Mladen Đordevic, Serbia: Film House Bas Celik, 2009.

The Living and the Dead [Živi i mrtvi], Kristijan Milic, Croatia: Olimp Produkcija, 2007.

The Next 365 Days [*Kolejne 365 dni*], Barbara Białowąs and Tomasz Mandes, Poland: Open Mind One, 2022.

The Oak [*Balanta*], Lucie Pintilie, Romania: MK2 Productions, 1992.

The Piano Teacher [*La Pianiste*], Michael Haneke, France: Arte France Cinéma, 2002.

The Return [*Povratak*], Živojin Živojin, Yugoslavia: Avala Film, 1966.

The Role of My Family in the World Revolution [*Uloga moje porodice u svjetskoj revoluciji*], Bahrudin Čengić, Yugoslavia: Bosna Film, 1971.

The Rules of the Game [*La règle du jeu*], Jean Renoir, France: Nouvelle Édition Francaise, 1939.

The Seventh Continent [*Der Siebente Kontinent*], Austria: Wega Film, 1989.

The Seventh Day, the Eighth Night [*Den sedmý – osmá noc*], Evald Schorm, Czechoslovakia: Filmové Studio Barrandov, 1969.

The Tribe [*Plemya*], Myroslav Slaboshpytskyi, Ukraine: Harmata Film Production, 2014.

Tilva Roš, Nikola Ležaić, Serbia: Kiselo Dete, 2010.

Touchless [*Bez doteku*], Matej Chlupacek, Czech Republic: Barletta, 2005.

Twentynine Palms, Bruno Dumont, France and USA: 3B Productions, 2003.

Vow [*Klyatva*], Mikheil Chiaureli, USSR: Tbilisi Film Studio, 1946.

Weekend, Jean-Luc Godard, France: Les Films Copernic, 1967.

Will Not End Here [*Nije Kraj*], Vinko Bresan, Croatia: Jadran Film, 2008.

WR: Mysteries of the Organism [*W.R. – Misterije organizma*], Yugoslavia: Neoplanta Film, Dusan Makavejev, 1971.

Notes

Introduction

1. https://www.vice.com/en/article/ppvwby/im-sick-of-pretending-i-dont-get-art, last accessed 10 September 2022.
2. https://www.vice.com/en/article/yv5jw5/i-went-to-art-basel-to-try-and-get-art, last accessed 10 September 2022.
3. See Quandt (2011: 18–29).
4. The double-standards which, similar to the West, existed in the Soviet Union as well, often blamed women for the attack and put drunk females or individuals with a sexual history at the forefront (see Morrison 2018).
5. In reality, regulations banned everything that seemed harmful to socialist political and economic interest (Kiss 2018).
6. Based on Friedrich Engel's hypothesis that the process of women's emancipation and equality are guaranteed by their high level of labour force participation, the eradication of private property, and the socialisation of domesticity, the Marxist-Leninist approach to women's wellbeing rested on equality with a man's right to work and the protection of mother and child (Brzozowska 2015). Equal wages, social security, education, paid leave of absence before and after childbirth, obstetrics hospitals, child-care centres and kindergartens, as well as development of services, canteens and maternity wards were all legislative actions to minimise the conflict between family obligations and occupational roles (David 1999). The Marxist legislation also aimed at 'finding a counterbalance between differing biological male and female roles' (Ibid., 6) by ensuring the political visibility of women (Raicoppi and O'Sullivan 2009). Despite these measures however, the socialist state apparatuses remained heavily masculine (Brzozowska 2015). With the motivation of disguising unemployment by long maternity leave, the regimes' pronatalist policy ensured women's social representation and role as 'married working mothers' (Verdery 1996: 67) and stressed the role of females as suppliers of the nations' future generation. Socialist structures thus functioned as an extended family – a '*zadruga*-state'– that composed of families tied to a 'patriarchal authority with the father Party as its head' (Ibid., 64). Nuclear relations and roles were embedded into a much larger social structure that made citizens dependent on the socialist father figure. Women's child-bearing task remained a female obligation towards the paternal state (Koncz 1995). Overall, the socialist gender ideology and Marxist

178   THE EXTREME CINEMA OF EASTERN EUROPE

biopolitics resulted in the maintenance of male dominance in the public sphere, and isolated women within the domestic realm and maternal world (see Sloat 2001; Brzozowska 2015). This marginal (domestic) dominance rested on the Foucauldian anatomy-politics of women's mechanical bodies. The introduction of new body politics regulations prompted socialist leaderships to take action and regulate or ban abortion (Legge and Alford 1986). The Eastern European pronatalist measures were all structured around patriarchal ideologies that looked at infertile women as deserters (Baban 1999) and their bodies as vehicles to convey and stabilise Marxist ideology (Kligman 1998). As Harsányi ironically highlights, women were depicted as 'an improbable cross between an ideologically distorted peasant model and a stereotypical Stakhanovite worker' (Harsanyi 1992: 48). Marxist body politics not only controlled women's reproductive acts as well as looks, but by doing so, they widened the gender gap and strengthened women's isolated position. As Fischer adds, while female sexuality was considered 'necessary evil', a sign of (...) danger and moral decay', men's sexuality was vaunted (Fischer 1998: 174). In extramarital sexual cases, it was often the women who were charged with prostitution and acquired a criminal record, while men went unpunished (Fischer 1998).

7. Almost identical to the ballad of Arges monastery, the Hungarian *Kőmíves Kelemenné* also tells the story of the walled-in wife.

Chapter 1

1. Interestingly, many of these films received state prizes, while filmmakers were often sent abroad to represent Yugoslavia at art film festivals. In this way, the government sent the message that the conflict around these films was not about politics, but art (see Vukovic 2018: 77).

2. It is through this pictorial depiction of abuse that Schorm criticises the atrocities of the Czechoslovak regime – especially in the post-Velvet Revolution climate. With its apocalyptic vision, the film has also been negotiated as an allegory of the Soviet invasion (Hames 2009: 84) and an answer to the radical abolishment of reforms in 1968. However, as Hames notes on the wave's political role that 'cannot be denied', he also mentions that, 'the films offer much more than a coded attack on the government' (Hames 2006: 74). Schorm's film features Biblical parables, and conjugates sacred and profane symbols while questioning mankind's very moral attitude. As the villagers are locked up in the village, the community is forced to practise self-determination and self-regulation, thus building up a miniature paternalistic society. Under the pressure of fear, stress and uncertainty, the villagers start to victimise themselves and commit a series of aggressive physical acts. Schorm's parabolic vision can be interpreted as a critique of communism's very idea of equality as, instead of supporting each other, the experiment's participants attack and hurt their fellows. The film this depicts mankind's very nature as depraved, corrupt and filled with iniquity, thus universalizing the film's primary message of communist coexistence.

NOTES   179

3. Muehl founded this Reich-inspired collective in 1972, hoping to replace bourgeois institutions with unlimited sexual emancipation and new forms of art that would be direct manifestations of the life force itself (see Sterritt 2007).
4. See for instance Hamblin (2014), Mihailović (2014), Goulding (1990), Mortimer (2009), Owen (2014).
5. For instance, The Milky Way commune recalls Buñuel's film of the same name (*The Milky Way/La Voie lactee* 1969).
6. The actress Carole Laure who plays Miss Canada felt pressured on set to perform sexual acts and she quit the production after shooting the penis-sequence (Smalley 2013).

Chapter 2

1. In Eastern Europe, over 70% of the assets are foreign-owned (see Lane 2010: 232).
2. Also, as Sloat notes, because socialist governments considered emancipation a state ideology and emphasised women's liberation within the communist ideology, many believed the women's movement was unnecessary and even humiliating (Sloat 2001).
3. The implementation of gender equality in forms of labour laws (Hungary, Bulgaria), Gender Equality Acts (Romania, Lithuania) and other anti-discrimination legislations created an even more favourable maternity situation for women and failed to address women's discrimination – even in the post-EU era (Sloat 2001). Because gender discrimination is not politically recognised, as is the case, for instance, with Hungary, the social change bolstered conservativism.
4. As Hughes (2000) points out, the post-Soviet Eastern states have become major suppliers of the global sex industry: their number is estimated to exceed 500,000 within the European Union. Because of their cultural-national heritage and Eastern European background, sexual workers from the former Soviet Union are often called 'Natashas' (Ibid.). Being a 'Natasha' not only refers to the women's role as subordinated to sexual power, but alludes to one's objectified, transnational identity. Coming from the post-socialist area of Europe, in the eyes of the exploitative power, the 'Natashas' are deprived of their citizenship (Ibid.). Instead, they are treated as coming from a universal, Eastern European sphere which is accompanied by images of poverty, economic hardship and prostitution.
5. In the Soviet colonialist epoch, female sexuality and motherhood were appropriated as symbols of oppressed nationhood (see for instance the Polish prison films *Interrogation* [1982] and *Custody* [1985] where mothers are incarcerated, tortured and deprived of their children [the future generation that could bring political change]).
   They eventually supererogate themselves to the state, the male power. The socialist political structure thus becomes itself the parent, one that

appropriates the future generation by violent means. The oppressive male apparatus that interferes in the sexuality of women brings forth images of the socialist pronatalist measures and one's obligation towards the paternal state. The recurring motif of rape only exacerbates this subjugated position. Whether it is a concrete, transgressive deed or an abstract act, its ideological critique of the actual political establishment is clear. That is, women, as symbols of the nation get violently harassed, raped and eventually killed in these films. The transgressive trajectory of images in these productions differ in terms of their detailed representation of sexual assaults. While we find several films that signal rape but do not portray it, in the selected examples rape reaches a radical imagery that eradicates any desire in the spectator (see Batori 2020).

6. See for instance Márta Mészáros's *The Fetus* (*A magzat*, 1993) and Dorota Kędzierzawska's *Nothing* (*Nic*, 1998), both of which focus on pregnant women who are unable to raise their own children. In *Nothing*, the mother kills her child, while in *The Fetus*, the female protagonist is considering giving her child up for adoption.

7. Several further examples reflect upon the emasculation process of men by displaying vulnerable, fallen male figures who cannot establish themselves in the new consumerist market. These 'drabness films', as Iordanova terms it (2013: 26) – such as Eduard Sachariev's *Belated Full Moon* (*Zakasnyalo palnolunie*, 1996) and *Wagner* (*Vagner*, 1998), *Look Forward in Anger* (1993) – display the socio-economic hardship of the capitalist transition and men's instable position within it while portraying extreme violence on screen.

8. The mise-en-scéne of the sequence shows close resemblance with the nine-minute rape scene of *Irreversible* (Gaspar Noé, 2002).

9. https://www.imdb.com/title/tt0304776/reviews?ref_=tt_urv (last accessed 12 September 2022).

Chapter 3

1. In a similar vein, Italian mondo documentaries of the 1960s and the cycle of Italian cannibal films in the 1970s and 1980s can be seen though the lenses and value of pre-filmic veracity (i.e., real or staged animal cruelty), which they used to form an evolving criticism of white imperialism (see Bernard 2016, 191–207).

2. https://www.imdb.com/title/tt0218871/reviews?ref_=tt_urv (last accessed 12 September 2022).

3. One cannot be dissected without the socio-cultural context of Seidl's dog or Reygadas' birds or pigs. As Wiegand (2017: 250–60) emphasises, killing animals which, irrespectively of the camera's presence, are intended for slaughter, foregrounds certain cultural food taboos. In Eastern Europe for instance, the slaughter of the family pigs once or twice a year is a celebrated

NOTES

181

event which brings together the family and as such, it functions as a culturally well-known and accepted practice. From this point of view, the killing of the pig in *Benny's Video* has less of a shock effect on someone from the region than on a spectator from a West-European country. Wiegand comes to a similar conclusion when arguing that the shock value of the infamous turtle-killing in *Cannibal Holocaust* depends on taste economies, for such killing is an accepted practice in some parts of the world (see Wiegand 2017: 156–258). Wiegeland thus proposes that animal slaughter be 'only considered acceptable when abiding by cultural food taboos dictating *which* animals may be eaten' (Wiegeland 2017: 261, also see De Luca 2016: 228–9).

4. Given the patriarchal-sexist set up of post-transformation Eastern Europe, it is less of a surprise that nonhuman-animal metaphors target women. Following the centrally planned agricultural system, the introduction of a capitalist market economy set Eastern Europe on the path of creating market economies based on private property. The restructuring of the marketing system and agricultural production had a deep effect on the agriculture of the region. Because the large-scale livestock and crop cooperatives were not suited to market-based private agriculture, the creation of private farming was one of the most difficult tasks of the transition period (Csaki and Tuck 2000: vii). The liberalisation of prices and the privatisation of farming structure went hand in hand with social and political changes. The need for educational qualifications led to a steady outflow of young people, especially women, from agricul-tural areas (Banski and Mazur 2021: 9). The changes in the price relationship between agricultural produce and production also incumbered the profitability of farming. As a result, agricultural production was mainly made possible by direct payments, subsidies and grants of external origin which, following the accession of the post-socialist countries to the European Union, further reduced the diversity of farming operations (Banski 2018). The first years of membership were characterised by a decline in the area of agricultural land. The development in the settlement network around large agglomerations, the growth of technical infrastructure and the competition in the food sector which neglected poorer lands all had unfavourable consequences for the efficiency of production (Banski, 2018: 549–50). For the deeply agriculture-oriented Eastern European region, privatisation led to a deep decline in output. As McInteryre has put it:

> The widespread assumption that Eastern European and ex-Soviet populations enthusiastically await the movement to recognizable forms of market capitalism has often been based on a simple mistranslation: the word privatization has been read to mean "private" ownership in the American sense of the word, while being understood by many Eastern European and ex-Soviet respondents to mean "no longer totally owned and/or controlled by the national-level gov-ernment." In agriculture the term can mean the establishment of more "real cooperatives," rather than the autonomous family farming assumed by Western economists. (Emphasis original, McIntyre 1992: 92)

182   THE EXTREME CINEMA OF EASTERN EUROPE

As Bansky summarises:

> The liquidation of the socialist cooperatives and state farms caused in many cases disrepair or complete destruction of farm buildings, infrastructure, equipment, livestock, irrigation systems, etc. Besides, in many cases the sales market collapsed, which forced many farmers to get directly involved in distribution and sale of agricultural products. This brought about a worsening of labour productivity. Many newly established farms with smaller acreages produce first of all for their own needs and do not constitute competition for the limited group of the truly commercial farms. They are doomed to marginalisation and gradual decline. This concerns also some of the cooperative farms, established by the owners of small properties, devoid of appropriate capital and experience. Members of such cooperatives frequently live in towns, far away from their property, and are thus only "loosely" tied to this property. (Banski 2008: 18–19)

5. I am aware that the countries of Eastern Europe are characterised by different agro-ecological conditions and directions of agricultural production, especially in plant production. Still, as Bansky has pointed out, the very fact that the region belonged to the Eastern Bloc means that the socialist model of production and centralised agricultural system interconnects the countries. Also, in terms of livestock husbandry and animal production, the differences are relatively small (Bansky 2008).

6. As Bansky emphasises, the Central European region disposes of a great potential in the domain of agriculture: 'According to the data from FAO, in 2003 these countries disposed of around 48.8 million hectares of agricultural land, that is – of every fourth hectare under farming in the European Union' (Bansky 2008: 3). Poland, Hungary, the Czech Republic, Bulgaria and Romania are believed to contain altogether around a third of all the arable land of the European Union (Ibid.).

Chapter 4

1. Available from https://www.imdb.com/title/tt0348529/reviews?ref_=tt_urv (last accessed 10 September 2022).
2. See Kovács (2008: 62–81), Galt and Schoonover (2010: 1–8), Kaplan (2010: 285–303) and King (2019: 50–62).
3. As Breillat explains:

> Eroticism is 'shameful and repulsive': I don't know what an erotic woman is. I don't know what eroticism is. Desire is much more violent, much cruder and more beautiful. Me, I hate eroticism; as a woman, it would humiliate me. Pornography is a manifesto. I have the right to make pornography. And it's not pornography; it's art because it tells something and it removes preconceived ideas; and these preconceived ideas that have been repeatedly hammered into us need to be removed ... Why would you say, that in order for it to be art, it mustn't be pornography? Does that mean that if I film someone drinking water or a coffee, that I am making art? But if this person is making love and when we see the sex, I'm making pornography? (Breillat in Maas 2019)

NOTES 183

4. When asked why she titled the film *Anatomy of Hell*, Breillat gives the following explanation:

> There's a fundamentalist view of women's bodies in our culture. Taken to the extreme, it makes even hair become obscene. If you cover something with a veil, you make it obscene. I wanted to show the most difficult thing to look at in order to inoculate the viewer, as if with a vaccine. It becomes impossible to say that something is obscene if we change the aesthetic codes. (Breillat in Chocano, 2004)

5. Breillat for instance states that the laughter of the audience during the screening of *Anatomy of Hell* comes from our own discomfort of bodies and expresses our own fear (see Chocano 2004).
6. Scholarship on Eastern European exploitation cinema is basically non-existent. One of the reasons is the strict socialist censorship which supervised production and screening and while focusing on topics that support communist ideology, it favoured propaganda to genre cinema. Also, the focus of most Eastern European film scholars is still on arthouse cinema who often consider grindhouse films part of lowbrow culture.
7. Available from https://www.zilnikzelimir.net/marble-ass (last accessed 10 September 2022).
8. https://www.bbc.com/news/av/stories-60839456Z (last accessed 27 March 2022).
9. Other articles praise the film as one of Žilnik's greatest works which stands for 'an enduring masterpiece of empathy' (Tot 2020), 'a pioneering LGBT film' (BBC), and 'a raucous, colorful film characterized by macabre humor' which deserves more visibility (Niebuurt 2021). For portraying two real-time sex workers, Todorovic even identifies *Marble Ass* as docudrama, and she praises the director for his thirst for realistic representation:

> Characteristic of Žilnik is that he tends, unlike Hollywood productions, to not use film as manipulation and stunning weapon, but quite the opposite – as a tool to deal with the most important problems of society ... The central topic of all Žilnik's films is reality as it is ... Without any judgments, mockeries, ridiculing and insulting, without moral judgment, Žilnik made a film about Merlinka's life, performance, and sexual identity. (Todorović 2021)

10. Baklava caused many changes in Bulgaria: the deputy director of the State Agency for Child Protection was fired. The government established special commissions which focused on juvenile issues and TV shows started to make visible Bulgaria's orphaned children. The government even raised the financial support for abandoned children (see Los Vulgaros 2007).

Chapter 5

1. In *Zone of the Dead* (*Zona Mrtvih*, 2009), the zombies eat Western scientists.

184   THE EXTREME CINEMA OF EASTERN EUROPE

2. The tortured and intimidated image of women fuelled the wars by alluring to the patriarchal understanding of women as property and men's responsibility to protect them (Kesić 1999: 189). It also served a sex-specific political function with the intent of impregnating the enemy's female individuals and betray that nation (Thomas and Regan 1999). Aggravating the trauma of the victim, rape survivors, as Isa Qosja's *Three Windows and a Hanging* (*Tri dritare dhe një varje*, 2014) demonstrates, often became symbols of betrayal and had to face social rejection from the community and family (Hashamova 2012). As a result, many women were killed by their families or have committed suicide (Hashamova 2012), while countless survivors experienced clinical depression and psychotic episodes (Thomas and Regan, 1999).

3. Kusturica's *Underground* (1995) has been discussed as an example of this tendency (see Žižek 1997; Longinović 2005; Rivi 2007). Murtic for instance argues that the film represents a 'place where a man, in between hedonistic orgies, in an almost natural manner, is ready to slaughter another man' and where a woman is 'either seductive and consequently a fatalist subject, or she is an irrelevant signifier pushed into the scene's frame only for the partial fulfilment of a (West European) aesthetic fetish' (87).

4. This is not to say that the post-war cinemas of the region solely focused on the topic/climate of war and/or did that in a self-Balkanised way. Migration caused by the post-socialist economic hardship (*Tomorrow Morning*, Oleg Novković, 2006), *Nowhere* (Predrag Velinović, 2017), and the disintegration of Yugoslavia (*Honeymoons* [2009], *The Box* [2011]) or by the bombing of NATO forces (*The Wounded Country*, Dragoslav Lazić, [1999], *Sky Hook*, Ljubiša Samardžić [2000], *War Live*, Darko Bajić [2000], *Mamarosh*, Momčilo Mrdaković [2013]) and post-socialist crime, violence and corruption were also shared topics (see Rankovic, 2019: 103–12). The trauma of the war victim (*For Those Who Can Tell No Tales*, *When Day Breaks*, *Snow* and *Grbavica*) and the trauma of the perpetrator (*Remake*, *The Living and the Dead*, *The Blacks*, *The Enemy* and *The Witnesses* [*Svjedoci*], Vinko Brešan, 2003) have also been a common approach to the topic of war (see Jelaca 2016). Thanks to the overall democratisation of the Western Balkans and the international producers' determination for a more balanced point of view of the conflicts, the recent years brought about numerous films which reckon with the stereotype of Homo Balcanicus – or, as Mylonas (2003: 4) puts it, '*Homo Serbicus and Femina Serbica*' – and focus on post-war transitional realities and traumas.

5. See for instance *Halima's Path/Halimin put* (Arsten Anton Ostojić, 2012) *Snow/Snjeg* (Aida Begić, 2010) or *The Melon Route/Put lubenica* (Branko Schmidt, 2006).

6. By erasing the capital letter, Longinovic emphasises the vampiric representation of 'the serbs' as 'the monolith of ethnic hatred' in the global media. At the same time, the collective phantasm of 'the serbs' highlights the way the

NOTES   185

global media coverage strengthened the vision of 'the serbs' as an essential, monumental and historically stable entity (Longinovic 2002: 48).

7. Frey (2016: 161–5) defines three main narrative themes that form extreme cinema's 'explicitly sexual art film' trajectory. The first one which he calls 'Amour Fou Scenario', chronicles a sexual relationship which becomes obsessive and pathological over the time. The story, narrated in an episodic form and set in a claustrophobic place, concludes with the end of the relationship and/or the psychological or physical decease of one partner. Films like Bernardo Bertolucci's *Last Tango in Paris* (*Le Dernier Tango à Paris* 1972), or Nagisa Ōshima's *In the Realm of the Senses* (*Ai no Korīda* 1976) are examples of this narrative form. A variation of the 'Amour Fou' plot, the 'Sex Addict Scenario' reduces the relationship of the protagonists to sex addiction which, as seen in Lars von Trier's *Nymphomaniac* (2013) or Sacha Polak's *Hemel* (2012), eventually annihilates the main character's relationship with his/ her partner and/or family. The third, 'Initiation Scenario' focuses on a self-discovery journey which, as seen in Catherine Breillat's *Fat Girl* (2001) or *Romance* (2004), happens through sexuality.

8. Spasojević's statement strongly corresponds to Featherstone's 'Serbian Being-in-the-World' theory (2013: 136) which reads the film as a sociohistorical critique of the Western market that positions the Serb as a sadistic other because 'it needs the shitty other to stabilize its own civilized identity [and because] it is possessed by its own carnographic culture of hypersexualized extreme violence' (2013: 131). The image of Serbia 'as the shit of European civilization' thus overshadows (and justifies) the West's neocapitalist, 'normalized brand of sadism' (Ibid.).

9. https://www.quora.com/Have-you-ever-watched-A-Serbian-Film (last accessed 21 October 2022).

10. https://www.imdb.com/title/tt1273235/reviews?ref_=tt_urv (last accessed 22 October 2022).

11. Critics are similarly polarised when it comes to the violent imagery of the film. Acknowledging Spasojević's intention for a political statement, many critics argue that the director 'exceeds the level of violence necessary to exercise his main point' (Smith 2022) and that 'subversive political statement or not, it's such a stinking pile of trash that viewers will need a lifelong shower after enduring it' (Kern 2011). Others defend the 'sinister ideas', production value and 'sheer competence' that sets it apart from other extreme films (Harlan 2022) and accentuate the superficiality of people who are blinded by the imagery (Lanthier 2011) and don't understand the political message (Seibold 2022).

12. *A Serbian Film* is a self-financed independent production and the Serbian government had no hand in its making (see Klapka 2014).

13. As Chowen describes his experience: 'Though I'm not all that hard, or too cynical, I still tend to ignore most marketing campaigns that claim their movie to be "better than" or "more shocking than" another film. When *The*

186 THE EXTREME CINEMA OF EASTERN EUROPE

Life and Death of a Porno Gang boasted that it was "more powerful than *A Serbian Film*" and "one of the most controversial video releases of the year", however, I listened and immediately felt the urge to review this movie' (emphasis original, Chowen 2012).

Chapter 6

1. Of course, the list is not exhaustive – the number of films representing violence against women would exceed the limits on the present study. Rather, it aimed at outpointing some examples from the present and past decade that use extreme violent graphic and shock aesthetics to raise awareness of the current socio-political and economic crisis in the region.

Index

9 Songs, 4–7, 28, 76

A Hole in My Heart [*Ett hål i mitt hjärta*], 1–4, 7
A Serbian Film [*Srpski Film*], 11, 21, 98–9, 106, 115–24, 131, 140–1, 143
Alone [*Sami*], 20, 77–80, 83, 140
Anatomy of Hell [*Anatomie de l'enfer*], 5, 20, 66, 82–6, 92, 98
Angel Exit [*Andel Exit*], 20, 73–6, 79

Baklava, 20, 86, 92–8, 140
Balkanisation, 104–8, 111, 113, 125
Benny's video, 66–7, 181
Bibliothèque Pascal, 21, 127, 134, 136–8, 141
Blacks, The [*Crnci*], 105, 184
Breakfast with the Devil [*Doručak sa davolom*], 23–4

Carne, 63–6
Clip [*Klip*], 106, 131
Clockwork Orange, The, 3, 8
colonialism, 14–15, 18, 43–4, 68–9, 72, 80, 139–40
Conjugal Bed, The [*Patul Conjugal*], 20, 45–8, 61, 140

Delta, 130–1

emasculation, 17, 20–1, 39, 40, 44, 45–8, 50, 58, 127, 130–6, 139, 140–1, 180
exploitation, 2–11, 14, 20–1, 38–9, 43–5, 53, 60–1, 66, 80–94, 122, 124–6, 138, 140–3

Fat Girl [*À ma sœur!*], 6–7, 53–4
feminism, 41–3, 59,

Greek weird wave, 62

Handcuffs [*Lisice*], 23–4
Hemel, 6
Hidden [*Caché*], 66
Horoscope [*Horoskop*], 24
Hostel I–III, 117, 121
hypermasculinity, 40–1, 103, 138, 143

I Stand Alone [*Seul contre tous*], 20, 65
In a Year of 13 Moons [*In einem Jahr mit 13 Monden*], 62–3
In the Realm of the Senses [Ai no korīda], 6
intermediality, 6, 106–8, 111, 119–23, 126
Irreversible [*Irréversible*], 53–4, 180

Japón, 20, 68–9

Last House on the Left, The, 86
Last Tango in Paris, 8, 55
Life and Death of a Porno Gang, The [*Život i smrt porno bande*], 21, 99, 106–26, 136, 140

Marble Ass [*Dupe od mramora*], 20, 86–98, 140
mondo, 65, 76, 81, 180
motherhood, 46, 48, 69, 74, 77, 79–80
Muehl, Otto, 28–9, 31

nationalism, 16, 44, 91–2, 99–106, 114
neoliberalism, 4, 10, 13, 15, 18–19, 21, 37–8, 41, 44, 50, 54, 63, 76, 115, 121–3, 128–36
Night of the Living Dead, 87
Nymphomaniac I–II, 6, 185

188   THE EXTREME CINEMA OF EASTERN EUROPE

patriarchy 15–18, 26–7, 40–1, 44, 48, 53–4,
  58–9, 72, 76, 89, 90, 92, 97, 100, 102–5,
  109, 130–3, 141, 177–8, 181–4; *see also*
  patriarchal structures
Pleasant Days [*Szép napok*], 20, 48–9,
  50–61, 70, 140
pornography, 1–5, 16, 26, 34, 36, 42, 47–8,
  53, 55, 57, 60–1, 84–5, 93–100, 107,
  114–17, 121–2, 125, 127, 131, 140–3
post-colonialism, 13, 16, 19–20, 44, 52,
  112

rape me / Fuck me [*Baise-moi*], 6
rape, 2, 12, 16–19, 22–5, 33, 35, 42–3, 45,
  48–9, 51, 53–9, 64, 68–9, 70–2, 78, 93,
  96–7, 102–3, 109, 110–19, 122, 124–5,
  130, 132–4, 137–8, 139,
  140–1
realism, 4–7, 9, 24–6, 32, 44, 54, 62, 66–7,
  80–3, 123, 142
Red Wheat [*Rdeče klasje*], 23
Reich, Wilhelm, 25–8, 34, 179
Romance [*Romance X*], 5
Rules of the Game, The [*La règle du jeu*],
  62–3
Ryna, 21, 127, 131–4, 136, 138, 141

Seventh Continent, The [*Der Siebente
  Kontinent*], 65
sexism, 42, 44, 53, 55, 97, 100–1, 105, 181;
  see also misogynism

She-Shaman [*Szamanka*], 20, 54–61, 140
Slovenian Girl [*Slovenka*], 2, 127, 134–41
snuff, 10, 21, 79–81, 99, 107, 109, 110,
  113–18, 122, 126, 141
Sombre, 5, 7
Somnambulance [*Somnambuul*], 20, 70–80,
  140
subjugation, 21, 44–5, 48–9, 53, 56–7, 70,
  101–2, 113, 127, 131–8, 141
supererogation, 16–7, 25, 45, 127, 130,
  138–40, 143
supererogation, 17, 45, 127, 130, 138–40,
  143, 179
surrealism, 35–6
Sweet Movie, 3, 20, 28–36

Taxidermia, 11
Tribe, The [*Plemya*], 19, 131
Tilva Roš, 99, 106
Tito, Josip Broz, 23, 89, 100
Touchless [*Bez doteku*], 20, 127, 130, 133–8,
  141
transvestitism, 89–91
Twentynine Palms, 7

Vow [*Klyatva*], 26

WR: Mysteries of the Organism [*W.R. –
  Misterije organizma*], 26–8

Yugoslav Black Wave, 100, 126, 142